DEMON RIVER
A PURÍMAC

DEMON RIVER
APURÍMAC ≈

The First Navigation of
Upper Amazon Canyons

J. Calvin Giddings

UNIVERSITY OF UTAH PRESS
Salt Lake City

LIBRARY OF CONGRESS CATALOGING-IN-PUBLICATION DATA

Giddings, J. Calvin (John Calvin), 1930–
    Demon river Apurímac : the first navigation of upper Amazon
canyons / J. Calvin Giddings
        p.   cm.
    ISBN 0-87480-525-2 (alk. paper)
    1. Apurímac River (Peru)—Description and travel.
    2. Kayaking—Peru—Apurímac River.   3. Indians of South
America—Peru—Apurímac River Region.   4. Giddings, J. Calvin
(John Calvin), 1930–   —Journeys—Peru—Apurímac River.
I. Title.
F3451.A6G53   1996
918.52'94–dc20   96-18666

CONTENTS

CONTENTS

PREFACE

In the violent rapids live evil river spirits; in the swirling whirlpools that pull under vessels and men dwells the demon of the abyss. One ought not to go by boat at night . . .

Hans Reiser

ROCKS, ROCKS, UNCOUNTABLE ROCKS. Rocks in the river, rocks on the shore, rocks up the hillside. Big rocks, like houses. Thick and close, like jungle trees.

Demon rocks. Rocks ripped from the heart of the Andes. I have seen nothing like them anywhere. And they go on and on and on, marching like an army of giants down the lonely canyon. The whole river plunges madly by and through such rocks.

On most river shores rocks come to your knees, your waist, your head. You can see over them and view the clean sweep of beach. Here such rocks are the pebbles. The rocks on these shores block your view like mountains. If you want to see, you have to climb to the top of one, as you would a peak. They dominate your thoughts and actions like a herd of restless elephants. They paralyze your mobility like waist-deep molasses. They jade your perception of distance, because nearby objects become remote and hard to reach.

Much of this book is a story of rocks and different ways to get past them. To get anywhere on shore, we crawled between them and over them, like ants. To go down the river torrent in our kayaks we tried to maneuver between them, but we sometimes got caught in their deep backflushes, and we sometimes slammed into them. We often capsized, and when we couldn't eskimo roll to get upright again, we would have a nasty swim down through the rocks. It could be life-threatening.

The watercourse along which these rocks lay is the Apurímac River, in southern Peru. It is the source of the Amazon. Its deep canyon, entrenched at the core of the Andes, is geologically young and rough-cut. The rocks have not yet ground down to a civilized size.

No one had succeeded in getting down this incredibly difficult canyon until our expedition accomplished the feat. This book is an account of the first navigation of the deepest chasms of the Apurímac.

The heart of this book is the adventure of challenging Amazon waters, deep canyons, and big rocks. However, the Apurímac has more to offer than our adventure. It cut through the heart of the empire of the Incas, and it profoundly influenced their kingdom and culture. For this reason, I have chosen to tell more about the river and the Incas in Appendix 1. I have also told, in Appendix 2, about other explorers who have challenged the river. In Appendix 3 I describe the basic elements of kayaking and river hydraulics to help the nonkayaking reader understand the action behind this adventure story. Appendix 4 is a summary of the 1975 expedition document that was central to defining the nature and conduct of the expedition.

These appendixes may prove interesting to the reader. With or without them, the reader is invited to share the story of this Amazon river odyssey, set among the big rocks of deep Andean canyons.

ACKNOWLEDGMENTS

I THANK, FIRST OF ALL, my fellow expedition members who contributed to the success of both 1974 and 1975 Apurímac expeditions. My warm thanks extend particularly to Jim Sindelar whose actions on behalf of the 1975 expedition often approached heroic proportions.

Numerous individuals read and criticized various drafts of the manuscript, helping improve the narrative at each stage of revision. These individuals include Leslie, Steven, Michael, and Val Giddings; Irene Thomson, Elizabeth Keate, and Elise Peterson. Woodruff Thomson edited the entire manuscript and provided useful comments as well.

Additional thanks to Julie Westwood for typing the manuscript and to Alexis Kelner for preparing the maps. The efficient work of Mick Gusinde-Duffy and Rodger Reynolds of the University of Utah Press in guiding the final editing and production of the book is gratefully acknowledged.

Finally I would like to thank my family, especially my wife, Leslie, for encouragement and help at every stage of writing, editing, and preparing illustrative materials for this book.

DEMON RIVER
Apurímac

It is the largest river there is in Peru, and the Indians call it *Apurímac*, which means the chief or prince who speaks, for *Apu* has both significations, being applicable to leaders both in peace and war. They also give it another name, which fits it better, and that is *Ccapac-mayu. Mayu* means a river. *Ccapac* is a title they give to their kings, and they applied it to this river to show that it was the prince of all the rivers in the world.

Garcilaso de la Vega

At the center of the river, a dorsal spine, a wall of crests of waves, toward which we are swept irresistibly . . . a liquid curtain, boiling and menacing. We are swept there broadside. I realize for the first time in the trip we would capsize—I find myself in the water, near the kayak, its keel in the air . . . I am horrified to see that Térésa is still in the overturned kayak . . . I finally get her out . . . she gets a firm hold on the boat. Then we are swept over another drop; I am torn from the kayak, knocked against a rock, sucked down interminably . . . buffeted about violently . . . carried by the current to the left bank . . . Térésa is nowhere in sight.

Michel Perrin

≈ RÍO APURÍMAC
Great Speaker of the Andes

I LIKE TO RUN WILDERNESS RIVERS, those marvelous trails of blue, gray, and white water vanishing into far-off canyons. I adore the whole experience: the wilderness setting, the beauty of the endless stream of moving water, the challenge of maneuvering my kayak through rapids, and the camaraderie around the campfire.

Exploring rivers—uncharted, unrecognized, unmapped rivers—that is my special passion. I love going around each new bend of an unexplored river, to see a new canyon open up, new rapids, new cliffs, new plays of light. Each is different, and every one is marvelous. Some have challenge enough to take your breath away.

I have experienced many marvelous river adventures, starting in the 1950s. In the 1960s and 1970s, with companions Roger Turnes, J. Dewell, Jim Byrne, and Les Jones, I made the first kayak descents of numerous canyons and gorges in the western United States, including stretches of the South Fork of the Salmon, Big Creek, the Falls River, and the Teton River in Idaho; Cross Mountain Canyon on the Yampa River in Colorado; and parts of the San Rafael, Escalante, Virgin, Muddy, Price, Bear, and other rivers in Utah.

By the early 1970s, I longed for a greater challenge, something more like the Grand Canyon of the Colorado. However, all the truly great canyons of North America had been explored decades before. Fine, I told myself, I will look at the great rivers on other continents. I would start by looking at the Amazon, the greatest river of them all.

My eyes wandered widely across maps of South America and came to a halt above the Andes Mountains of Peru. Unexplored rivers were threaded everywhere throughout the Andes. Most of their waters flowed into the Amazon River. I tracked down the source of the Amazon, its most remote tributary. Here I found the Apurímac River—my ultimate dream of an unexplored wilderness river.

I almost burst with curiosity. Would the river be navigable? Would it be dangerous? How much would the remote canyons and pueblos of the Apurímac be tainted by civilization? How did native people survive in a

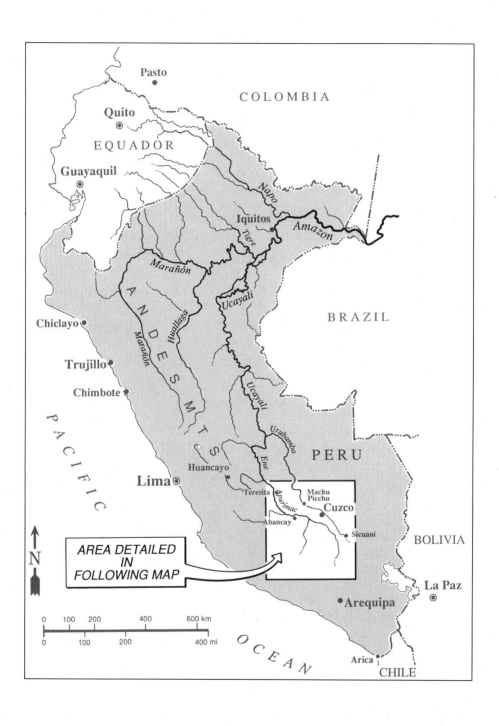

CHILE

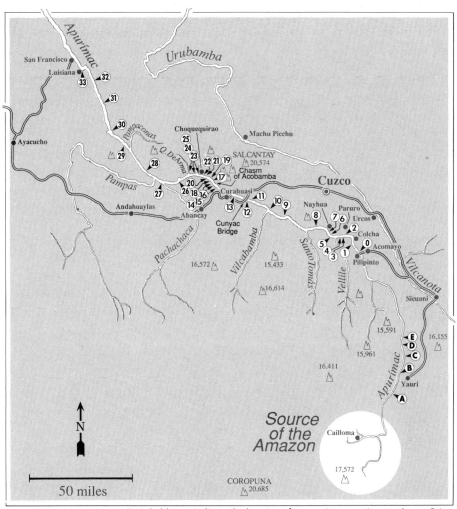

San Francisco

Apurímac

Luisiana ◢ 32
33

31

Urubamba

30

Pampaconas

Ayacucho

Choquequirao
25

Machu Picchu

Q. De Arma

24
29
23
28

SALCANTAY
22 21 19 ⛰ 20,574

27

Chasm
of Acobamba

20
18 16
26
14 15
Curahuasi
13
11
10
9

Cuzco

Andahuaylas
Abancay

Pampas

12

Nayhua

Paruro
Urcos

Cunyac
Bridge

8

7 6

2
Colcha

5
4 3 1

0
Acomayo

Pillpinto

Vilcanota

Pachachaca

16,572 ⛰

Vilcabamba

15,433 ⛰

Santo Tomas

Velille

Sicuani

⛰ 16,614

15,591 ⛰

15,591

E
D
C

16,155 ⛰

15,961 ⛰

B

16,411
⛰

Apurímac

Yauri

A

N

Source
of the
Amazon

Cailloma

50 miles

COROPUNA
⛰ 20,685

17,572
⛰

Encircled letters indicate the location of successive campsites on the ≈
1974 expedition. Encircled numbers locate 1975 campsites.

land sliced by hostile gorges and racing water? Did their way of life promise to endure? Hundreds of other questions coursed through my mind.

I read all I could find about the Apurímac. I found that the river is not only the source of the Amazon, but that it cuts decisively through the ancient empire of the Incas, its deep gorges blocking the expansion of the empire to the northwest. The Incas countered by spanning the river with a marvelous suspension bridge, immortalized by Thornton Wilder as the "Bridge of San Luis Rey."

The Apurímac is born in a trickle of meltwater in a snowfield in the Andes of southern Peru, at about 17,000 feet elevation. It flows 4,000 river miles to the sea, making it the longest tributary and thus the true source of the Amazon. The river starts cutting canyons and gorges at about 13,000 feet elevation and, flowing northwest, soon becomes deeply entrenched in the Andes. It remains in deep canyons for 300 to 400 miles, after which it emerges as a large easygoing jungle river at about 2,000 feet elevation. Except for the jungle river and a few short segments higher up navigated by French explorer Michel Perrin, the Apurímac canyons were unexplored at that time.

I was determined to see everything possible of this unique thread of uncharted wilderness. Modern kayaks would be the vehicle. Fast and nimble, these small boats can slice through rock-laced water and can be carried around unrunnable cataracts. Inside, they can hold food and gear enough to last for weeks, a month if pushed.

Nonetheless, detailed information was woefully lacking on the feasibility of kayak exploration. Were there impossible gorges and waterfalls in the deeper canyons? Were the rapids too severe for safe exploration? Encouragingly, I found that the Apurímac lost an average of only 40–50 feet elevation per mile in its upper and middle stretches, less in the lower canyons. Such gradients are usually not bad, not too violent. They are largely or wholly navigable, even with boats heavily loaded with food and gear. I envisioned a magnificent ribbon of water with continuous rapids, free of great cataracts—a recreational paradise. That was before I talked to Loren McIntyre, *National Geographic* writer and explorer, who told me about the ferocious Apurímac gorges, buried in one of the earth's deepest canyons. He wrote in the October 1972 issue of the magazine about a flight in which he "skimmed far down into the awesome Apurímac gorge, over a mile deep, where no vessel could survive the river's turbulence."

I had also not yet read Isaiah Bowman's scholarly book, *The Andes of Southern Peru*. The book, although published in 1916, represents one of the most complete surveys ever made of the geology of the Vilcabamba Range, through which the Apurímac cuts deep canyons. Isaiah Bowman found evidence of a powerful uplift in the region in late geological times. He noted its effect on the rivers: "Further proof of recent and great uplift is afforded by the deeply entrenched streams. After descending the long graded slopes one comes upon the cliffed canyons with a feeling of consternation. The effect of powerful erosion . . . is heightened by the ungraded character of the river bed. Falls and rapids abound, the river profiles suggest tumultuous descents."

More and more it looked like the Apurímac would be a demon river rather than a recreational paradise. "Demonic" not only for the difficulty of its rapids, but also because of its isolation and burial in dark, threatening gorges at the heart of the Andes.

The river sounded tough, but no one knew for sure. How difficult would the Apurímac be compared to the great rivers of North America? I would have to go to Peru to find out.

I expended great effort in the early 1970s on researching, planning, and organizing an Apurímac kayak expedition. I found that little was known about the Apurímac River and its canyons. Based on the meager knowledge gained, I set up tentative timetables for different segments of the river. The timetables were critical. They helped spell out food requirements and food supply problems. The amount of food to be borne impacted our ability to carry camp gear, first-aid supplies, and emergency mountaineering equipment such as ropes and carabiners. Our total cargo of food and gear was limited by the volume of our kayaks and by the loss of maneuverability of the boats when fully loaded. Maneuverability and load would in turn affect our rate of progress, which came back to influence our timetables and food needs. The whole planning process became a merry-go-round of guesswork, circling a core of uncertainty about river navigability and difficulty. Yet the planning process, no matter how uncertain, was necessary for even beginning to think about expedition requirements.

People would be the key ingredient to the expedition's success or failure. I searched far and wide for suitable companions, knowing that the essential fabric of expeditions is often torn apart by the inability of expedition members to handle the severe stresses and dislocations of expeditionary life. I looked for expert, safety-conscious boaters disposed to work cooperatively and unselfishly in a group setting. I also looked for those who could bring special outdoor survival skills such as mountaineering, wilderness rescue, first aid, and a knowledge of Spanish.

The net was cast widely, across North America. My search was based mainly on contacts I had made while on the board of directors and while president of the American Whitewater Affiliation. Even so, I found it extremely difficult to lure good people to the expedition. After all, those invited were being asked to take considerable time from their busy lives to join a costly and dangerous undertaking of uncertain outcome.

Plans began for a small survey expedition to the Apurímac in 1973. Hopes for a 1973 trip to Peru were abruptly dashed by a damaging dislocation of my right shoulder in the spring of 1973. I then drew up plans for a second trip to Peru in 1974. However, after a long search, I could find only one expert kayaker willing to go: my friend Roger Turnes, of Salt Lake City. We were too small a party for such a remote and formidable river, but I had already finalized plans. I had committed myself to a Fulbright professorship in chemistry at the Universidad Cayetano Heredia in Lima to begin in August 1974. We decided to proceed with an exploratory trip to the Apurímac in July.

Expedition strategy was crucial. I fretted over how to make our journey as safe as possible considering its inherent risks and our pitiful two-man strength. After looking again at my maps and documents, only one approach made any sense. Simply put, we would start in the highlands of southern Peru and, bearing northwest, proceed down the river as far as possible. Almost any river trip starts high and ends low, so this hardly seemed a novel approach. However, my reasons for choosing high river segments before low river segments had little to do with the logical progression of a river trip—and everything to do with Peruvian topography, hydrology, and demography.

Specifically, to the south, near the first trickling source of the Amazon, the river cuts across a high, bleak tableland. Here the Apurímac seemed at its safest. First, the volume of water was at its lowest. Second, the gradient in elevation was least; you can't have a lot of big rapids without a steep gradient. Third, maps of the highlands showed few indications of gorges or steep canyons, which could make escape from the river difficult. Fourth, small pueblos and haciendas were scattered across the barren landscape, providing a network of trails and roads for river access, for escape if necessary, and for resupplying food.

The obvious downside of the upper river was the intense cold of the highlands, where the river valley was elevated around 13,000 feet (4,000 meters) high in thin Andean air. (The chilling effects of cold splashing water can be severe in rapids.) The less obvious downside—discovered only later—was that the mapmakers forgot to show some gorges in the highlands, which were quite dangerous.

In any case, all my evidence suggested that the highlands were relatively safe and that the river after exiting the highlands bored into the earth with accelerating fury. Proceeding downriver, the volume of water in the river increased from new tributaries, the gradient of the riverbed heightened, the depth of the canyons increased, and road access became almost nonexistent. The intensity of Apurímac dangers reached a maximum in the great canyons of the Vilcabamba Range.

With this evidence, I decided we should start in the highlands somewhere above the pueblo of Yauri, where a road bridged the river. We would push on upriver as far as the road would take us. Here we would start our odyssey and begin to get some feel for the navigability of the Apurímac.

I worked out a timetable and planned our first food resupply, 100 or so miles downstream at Pillpinto. Other resupply points would be set up later.

It was now time to confront the Apurímac.

My family and I arrived in Lima on July 9, 1974. I spent four frustrating days in Lima seeking nonexistent maps, unavailable flow tables, and fragments of information about the Apurímac. The only consistent information I found was that the Apurímac Canyon was enormously deep and vertical—perhaps more so than any other canyon in South America—with a powerful river falling incessantly over giant rocks, hemmed in by uncomfortably close walls.

After all of my inquiries and all the foreboding responses, the Apurímac had begun to acquire, in my mind, a surreal demeanor—the character of a legendary demon river. On July 12, the Apurímac finally revealed part of its true reality and complexity. It became not a legend, but a real river carving canyons and gorges out of the Andes. On that day our flight from Lima to Cuzco crossed the great river and followed its course upstream. At first we traveled above an open canyon with some rapids that appeared navigable. Then in the distance we saw from the plane window a deep slash in the Andes, so deep that the river at the bottom looked like a watery thread beaded with tiny specks of silver foam where rapids roared.

I was dismayed at the sight. If we encountered unnavigable waters in a canyon of that depth and steepness we would be trapped, unable either to portage our kayaks or to climb out. All the somber reports that I had discounted, because river gossip is forever exaggerated, seemed mild compared to the harsh reality of that monstrous crack in the earth. My mind was besieged by doubts. To approach that remote and unearthly canyon with two mortal paddlers and their eggshell-thin crafts seemed unforgivable folly.

The plane sped on, and the Apurímac once again began to seem more hospitable. A few filaments of sandy beach lined the river in places, breaking the madness of the canyon. We veered away from the river, its mysteries left mostly intact, and flew on to Cuzco. That ancient capital of the Inca empire would be Apurímac headquarters.

We circled above the valley of Anta and slowly descended to Cuzco's modern airport. I arrived in the terminal building with my family, a great tangle of bags with mixed portions of family goods and river gear, and two awkward kayaks. No taxi driver stepped up to haul this mess to town. At this point an elegant gentleman named Carlos Zegarra came to our rescue.

Señor Zegarra ran the tourist machinery in Cuzco. His bureau exposed tens of thousands of tourists each year to Inca culture. His staff fielded questions all day long in a dozen languages about a thousand subjects, centered on Inca historical sites and accomplishments.

In perfect English, Carlos offered us transportation to town. He arranged our lodging and then introduced us to Cuzco. He did all of this for total strangers, based only on a letter of introduction obtained from the Fulbright Commission in Lima a few days before. I was beginning to learn the importance of letters of introduction in Peru.

After we settled into Cuzco, the business of the expedition took center stage. I was uneasy after sighting the Apurímac from the air and sought to learn more. I grew particularly impatient to see the river up close. I wanted to get a better feel for the canyon—its moods and its obstacles. I also wondered if I should return to Lima and arrange for a low-level flight along the length of the river to better appraise its risks. I hesitated because a flight would be terribly expensive, would succeed only with good weather, and would, at best, cause further delays.

As I weighed these options I thought about my children, Steve and Mike. I was both parent and sole custodian of these two boys, ages twelve and seven. I was the whole world for little Michael, but they both needed me in endless ways. I wished at that moment that I had never dreamed of this expedition. I also knew that deep within me the urge for such exploration could not be contained.

Finally, on Sunday, I would go visit the shores of the Apurímac. I had made arrangements with Alex, a taxi owner, to drive me to the river for reconnaissance. I would see the great river in a historical region, where it had been spanned centuries earlier by the bridge of San Luis Rey. Just above this ancient site, the road crosses the river at a place known as the Cunyac Crossing.

From Cuzco, already elevated two miles high in rarefied Andean air, the road snaked further upward toward the sky, through mountain valleys suspended like giant hammocks from rounded hills. I saw a truck that had plunged off the road into a tree, and I wondered what had happened to the occupants, for most trucks are loaded in back with Indian workers and families.

Well above 12,000 feet, we crossed an obscure mountain pass and began our long descent toward the Apurímac. Our route followed the ancient Inca highway leading to the Apurímac Canyon. I could imagine Inca royalty passing this way: I could almost hear the muted rumble of their trudging armies. The Spanish conquistadors passed through here too, seeking Inca gold, killing, pillaging, and bringing Christian faith to the "uncivilized."

11 ≈

The glory of the Andes was striking, so vertical everywhere. Ahead the lofty summit of Salcantay, over 20,500 feet high, was partly shrouded in clouds.

The dry hills and dull pastures gradually gave way to flowering plants and trees, as we descended toward the Apurímac. A beautiful legume, tall as a man, displayed yellow flowers. Farther on, reeds and semitropical broad-leafed plants became abundant. The Indians here eked out their existence on steep patches of land. Corn and potatoes would be grown when the rains returned. Nearby sat adobe huts with grass-thatched roofs. In front of the huts, an idle mingling of humans and animals sought out thin shreds of shade to protect them from the hot sun of these lower valleys.

The Indians of this land were terrified of cars. The road was wide, but an approaching car was a signal to the Indians to scurry with their possessions off the roadbed. Indian men with monstrous burdens on their backs, bent and tired, scrambled over rocks and through brush to safety. One poor woman, leading a mule, was near a steep embankment when our taxi roared around the bend. She flew down the embankment, almost tripping, trying desperately to pull her recalcitrant mule after her. The mule wouldn't budge. My driver, Alex, was not inclined to give an inch, despite my cry of "¡cuidado!" (take care!). I will never forget the look of wide-eyed terror on this woman's face as we arrowed by, missing her by inches. The cruel omnipotence of the automobile hardly seemed consistent with the graciousness of the Peruvian people.

I grew breathlessly expectant as we approached the canyon domain of the "Great Speaker." We came over a rise and suddenly the river was there, to the left. It was so unlike the terrible river I had imagined! Flowing gently, interrupted occasionally by mild rapids, it possessed a kind of soothing tranquillity. It was beautifully clear and reminded me of the Salmon River in Idaho. It carried less water than I expected, only a few thousand cubic feet per second—comparable to that of the Salmon River at low flow. However, its naked banks were testimony to its fury during the rainy season.

I rushed down the embankment to see and feel the waters of my dreamed-of river. The water was pleasantly cool, its clarity revealing the patchwork of rocks over which it flowed. The moss-like fragrance reminded me of rivers everywhere, and I suddenly felt much more comfortable about the dreaded Apurímac. The terrible inconvenience and expense of an aerial overflight did not, in the serenity of the moment, seem necessary.

We drove onward, across the Cunyac bridge and out of the Apurímac gorge, to a little pueblo called Curahuasi. Here I hoped to find someone to hike with me up into the hills to a canyon overview.

"Can I find a guide here?" I asked Alex.

"I will go," he exclaimed enthusiastically.

The pace was fast. I was hard-pressed to keep up with this bounding highlander from Cuzco. I could see in his movements a well-justified pride and confidence. After all, these hills belonged to him and his people.

We hiked to the top and came in view of one of the Apurímac's magnificent canyons. The river was 4,000 feet below, almost straight down, flowing between steep canyon walls. Here it did not look dangerous, but we could not see the river farther downstream. We saw, instead, much higher than we were, windy ridges and snow-capped peaks hanging above the descending gorge. I realized that the 4,000-foot-deep abyss falling away beneath our feet was but the entrance to the great canyons below.

We walked back to the car, my mind filled with thoughts about the enormous canyon and its uncertainties. I resolved that the expedition would go forward at the earliest moment, despite the nagging questions. The next step was to get back to Cuzco to continue with expedition plans.

Exploring is delightful to look forward to and back upon, but it is not comfortable at the time, unless it be of such an easy nature as not to deserve the name.

Samuel Butler

Only fools never doubt.

Alan Jay Lerner

I've never been lost, but sometimes I didn't know where I was for a few weeks.

Daniel Boone

≈ HIGH GORGES

Roger Turnes arrived in Cuzco the next morning, Monday, July 15. Our small expeditionary force was now in place. Though we were undermanned, the great river, Ccapac Mayu, lured us onward. We would give it our best effort.

Roger was a skilled kayaker and had accompanied me on a number of first descents of North American rivers, including the South Fork of the Salmon River and Big Creek, in Idaho. He was a powerfully built man of medium height. Roger always exuded good cheer, no matter how tough the problem we faced. He was easygoing, generally content to have others set goals and make trip decisions. Once he had a goal in mind, he held on to it tenaciously.

We spent the day preparing for our trip. We bought groceries, made last-minute arrangements with our driver, and sorted through our gear one final time to reduce its bulk. We had chosen high-volume kayaks—based on the Lettmann Mark IV line—with enough space to hold our gear. Most of the gear could be packed into two large waterproof vinyl bags, the larger one (the stern bag) forced under the rear deck and the smaller one (the bow bag) secured beneath the foredeck, in front of the paddler's feet. A few smaller bags and containers would be stuffed behind the seat.

Despite our adequate storage space, we had to cut weight ruthlessly to keep our boats maneuverable and portageable. We reduced first-aid supplies, clothing, and camp gear as far as we dared. We felt we must carry along a small amount of mountain-climbing gear, in case we encountered an unnavigable gorge. I wished we could bring more, because our five pitons, two carabiners, 100 feet of 3/16-inch rope, and various cords seemed no match for the harsh reputation of the Apurímac Canyon. But to cover every contingency would have required a burden we did not have space for, could not carry, and could not navigate with.

At 7:30 the next morning we left, our kayaks strapped on top of a taxi. Saying good-bye to my family was the hardest thing I had ever done. Visions of the awesome canyon had returned, sweeping away the comforting solace of the short, tranquil stretch viewed two days earlier. I once again doubted the sanity of my plans. However, I shared my doubts with no one. Outwardly, it was just another river trip.

We followed the road along the Vilcanota River, through broad valleys. This dusty byway was traveled mostly on foot—by families of Indians and their livestock. From the pueblo of Combapata, we climbed above the Río Vilcanota, out of the valley, to the treeless and windy tablelands above. Human habitation dotted even this inhospitable land and broke its sullen monotony. Herders tended their llama flocks in the rolling hills between pueblos. Even as our road climbed toward 14,000 feet, the Indians still clung to the desolate landscape.

A few hours later we arrived at Yauri, near the headwaters of the Apurímac. The streets were full of people, some in colorful costume; a fiesta was in progress. We checked in with the chief of police, to whom I had a letter of introduction from Carlos Zegarra. A small crowd gathered around. "How is the river?" I asked.

The joviality of the fiesta evaporated with my question. We were told in dark tones, "The river is not navigable. It is dangerous." The words "muchas piedras" (many rocks) were muttered several times.

It was easy to communicate with the inhabitants of Yauri. Almost everyone was approachable and spoke Spanish. As we moved into the hills, farther away from the main villages, Spanish would be replaced by Quechua. Communication would become much more difficult. Quechua is the language handed down by the Incas. It is the sole language spoken by most of the Quechua Indians in the backcountry of southern Peru, who consider themselves descendants of the Incas.

Having obtained all the information we could in Yauri, we moved on, up the broad valley toward higher elevations. A maze of unmarked roads criss-crossed the land. We proceeded, half-lost, never knowing when we would be turned back. The road was very bad, with many washouts and giant ruts that nearly stopped us.

Some time later we approached a small pueblo by the river. We photographed the llamas and the shy little girls. The Apurímac was already, unexpectedly, embedded in a gorge here in the highlands. It was very narrow but perhaps only 40 feet deep. It was an anomalous slice into black rock, breaking the endless monotony of the cold, dull plain.

Because it was late, we moved on to seek a suitable camp. We stopped at a place where the river emerged from its somber black gorge to splash and play across the pampa. We chose a campsite beyond a shallow embankment, a small distance away from the road, now so busy with the feet of Indians, llamas, dogs, and burros. A few bicyclers pedaled by, their wheeled vehicles seeming out of place on the ancient plain.

We began to unload in the failing light. The descending cold, the unbroken wind, and the dull brown treeless landscape were unbearably depressing. I wished that I had never planned this bizarre adventure, and it depressed me enormously to think of the car leaving us. Soon it would pass over a low hill, disappear, and we could not recall it. We would be surrounded by many but would know no one. The world we were accustomed to would become distant and unreachable the moment the car passed from view. I almost asked the driver to wait, to let us load again and leave this sad land. But I knew that plans gone this far must, by the strange nature of human compulsions, be pursued to the next level.

We thus found ourselves deposited with our gear on the cold plain in darkness. Our first concern was with fire. We then learned the terrible difficulty of trying to build and maintain a fire with dry pampa grass in the incessant wind. Our tiny smoldering grass fire needed constant attention, a circumstance that would certainly eat into our short days, which lasted only twelve hours here near the equator. We had brought very little fuel, in order to save weight; the price we would pay would be the precious time spent nursing our grass fires to life. We felt compelled to boil all of our drinking and cooking water before consumption, because illness had to be avoided at all costs.

After a warm dinner, we crawled into our sleeping bags to protect us from the frigid night air. The moonless dark and the penetrating cold deepened the black images of impassable canyons. I wished that my children were old enough not to need me anymore. My mind wandered to other remote places and other river adventures. I thought about the cold night that Roger, Jim Byrne, J. Dewell, and I were caught without food or gear in the Black Box of the San Rafael River, in Utah's great desert wilderness. I mentally reviewed the exhilarating run down Cross Mountain Canyon of the Yampa River, in our first descent of this classic western canyon. I thought about the big uncertain drops encountered on the Salmon South Fork and the first halting approach to nearby Big Creek Gorge, which ultimately gave us the most enjoyable whitewater in memory. I thought about the fast schuss with Les Jones down the upper Teton River, dropping 100 feet per mile, with a right arm still weak and unstable from my dislocation; the ice-cold morning on the nearby Falls River with fingers frozen, our lookout for the falls impeded by cold vapor condensing to thick fog in colder air; and the almost ancient memories of bashing down Wisconsin's Wolf River in an open canoe, none of us experienced enough to belong there.

I thought about these and many other adventures, all approached with anticipation. But this trip was different. This was more remote, it was in an absolutely bizarre and unknown land, the size of our party was pitifully small. And I was a father. But then I began to reason with myself. This was, in fact, just another river, with eddies, rocks, waves, and holes like the other rivers I had known and navigated. I listened, and I could hear the river less than 30 yards away, sounding unbelievably tranquil and calm. I went to sleep, suddenly contented and at peace with myself and the river.

W e were up at 6 A.M. the next day, Wednesday, July 17. This was to be the first day of our journey on the river. A feeble sun broke over low hills at 6:30. The air was 10 degrees Fahrenheit and the water 34 degrees, promising a cold run. The altimeter, with which we had hoped to trace our progress, was not working. From map sources, we knew that we were within 100 feet of the 13,000-foot level. To the best of our knowledge, we were the first to undertake a kayak journey on a whitewater river at such a high elevation.

The little road by our camp was used constantly by the Indians that morning, trekking upriver to pasture in the hills with herds of llamas and burros. This country looked badly overgrazed, utterly without green forage, and was dominated by the spiny defiant pampa grass, also called *ichu* grass. There was no wood here, so we lit some of the dry grass. The fire was hard to keep going. Finally, Roger dug out a small tin can filled with paraffin and cardboard, ignited it, and we enjoyed a trouble-free fire, while watching our only fuel disappear. We boiled water from the river for half an hour, then made tea and cereal—very tasty, and the world looked brighter. We were anxious to get out of this desolate land and to reach lower elevations where it was warmer; where we would see trees, smell flowers, and hear the buzzing of insects again.

Organizing and loading our gear was the first order of business. It was critical to distribute the gear properly among the waterproof bags. For one thing, we had to carefully balance our loads to keep our boats maximally responsive. Items like canteens, lunches, cameras, and film had to be accessible. At the same time, we had to distribute food and gear so that the accidental loss of one waterproof bag would leave enough in the other to permit our survival. Because of these complications, we departed late, at 11:30. This was unfortunate, since the day would shut down again promptly at 6:00.

An Indian arrived at the river to see us off. I took his picture straddling the back of Roger's boat. Roger enjoyed the camaraderie. He was always cheerful, yet had great strength when needed. He could survive this tough land if anybody could.

We launched from a pebbly beach and followed the river's meandering course through the pampa for two hours before lunch, paddling hard to regain time. There were many small, shallow drops, and our heavily loaded boats sometimes dragged over rocks. We saw several flocks of beautiful pink flamingoes, and a few ducks and cranes passed back and forth. Llamas grazed on the riverbank and in the nearby hills.

A herdswoman on a hillside half a mile downstream saw us coming and fled up the hill in panic and out of view. The same thing happened again. We realized that we must look strange to the Indians, dressed in our alien helmets, life jackets, and wet suits, but we still wondered at the deep and terrifying insecurity that would make the hill women panic at the distant sight of us.

After lunch we paddled another half hour in the pampa, then entered the first *quebrada* (gorge). This was narrow and deep, with walls rising straight out of the water in many places. It reminded me of Westwater Canyon on the Colorado, except that here the river was smaller. Some nice short drops developed. These mainly occurred where the walls were broken down, usually where a side gully entered. We were encouraged about our prospects below, for all the rapids so far encountered could be run easily or portaged if necessary.

We passed beneath a bridge, the scenic Puente de Santo Domingo, at 3:30. The bridge consisted of beautiful colonial rockwork spanning the narrows. Then we passed through more of this scenic gorge and its nice drops. We portaged one rapid because the rocks formed a twisting channel that our overloaded boats might fail to negotiate; our kayaks could not be risked without good reason. They were tough boats, made of high-strength S glass and epoxy, but with such loads they were constantly threatened.

We camped at 5:00 on a small, mossy tableland, 50 feet above the river. Again a fire was hard to build and maintain. Pampa grass supplemented by livestock droppings and endless coaxing finally brought our water to a boil, and we feasted on soup and dehydrated dinners. We secured our gear and entered the tent at 7:30 on this first evening. We had probably covered 15–20 miles, with a total drop in elevation of perhaps 200–400 feet.

Our first day had been successful. I hoped it would work out as well tomorrow. And now to sleep, for the candle was disappearing, and we needed to conserve our precious light.

We were up at 5:45 on Thursday morning, July 18. The temperature was a little higher, almost 20 degrees. The sun came up over a hill to the northeast at 7:00, breaking the stranglehold of the cold night and brightening our outlook. The sun was also needed to melt off the heavy deposit of frost on our tent and gear before we could pack up.

The tribulation of fire and the joy of breakfast were repeated. An old Indian emerged from a gully downstream and stopped at our camp. His eyes were clouded, and I imagined that he must have been blind, except that he seemed sure of his direction. His behavior was erratic and nervous. I thought he was deeply affected by chewing coca leaves, a staple of these windswept hills that numbs pain, fatigue, and cold. He knew a few words of Spanish, and I tried to ask some questions while taking his picture. He mumbled something incoherent, and we learned nothing. He then wandered off without warning, toward what objective we would never know. The low hills swallowed him up, an enigmatic figure etched deeply in our consciousness. But in reality this was his land, his home, and we were the enigmas, badly out of place, unadapted, uncomfortable in this harsh land.

The encounter with the old man had been remarkable, for most Indians, except near the villages, had resolutely avoided us. The men did not flee like the women, but they stayed clear, keeping a 100-yard buffer of bleak terrain between them and us. On a few occasions we had seen them watching us from some high ridge. They were silent sentinels, mysterious and aloof. Their behavior contributed to our feeling of isolation and remoteness.

We started down the river at 9:30, again surrounded by colorless hills. At 10:00 the canyon narrowed and another gorge took form. We soon came upon a difficult rapid, rocky and turbulent above, flushing through a strong reversal below. A ledge on the left accommodated our scouting and our photography. We navigated the rapid without mishap, but were thoroughly drenched by the cold, spouting water. We passed on, each moment more confident. We then approached a long rapid, amply wide at the top, which gradually narrowed to 20 feet in width. At its bottom, the entire river funneled abruptly into a thread-like channel between rock walls. From the top of the rapid, the channel below looked almost too narrow to allow passage of our kayaks. As I hovered near the lip of the rapid, I could see that the narrow passage below lacked strong turbulence, although the currents at its entrance were uncertain. Thinking that we could stop in some small eddy if we were misled by this strange formation, we entered the rapid. The cascading ended in a deep pool, and we saw now that the water entering the channel was fast but smooth. Hopeful but still uncertain, we aimed our boats toward the channel and maneuvered into its mouth. This place was incredible! A mere 4 feet wide, this crevice in the ancient rocks was accommodating the entire river in calm, unagitated flow! Elementary fluid mechanics told us that the product of the average velocity of flow and the cross section through which the river passes is constant: the same here beneath our boats as up- or downstream. The gentle flow meant that a large cross section, some gigantic deep channel, must be conducting the water underneath. Amazed by this natural wonder, but without time to linger and enjoy it, we paddled on.

The narrow crevice appeared to be a precursor of things to come, for the gorge was becoming narrower and more persistent.

Just past 11:00 we approached a large drop in the river. As the gorge was now narrow and confined, we couldn't see it all. There was a broken wall on the left, suitable for landing. We scrambled to a lookout and beheld the water below splitting over a rocky wedge thrust upward from the river bottom. The current divided, crashed into the wall, rebounded, narrowed, then dove violently off the toe of the wedge into a small pool. The violent twisting of the rapid made it too difficult for safe navigation. Here, however, things were different than above. The walls confining the rapid were solid and steep. No portage route was apparent. The water crashed past us as the grimness of our predicament gradually sank in. We had become trapped in the gorge! The "Great Speaker" was beginning to show its domination of this land.

Our first objective was a more thorough search of our surroundings. We climbed up the broken wall and reached an overlook. The narrow river disappeared around a bend, bound in by vertical walls. We could see this awesome gorge extending into the distance, and we had no way of knowing where it ended. The makers of our maps knew nothing of it either, for there was no indication of its existence—no markings that revealed its formidable vertical walls—on these worthless sheets of geographic scratchings. We decided to call it the Gorge of Pichigua, after a local name. (*See* Plate 1)

Halfway up the broken wall, a ledge extended down the canyon. We followed it, and found that it widened and carried us past the rapid. Then the ledge ended abruptly, 30 vertical feet above the river. We peered down and saw some sloping ledges below, ending in a churning pool of water. To attempt this route would entail, first of all, lowering ourselves and our boats to the unstable ledges, and then arranging our boats, bodies, and gear with the constant threat of something vital slipping off into the river. Finally, we would have to launch into that turbulent pool from the narrow sloping toe of the ledge, the back of our boats clinging by friction, hopefully, to the rock. The front of the boat would be bobbing up and down in the tumultuous water, threatening to break the boat free. It was a terribly grim prospect. If we failed, if we so much as dislodged a paddle into the water, or if we slipped off the sloping ledge before fixing the spray covers onto our kayaks, we would face the loss of our gear, a probable swim in that cold gorge for an uncertain distance, and a cold night that, unprotected, we might not be able to endure. If we succeeded, what further problems would we find below?

The alternative to this portage was equally grim. We could climb out of the gorge past the broken wall, and out of the canyon above. But where would we go? We could see no place below to reenter the river. We would have to trek blindly down the serrated canyon rim with our heavy burden of loaded boats, hoping that eventually we would find access to the river again, hoping that no impassable side canyon would block us. We could also strike out for the main road, abandoning our boats. But the river had cut a solid wall in that direction, decisively blocking such a plan. Our only egress was toward a great barren roadless area to the west.

Facing the terrible dilemma was agonizing. We searched the cliffs, the horizon, and our minds for a better choice, but discovered none. Roger wanted to try the portage. At first I rejected the idea as too risky. But the more I thought about the grueling alternative, the better I liked the portage. A choice, almost, of necessity.

We dug out the thin nylon rope that was stashed away in our gear for such emergencies and moved our equipment to the end of the ledge. I lowered Roger over the rim, down to the sloping ledges below, then passed the boats and gear down to him, secured at the end of the rope. I clambered down last, Roger supporting me from below.

Who would go first? The first one to launch would confront the full uncertainty of the venture, but the last to launch would have to work alone, with no possibility for obtaining help should it be needed. Roger offered to go last. I agreed under one condition: that he would not attempt to secure or stabilize my boat from behind as I entered, so that my launching would test the feasibility of his own.

I edged down the sloping shelf beside my boat, as far forward as I could go. I extended my right foot in front of me, up over the back edge of the cockpit, onto the floor of the boat. None of my weight was applied to the boat yet. I lowered my center of gravity by dropping my weight back onto my left arm, supported on the ledge behind. I put my left foot into the cockpit, now accompanied by some inevitable weight. The boat rocked on the sloping shelf but did not slide off. Now I faced the most delicate maneuver: getting my full weight into the narrow cockpit. I pushed forward off my extended left arm, pushing my body

≈ Roger Turnes cautiously enters his kayak on an unstable ledge after a hazardous portage that involved roping down the cliffs above him. The boats had to be lowered to the ledge on ropes.

forward, up and over the deck. My center of gravity was at its highest, but I slid in quickly to make that moment of instability as brief as possible. Success! I was seated, and despite my added weight, the back of the boat still clung firmly to the ledge.

Now, to the next urgent problem. The bow of the boat was bobbing from the surges of turbulent water, and I had to affix the spray cover quickly before the boat rocked loose or capsized from the incessant agitation of the currents. I worked frantically. The boat remained attached to its fragile anchor long enough, and I completed the task.

The final problem was a wall directly in front of me. The strong current ran directly into the wall, from right to left, and I had time for only a few hard strokes on the left to pull clear. I wished the kayak had been facing upstream, but entering the boat in that orientation would have been impossible. With nothing more to delay me, nothing to gain by waiting, I pushed off my weak frictional anchor, leaned heavily left, and pulled hard on the left blade, out into the current. I cleared the wall by a few scant feet and paddled across to an eddy on the other side of the gorge. Here I parked in the stilled water and turned to watch Roger as he attempted to repeat the process. He followed each agonizing step, and finally he too was successful. He joined me in the eddy. We were exuberant in our victory!

Our exhilaration was short-lived, as we again faced reality. Two hours had elapsed, and we had gained only 50 yards. We surged on, into the depths of the gorge.

A few blocks downstream we found that the river disappeared to the right. We landed on sloping ledges to get a better look. The rapid immediately below us was simple enough, but 30 or 40 yards ahead, we saw the river drop onto a giant rock in mid-channel. It rebounded to the right, then disappeared from view! It obviously struck the wall of the gorge, for we could see the frothy tailwater emerge below. But we could not see where water and wall collided. We didn't know what obstruction might lie in this turbulent interface, and worse, we had no way of finding out. Perhaps, just possibly, this rapid was runnable, but how many more would there be? Our prospects and our optimism sank to new depths.

Again, agonizing choices. We could blindly run the rapid, hoping that it was not impossible, hoping that the drops below were not impossible either. Was there any way around? We could not portage, but we saw prospects for a frigid "half-portage." Starting just above the blind rapid, a ledge on the left-hand wall passed down beyond the turbulence, then ended abruptly, 8 feet above the water. We thought it would be possible to carry our boats along the ledge, past the rapid. We would then tie off our cockpits in order to seal out the water, drop the boats in the river, jump in after them, and swim them to a landing spot where we could reenter. We had done this maneuver to skirt a waterfall on the San Rafael in Utah, but there the water was warm and the landing in view.

With either choice we had to confront the question, what then? This canyon seemed to be getting more difficult, and we needed, more than anything else, to find out what was below. We must try to climb out of these somber depths, up to the canyon rim, so that we could determine once and for all whether there was any hope of getting through this relentless gorge.

25 ≈

Climbing out on the right, above the ledges on which we stood, would be best. I tried this and got part way up, but the handholds were sloping and the rock was crumbly. I then directed my attention to the other side of the river, although this did not promise to be simple either. I had to ferry across, just above the lip of the upper rapid, and disembark on steep rocks. I was able to do this, but was getting tired. I still had to wrestle my loaded boat up the almost vertical wall, onto a sloping shelf where I could anchor it. Roger could not help, because the landing was too small to accommodate two people. This arduous task drained my energy, already depleted from a trying day. I rested a few minutes, felt better, then began scrambling up the broken wall of the gorge. Even after leaving the gorge the canyon was very steep. However, there was nothing dangerous about it, and I trudged upward, now alone with the cold wind, the sweeping slopes, and endless miles of dry pampa grass.

As I went higher, more of the gorge revealed itself. First I saw two major rapids downstream, which I estimated to be difficult but not impossible. The gorge then disappeared to the right. Finally, as I reached the canyon rim, I saw the river emerging in the distance between gentle, rolling hills. The terrible confinement of the gorge was broken! A side canyon entered from the right, and at that distant spot a white sandbar glistened in the afternoon sun. Never had I seen a pile of sand with such heavenly appeal; it was truly a vision of Camelot. But could we make it that far before nightfall?

I could see most of the river now, but I could not see a stretch beyond the right bend. That segment, like the blind rapid below, would remain obscure until the irreversible moment when we must commit ourselves to its passage.

When I returned, Roger was rested and anxious to start. He wanted to run the rapid directly. We reasoned that barring some unusual, hidden trap in the blind rapid, at the very worst we would end up swimming. If we did the half-portage along that left ledge, we would be forced to swim in the cold water as a matter of necessity. We would try the rapid; with luck, there would be no swimming at all.

We paddled through the first minor rapid. We were committed! There was no way to return from this point. Roger swung to the left wall, stepped out of his boat momentarily to get the best possible view of the rapid, then plunged forward. His boat dropped toward the midstream rock, twisted violently right, then disappeared. After seconds that seemed like years, he drifted out below, a broad grin on his face. I followed. Events transpired so fast that there was barely time to respond to them. The falling, twisting current dictated the course of action: straight over a substantial drop, an abrupt turbulent thrust to the right toward the cliff, then a crashing rebound directing water and boat back downstream. A quick drawstroke on the left to avoid a jutting section of the wall brought me out into the pool below. We laughed. We laughed because of the broken tension. We laughed at the strange canyons, the thrilling rapid, our bizarre day.

The day was not over, although it was getting late, past 4 P.M. We must hurry. We paddled on, toward the large rapids that I had spotted earlier. The first was simply a big drop, clear on the right. At the bottom was a large hydraulic hole, then the current pounded into the right-hand wall. I led this time, inasmuch as I had glimpsed the rapid from above. I found a perfect course, was buried momentarily in the hole, then drew quickly away from the right wall. Roger was a little off to the side, dropped over an enormous rock, and was capsized by the frothy hole. He rolled up immediately and drew successfully away from collision with the wall.

The next large rapid was wider and very rocky. We could scout this one from the side, but it didn't help much. There was no good path through. Roger chose one route, and I chose another. Neither route was very successful as we ground down over the rocks. But they were successful enough, since we were still upright at the end, and we hurried on. One more substantial drop, a few smaller rapids, then that ominous right bend around which I could not see.

Would the "Great Speaker" spare us, or would it, so near the end, in a dramatic display of domination, arrange some impassable blockade to end our silly, mortal voyage? We rounded the bend cautiously, hopefully. We glimpsed rapids ahead, but as our view crystallized, they took on a gentle, friendly demeanor. There were no more great barriers! That beautiful, forgiving river—we loved her!

The good news was very timely, for it was late and we were getting cold. Roger, in particular, was chilled from his immersion. We paddled through the few small rapids, and the canyon gradually widened. An old, weathered suspension bridge loomed high above the river, passing from one wall of the gorge to the other. It was a footbridge, but its loose boards and gaping cracks made us wonder how anyone dared walk across. I remarked to Roger that I would rather swim the gorge than walk across that creaking, sagging bridge!

Soon we reached the sandbar that had attracted me so magnetically that afternoon. The sun was just going down, and we hastened to establish camp. The usual problems with fire were compounded by descending darkness. Roger was chilled, and I had a badly irritated eye— perhaps from a piece of grit.

There were footprints on our sandbar. They led to one end where, beneath a cliff, sand had been dug out and later replaced. "It looks like a grave to me," suggested Roger. I shuddered in the gathering gloom of night, an involuntary shudder, for I realized how little I knew of the customs of these elusive highlanders; their beliefs, their burial sites, the ground they might hold sacred, upon which strangers should not tread, the possible punishment for infractions. Our sandy refuge—our Camelot—was tarnished by these dark thoughts.

We reviewed our broader predicament. We had made only about 6 miles today. Yet the maps suggested that these upper canyons of the Apurímac were far simpler to navigate than the lower canyons, which now lay ahead of us. The average gradient of the river was less steep here, and the canyons were far shallower. The maps did not show the awesome gorge that we stumbled on today. All our evidence suggested, then, that it was likely to become more dangerous and more grueling as we moved downstream.

Nothing outweighed the resupply complication in our minds. We had arranged to be met next Tuesday morning with fresh supplies, about 100 miles downstream. I wondered what dream world I was in when I made such plans! Up here, in this real world of short days, constant cold, and endless struggle with Apurímac meanness, our progress was only half of that projected—only half what I would expect on a North American river of similar size and gradient. It might get worse.

The bearer of our supplies, either our cab driver or another driver he designated, would wait for us a day or two, then would leave. We would surely miss him now and miss the vitally needed provisions. Without them our trip would come to a halt.

Perhaps, then, we should leave the river! Where and how? I could not locate our position precisely on these questionable maps, and we didn't know how far it might be to a road. Presumably there was a bridge somewhere ahead, but the maps disagreed.

I asked Roger, "What do you want to do?" He replied that he would do whatever I thought best. We would sleep on it and decide tomorrow.

We were up at 6:45 Friday morning after a sleepless third night on the river. The pain in my eye had become excruciating. Roger looked, but could see no irritant particle. We applied some ophthalmic ointment, and the eye began to feel better.

Today we must get our bearings! After breakfast I hiked high above our camp with maps, altimeter, and compass. I reached a good vantage point, but no landmarks could be found matching those on the maps. Nothing made sense. The compass was erratic and seemed to have joined the altimeter in failure.

The Indians were an incredible frustration as well. They must have known every square foot of this country, but we could not approach them. Some of them stared at us from distant ridge tops. Sometimes we heard them without seeing them, for they whistled loudly and beautifully as they walked the steep trails over these otherwise silent hills. They were like ghostly images from another world.

With this added failure to determine our location, I became convinced that we should leave this canyon at the first good opportunity. We could seek more information, perhaps in Lima, and still have ample time to come back here for more exploration. We hoped there was a bridge somewhere below. If we could find one, it would greatly simplify the task of getting back to civilization when we left the river.

We launched again, glad to leave this haunting sandbar, hoping to find clues of our whereabouts downstream. We resolved to be more careful, not to enter any gorge unless we could see some route which could be used for an emergency exit. Yesterday was close enough. We shuddered in the realization that with only a few small ledges and rocks in slightly different positions, it could have been a day of tragedy.

The canyon was getting deeper again, and the telltale fragments of rock wall that tended to grow and solidify into full gorge formation were beginning to appear. We moved forward cautiously as we entered a gorge of magnificent proportions and color. None of the dreaded, impassable rapids developed, and we settled down to enjoy ordinary rapids and extraordinary scenery.

Later we surprised two Indians fishing from shore. They were too astonished to flee. Finally we could hope for precious clues as to our surroundings. "How far to the next bridge?" I asked in Spanish.

"Three hundred kilometers."

I tried again, testing: "How far to the nearest school?"

"Three thousand kilometers." The test had clearly failed. The men probably knew very little Spanish. After a few more attempts to communicate, we moved on downriver.

The canyon broke down, and we entered another. This, too, was a beautiful gorge, free of problems. We emerged into rolling hills and immediately encountered a stupendous rapid. It was long, studded with rocks everywhere, and ended in a boat-breaking cascade. We began the tedious process of lining and portaging our boats around. It was hard work, but we were happy; after yesterday, we were glad to be able to choose such a straightforward portage, even if it involved strenuous work.

It was late, and we had to seek a campsite. We entered another gorge, but it was short. On the other end was a high gravel bar, narrow and rocky, but adequate for a camp at this late hour. The steep ground above our campsite had been cultivated, and some stubble from last year's crop remained. It was easier to burn than pampa grass, and we soon had a small, persistent, and wonderful fire.

High on a ridge we saw some buildings and corrals. Far-off human figures, made small as ants by the intervening distance, strolled to the end of the ridge, where they could keep us in surveillance. We were getting used to this now and paid no special attention. We went about our camp preparations. Then I looked up and saw a man standing on the bank immediately above our little gravel bar. His garb was not typical of that worn by the highland Indians. A button sweater and shirt replaced the ubiquitous poncho, and he was wearing heavy laced boots and a gray narrow-brim hat. "I am the owner of the hacienda up above," he told us in perfect Spanish, pointing to the ridge. His greeting was amicable, despite my sudden concern that we might be trespassing on his farmland.

We sought information from him. We learned that there was no

Apurímac bridge in this area. No matter; he was a schoolteacher and would arrange to have his students carry our boats to the nearest road tomorrow, which was a Saturday. We were to visit the hacienda in the morning to make final arrangements.

We finished our camp chores and food and turned in for the night. It had been a good day, and prospects for finding a way out were improving.

Rising early again the next morning, we finished breakfast, then started off for the hacienda. We left the tent standing so that the sun would strip off the frost. A half hour later we arrived amidst noisy greetings by dogs, cats, chickens, and kids. El Señor, the owner, welcomed us and showed us around. It was not a terribly prosperous place, having to face, I suppose, the stunted growth of crops and grass occasioned by these windy frost-covered hills. Only the Señor wore shoes. But the eight or ten people looked well fed; a small herd of dairy cows in the corral certainly provided them with needed protein. The buildings were small but well-thatched. And the vista was superb; one could look down on the Apurímac cutting ever deeper into Andean rock.

After a while we discussed the boats and negotiated a fee for the porters. Then abruptly El Señor told us: "It will be easier tomorrow."

"Why tomorrow?" The answer was not clear. But his mind was made up, our pleas were to no avail. We had seen before how mañana can follow mañana, and we did not feel confident that tomorrow would, in fact, be any better. Besides, we had mixed emotions about this; we would like to run all the river possible, despite the constant threat of impassable canyons. We decided to continue down the river for now. El Señor told us that a pueblo could be found in the hills above the river, if we proceeded through the next canyon. Perhaps we could hire porters there. "And the rapids?" we asked.

The expected answer: "Very bad." We gave the girls and women some small mirrors and were given a large wheel of cheese in return. We said "adios," and hurried back to camp. We had lost valuable time and did not leave until 11:30.

Within minutes, still in sight of the hacienda, we found a small falls in the river, and had to portage over giant boulders. We then entered a narrow canyon on placid water. Another abrupt drop, another difficult

31 ≈

portage, more calm water. Our afternoon passed in such repetitions, at a correspondingly slow pace. Roger, in exasperation, ran one of these drops, plunging over a chute and through a sieve of giant rocks. This one worked out okay. The biggest threat was that we might break our boats, despite their tough S glass construction.

Altogether we had to make five or six of these exhausting portages. If the violent drops could only have been spread out evenly over the long stretches of calm water between, the paddling would have been most enjoyable. It was not to be.

Later in the afternoon of this fourth day we encountered a massive, almost endless, boulder field. Enormous rocks, many as big as a house, had tumbled down from the hills to cover the valley and fill the river. It was incredible. We could barely climb from one to another. The river sank almost from view between the rocks, roaring around the bases of these monsters in a frenzied effort to get past. The river and the boulder field dropped around a right bend, still locked in rumbling battle. We had no way to know how long this travesty would last. An Indian youth sat high on the right bank, and we imagined he must be enjoying our predicament.

We began scouting for a passage down the left bank, making our way torturously from one giant rock to the next. We went perhaps 200 yards and stopped to rest, no end in sight. We then looked around and were startled to see the Indian youth racing down the hillside on which we had seen him peacefully resting a short while before. He was headed directly for our boats. No doubt he knew a pathway across the river, walking on top of those giant rocks. Our camera gear, our paddles, our boats and supplies, our passports and money, were all lying idly on the beach, perfect game for theft or mischief. What if he pushed the boats into the water? They would be pulverized on those monstrous rocks. We had been very careless; in the past we had usually left one person near the boats.

Although near exhaustion from our difficult day, we scrambled desperately toward the boats and the youth. Our outlook was grim, for the youth was nimbler than we, and totally acclimatized to these breath-taking elevations. We split up, Roger going straight toward the boats over the bigger rocks, while I headed right on a longer but hopefully smoother path. Each step became almost impossible, each breath an agony. We pushed ourselves absolutely to the limit of our endurance, knowing the grim consequences that might accompany too late an arrival. Finally, as I rounded a corner of boulders, by now even with the boats, I saw the youth trotting far up the river bank, not a care in the world! The whole scene was now obvious. This poor scared youth simply wanted to cross the river to the other side and felt too shy to do so while we were near. He waited and crossed after we had passed a safe distance beyond!

Words cannot express our sense of frustration. The rapid was not scouted, and we were exhausted and discouraged. Also we had begun to worry again about our whereabouts. We didn't want to pass the pueblo and plunge into those deep canyons without knowledge or supplies.

We developed an alternate stratagem. We would carry our boats to a high bench on the right side. From there we could see the river below. We could launch again, if feasible, shortcutting the right-hand bend of the big rapid. Or we could keep going up into the hills in a vague search for the pueblo and the highway.

The narrow gully leading out of the Apurímac gorge was steep and tiring. We arrived on the grassy benchland a half hour later and climbed a low hill to view the furious scene at our feet. The river plunged past rock after rock, downward 100 vertical feet, through a tortuous labyrinth a quarter of a mile long. The water was sieved through a few more scattered rapids, then disappeared around a bend.

Now we had to make our choice. The climb back down to the river looked difficult, beset with steep ledges. If we followed the path away from the river, the possible problems involved in getting to the nearest road and back to civilization were uncertain. Neither choice was very good.

Tired and discouraged, we decided to leave the river. It would crash and flow nearly 4,000 miles to the Atlantic, through great mountains, deep gorges, and green jungles. Countless tributaries would join it, and this raucous youth would become the Amazon, the greatest of all rivers.

For our part, we would test those cold, gray hills with our heavy loads. An aged woman at an hacienda told us that the trail we had found led to the pueblo. We trudged onward and upward until dark. We pitched camp beside the trail on a high pampa, amid scattered but now dormant fields. The wind blew ferociously through a pitch-black night. The tent shuddered and acted as if it was preparing to take flight. We were soon unable

≈   Roger Turnes in the back of a highland truck on the way to Sicuani and Cuzco.

to care, for the steady exertion had taken its toll. Besides, we felt that if these austere highlands intended harm, they would already have chosen the high Apurímac gorges to administer the judgment. We were beyond the river's grip now and could finally sleep in peace.

On Sunday morning we hired two men and a boy to help carry our boats to the pueblo. It was a long trek, lasting most of the day.

The little pueblo was in turmoil. The town doctor, apparently an alcoholic, was fighting off the ridicule of the villagers. Bickering and arguing went on into the evening. That night we were put up at the government post. On Monday morning we departed, with four durable barefoot "hombres" carrying our heavy boats. We reached the main road in the afternoon, caught a truck to Sicuani, and then took a cab to Cuzco. We arrived late Monday night, barely in time to intercept the car taking fresh supplies to our Apurímac rendezvous.

My plan to return to the Apurímac after gaining more information did not materialize. Roger felt compelled to return home, since his wife had been ill. I cannot say that I was bored in Cuzco; the city and its surroundings were too marvelous for that. I had time to pursue some environmental studies that I had come here to make and to improve my Spanish. But staying in Cuzco several more weeks, before my appointment in Lima, was a frustration. The worst was that I had two boats and some of the world's great rivers nearby, but no one to explore them with.

Months later in Lima, now city-weary, I recaptured a glimmer of Apurímac madness. I began searching for more information. At Peru's central mapping institute, I painstakingly pieced together a broken quiltwork of aerial photographs of the Apurímac valley. Some major links were missing, and crucial details were obscured by distance, oblique viewing angles, and intervening gorge walls. But before me, for the first time, was an overall view of the Apurímac canyon system.

Amazingly I saw few repetitions of the narrow gorge that had trapped us in the highlands. The deepest gorges lay in the canyons below Cunyac, where the explorer Perrin had briefly ventured. But scattered up and down the river were flecks and streaks of solid white, which could only mean enormous rapids. I concluded that the canyon was lashed by unrunnable cataracts that would force us into back-breaking portages, perhaps over entire mountains. Despite the problems, however, I was convinced it could be done.

R ivers are a constant lure to distant adventure. . . . We
left all . . . behind us and entered nature with one stroke
of the paddle.

Henry David Thoreau

O f the gladdest moments in human life, methinks, is the
departure upon a distant journey into unknown lands.
Shaking off with one mighty effort the fetters of Habit,
the leaden weight of Routine, the cloak of many Cares,
and the slavery of Home, man feels once more happy.
The blood flows with the fast circulation of childhood.
Excitement lends unwonted vigour to the muscle, and
the sudden sense of freedom adds a cubit to the mental
stature. Afresh dawns the morn of life; again the bright
world is beautiful to the eye, and the glorious face of
nature gladdens the soul. A journey, in fact, appeals to
Imagination, to Memory, to Hope—the sister Graces of
our mortal being.

Richard Burton

≈ BACK TO THE APURÍMAC

Back in the states in the spring of 1975, I started organizing Apurímac Expedition II. I decided that this expedition would start at the pueblo of Pillpinto, at an elevation of about 9,300 feet and about 70 miles below the point we exited the river in 1974. I worked out prudent procedures in writing, to which every expedition member would agree, by signature, in advance (see appendix 4). This way, I thought, the ground rules would be clear at the beginning and misunderstandings less likely. "This will be a cooperative venture, a team effort," I wrote. "We will aid one another in all long portages." And "If someone hangs up on rocks, it is everyone's concern to get him off." I emphasized safety, particularly after our close call in the highlands: "We will enter *no* gorge without positive knowledge that an exit of some kind exists. . . . We will portage difficult rapids if there is any question about safety."

Safety takes time, and I worked out a timetable generous enough to allow for safe on-river procedures, photography, and shoreline exploration. Two weeks were allowed for the first section, above the resupply point at the Cunyac Bridge. Four weeks were allowed below Cunyac; three weeks for the difficult section where the river plows through the Vilcabamba Range, and one week for the jungle canyons below.

My pressing task now was to find the right people—people with abundant skills and strengths, especially in the areas of cooperation, teamwork, tolerance, level-headedness, and care against recklessness. I approached first some longtime Utah friends, including Roger, but expense and other obligations ruled them out. Another obvious choice was Jim Sindelar, with whom I had worked as an officer of the American Whitewater Affiliation; he had served for many years as executive director. Jim enthusiastically came west from Concord, New Hampshire, to run a shakedown cruise on the Salmon River in the early summer of 1975; with him came Gerry Plummer.

Jim was an engineering technology professor at New Hampshire Technical Institute. A man of medium height, he was a powerful boater and a strong and competent outdoorsman. What he lacked in expeditionary experience he more than made up for with his numerous strengths: a logical mind, practicality, ingenuity, and integrity, combined with an inner calm overlaid with gritty determination. Most importantly of all, he was a warm and considerate human being, helpful and caring to those around him.

His friend Gerry was a bearded dynamo of energy. He moved and talked rapidly, as if constantly needing to unload excess enthusiasm. He had been a piano accompanist for the chorus of the Boston Symphony Orchestra until he decided to abandon the grind and enjoy music and mountains in Colorado. He later went into telecommunications.

I invited three other men to take part in the expedition. I had met Chuck Carpenter years before and had mentioned Peru to him then. He was intensely interested in Latin America and was a skilled boater—he had served as a professional river guide in the Grand Canyon. Chuck was tall and tough, with a wry sense of humor, a rigorous sense of independence, and the ability to spend time by himself, engrossed with nature. I had known Dee Crouch, a Coloradan, for years, but had considered him too impulsive for this undertaking, where we would emphasize safety and conservative boating. I called him to get his recommendation for someone with medical expertise, sensed his great interest in the expedition, and ended up asking him to join us. Then Dee introduced me to Steve Pomerance, also from Colorado. Steve knew Spanish and was, according to Dee, a strong boater and an experienced mountaineer.

Others were interested, but they were forced by circumstances to back out, leaving the six of us. Our small team abounded in crucial skills: whitewater kayaking, mountaineering, survival, first aid, field repairs, conversational Spanish, and general outdoor and expeditionary experience. So we began the business of assembling our supplies and gear.

Back to the Apurímac again. Back to charging water and narrow canyons in a land ruptured by great mountains and sprinkled with the broken ruins of Inca civilization.

I bade yet another farewell to my family and staggered into the airport with great piles of gear. Soon I was airborne for Los Angeles, where

I would catch a flight to Lima. Our boats and supplies were tucked deep in the belly of the big jet aircraft; if anything had been forgotten, it was too late now. But it felt good to know that nothing more could be done; to lean back and relax and catch up on sleep lost over months of dogged preparations.

Chuck Carpenter joined me in Los Angeles. He had left the Alaska pipeline a few days before, to return to southern California for his final preparations. We would meet the others in Peru in two days, on Saturday, August 30. We winged across the equator in the darkness of night. We circled Lima, 12 degrees south latitude, as the first rays of sun speared across the dry coastal hills. Then we plunged down into overcast skies.

T he first challenge was clearing customs. Our burden of strange gear and 13-foot-long boats would certainly draw attention. Customs officials are always unpredictable, but here they are additionally sensitive to large piles of unusual paraphernalia, because they think that every traveler is trying to circumvent steep Peruvian import taxes.

"Where are you going with these boats?" the official asked us.

"To Cuzco, to run the Apurímac River," I replied and produced letters to verify our intent.

"We are mountaineers," Chuck added, feeling that identifying with that somewhat more common group would help pigeonhole us in the official's mind. The official scratched his head, perhaps trying to figure out how we would get to a mountain top with four-meter boats. He looked puzzled, but since he evidently couldn't think of any harm that we might do his country, he let us through.

Next we went over to the air cargo office of Faucett Airlines, to air freight our kayaks to Cuzco.

"It can't be done; they won't fit in," we were told firmly by an officious looking clerk.

"But I did it last year," I retorted in disgust. Then I asked, "Have your planes shrunk?" Long consultations, a shuffling of paper, and finally our boats were tagged for Cuzco, once again our Apurímac headquarters.

We sped toward downtown Lima, a long list of arrangements to finalize in the short two days before we ourselves would depart for the ancient Inca capital. Many of the friends I had made in Lima the year before were ready and willing to help us: Doctor Antonio Luque, Marcia Koth de Paredes of the Fulbright Commission, and the wonderful Merino sisters, Marta and Liliana.

A chain of communications was set up in case some emergency arose in those canyons. We talked to Rebeca Menacho, a representative for Faucett, who would request that Faucett flights over the Apurímac monitor the frequency of our emergency transmitter. Leon Miles Johnson, of the American Embassy, agreed to relay any emergency signal on to other agencies and to our families.

"Not too much could be done in an emergency," I told him. "Many of the canyons are too sheer even for helicopter rescue."

"Don't worry," he replied, "there aren't any helicopters in the area anyway. Even out in the jungle, the American helicopters once used for oil exploration are mostly gone now."

We discussed the possibility of Peruvian military aid in case of disaster, but of course they would not be responsible for us. It was clear that if some tragedy should overtake us, we would have to count on our own resources. The likelihood of any other help would be extremely remote.

And we sought more information. Although I had researched the Apurímac extensively the year before, so little is catalogued about this corner of the world that I felt compulsive about following every lead, hoping to unearth some new nugget of knowledge, perhaps some fleeting reference to an unknown twist in the canyon or an impassable gorge that might, in the end, decide our fate. We visited the Geographical Society office and library and the Instituto Geográfico Militar, in addition to several wilderness guides and tour operators, but no new information surfaced. That night, however, in a Lima newspaper, I found a wisp of information that totally confused us and cast a dark shadow over our hopes for a successful expedition.

The Apurímac River was the subject of a short editorial wired from Cuzco. Flooding on the Apurímac had evidently caused landslides around Colcha, and the whole town was to be moved to another site. But Colcha was only a few miles down the canyon from our starting point! What kind of strange deluge could be coursing down the river now, still in the dry season? But, wait, when did the flooding occur? In the last rainy season, or yesterday? The words of the editorial closed without offering any clarification.

The most fundamental premise of this expedition was that the river would be attacked at a stage of low water. I had read about the river's great floods, gushing madly out of the water-soaked highlands in the rainy season. Back in 1909, in the month of February, when the whole countryside was under siege by pelting rain, Hiram Bingham had crossed the Apurímac on a fragile bridge below Choquequirao (see chapter 11). He was awestruck by the river: "We . . . stood in complete amazement at the sight of its tumultuous rapids, two hundred fifty feet across, tearing through the canyon at a fearful pace, throwing up great waves like the ocean in a north-east storm. An incredible mass of water was dashing past us at a dizzy speed. We learned that the river had risen more than fifty feet on account of the heavy rains." It was clear that the Apurímac was not to be trifled with in periods of torrential flood.

The fact is, we didn't even care to challenge the Apurímac on a receding flood. For a river as big and formidable as this, racing through narrow, unknown gorges, even intermediate levels of water are too high for safe exploration. One simply loses control of one's destiny. Racing currents outstrip paddling velocity, and trajectories are increasingly fixed by the river. Rapids become longer and the calm intervals shorter and more hurried. River crossings take longer, and working to shore is more difficult. Hazards are better concealed by the big waves. Threads of shoreline that might serve as conduits for portage disappear. Accidents, should they occur, become potential disasters, because no one can help in the midst of great turbulence. And the slow, tedious process of reaching a more distant shoreline may be fraught with the additional hazards of not making it in time above an approaching cataract or gorge.

My long-standing goal was to attempt navigation at the lowest possible water level, and I had scheduled the trip near the end of the dry season to realize this goal. But I knew that Andean weather is among the most unpredictable anywhere. Almost exactly a year before, I had seen snow and rain engulf the entire highland region around Cuzco, and the first snow in decades carpeted Cuzco streets.

Now we had to face the terrible dilemma posed by this editorial. Frantic phone calls were made, but no one seemed to know if the

Apurímac was flooding. The weather around Cuzco appeared to be normal, but the most remote basins of the Apurímac were beyond the reach of our surveillance. Our investment in the expedition was now extraordinary, and a major part of it, the costly flight to Peru, had already been made. The other expedition members would be starting the long flight across the ocean to join us within twelve hours. "Should I try to wire them and save them the expense of a useless round-trip ticket?" I asked Chuck. "But then, if it actually isn't flooding, it will completely mess up our plans, and that, too, will be costly."

Chuck and I pondered the question and finally decided, in view of the normal weather pattern around Cuzco, that we would risk continuing the expedition.

As if the excitement of the reported flood was not enough, we also experienced a revolution. Thursday night in the central square, on the old stone steps of the Plaza de San Martín, I saw a large crowd surrounding a fiery protest speaker. Strange, I thought, because such a level of overt outspokenness is discouraged and even suppressed. Then, passing that way an hour later, we saw troops of police rounding up bystanders, beating them about the heads and bodies with billy clubs, and loading them in stake-bed trucks.

The next morning, a new president was announced. General Francisco Morales Bermúdez would replace General Juan Velasco, one of the most enduring and anomalous heads of state in all of South America. A military rightist turned military leftist, Velasco had championed the cause of the lowly *campesinos* (field-workers) and had launched a vitriolic campaign against the United States and all that it stood for. He had gone so far as to oust even the Peace Corps the year before. He was thought to be powerful, decisive, invincible . . . but suddenly here was a new military officer at the top.

Although General Morales had belonged to the inner council of generals, no one knew his intentions, and the people of Lima were understandably nervous. Many shops were closed and shuttered. Tanks were expected in the streets. There were hints that the airport might close. The static tension, the pervasive feeling of blank helplessness and withdrawal, were outside my experience. But the new president ended up with all the cards; there was no challenge from Velasco. The anxiety evaporated.

Later that night, we drove to the airport to meet the others with whom we would share this perhaps questionable expedition. Looking through the chain-link fence into the poorly lit cargo area, I glimpsed my newly arrived friends working over a great pile of gear. But who was there? Gerry Plummer had shorn his long hair to avoid provoking intolerant police and looked totally different in the dim light. I could make out Jim Sindelar and Dee Crouch, but I couldn't see Steve Pomerance anywhere.

"You won't believe this," Dee said a bit later, in obvious disgust, "but Steve dropped out. I had to redivide all our gear last night."

This was a shock. Steve was probably the strongest mountaineer among us, fluent in Spanish and a strong boater. Fortunately our team of five still had reasonable depth in these skills, so that his loss weakened us a degree but left no gaping holes.

I remarked to Jim, "What a beginning! Two days into the expedition and we're already caught up in floods, revolution, and abandonments."

This time the customs officials could not resist those strange, monumental piles. They wanted to tax the boats. "But we are on an official expedition," I argued, pulling out a letter from a Peruvian tourist official. "We will be engaged in scientific studies of the valleys of the Apurímac." A great, confused milling of customs officials ensued, until the logjam broke as rapidly as it had formed. The gear was released without further problem.

We were now deposited in the middle of Lima's modern air terminal with our piles of luggage and three kayaks, but the air cargo office was closed for the night. "I'll stay here and watch the gear," Jim offered. "Me too," Gerry joined in. The rest of us, including Dee's wife, who had come with him for a vacation, returned to town to get a night's rest.

The next morning, August 31, we shipped the boats off; then we boarded the plane for Cuzco, ready to launch the next step of our expedition. We cut through the low coastal clouds engulfing Lima, then up and over the foothills to the high lake-dotted plateaus of the cordillera. We sped across Ayacucho, a historic mountain town on whose outskirts the decisive battle for independence from Spain was fought in 1824. Then, finally, we entered the domain of the Apurímac.

I was allowed in the cockpit as we once again streaked across the canyon of the Apurímac. On previous trips to Cuzco, I had never been able to see more than broken ribbons of water down in the inner canyon. This time I saw a new stretch, very narrow but possibly navigable. Then the river suddenly hid beneath the clouds, and the secret of that monumental canyon—so tantalizingly close—was withdrawn once more.

Sunday in Cuzco was marked by the music of the beautiful cathedral bells. Visiting our friend from last year, Carlos Zegarra, chief of tourism in Cuzco, we found out, to our relief, that the Apurímac was not flooding.

In Cuzco we set up operations in the Virrey Hotel. Raul, the manager, gave us space to spread everything out. First we split our gear and food into two great piles, one to go with us and the other to await our return from the Cunyac Bridge for resupply. We then divided between us, on an equal-weight basis, our community gear: stove, ropes, tents, medical kit, special photographic gear, maps, altimeter, thermometer, repair kits, tools, spare paddles, and so on.

In the evening we sallied forth into marvelous Cuzco. Chuck and Dee located the proud owner of a truck and bargained for transportation to Pillpinto. Amid free-flowing beer and vows of eternal friendship, a rock-bottom price was fixed, much lower than I had estimated.

"Don't worry about transportation," Dee assured me buoyantly. "We'll handle this problem."

"Okay, fine with me," I said. "I'm glad to be relieved of this one problem, but that price sounds too good to be true."

Next morning the truck failed to make its appearance. A frantic call to an intermediary in those delicate negotiations revealed that "the driver changed his mind. He won't go!"

Five expedition members then scattered in five directions, in search of a vehicle large enough, and a driver sober enough, to take us. Raul, wonderful Raul, saved the day. He telephoned a friend of his, a schoolteacher, who had a Volkswagen microbus, a top rack, and a free day. He agreed to take us.

In Urcos we stopped at the Sunday market to buy fresh vegetables and fruit, which we were sure would be our last for some time. Hours later we chugged up through dry, cold hills to a 13,000-foot mountain pass. Then we crossed into the valley of the Apurímac. Down the other side we rolled, seemingly forever. On a thin shelf of road cut into the raw mountainside, we gradually descended into warmth, where trees grew, flowers bloomed, and bees hummed. A toy-like cluster of tile roofs and glistening lime-washed walls deep in the valley below grew into beautiful Acamayo, the principal city of the region. But we continued on, past dull Acos, down to the Apurímac.

A ribbon of clear water traced its way across the valley. Foam-flecked and placid, the river was most definitely not in flood. The afternoon had fled, and we quickly unloaded our gear and established camp on a nearby beach as the driver left. Some straggling travelers passed by in the fading dusk, staring incredulously at our strung-out array of sleeping bags, boats and paddles, and innumerable supply bags. That night, I am sure, the whole valley buzzed with the news of our arrival. I could imagine their amusement: "Those crazy gringos want to run the river. Tomorrow we'll have the greatest circus we've ever seen!"

That night we talked yet again about the forthcoming expedition.
"How do you feel about it compared to your expedition last year?" Dee asked me.

"Good," I said. "Down here it's warm, and you aren't constantly freezing, which is a big problem higher up. We are also much better informed now on the canyons below. And the group is so strong—fantastic talent and strength. My only concern is whether we can hang together to use all of our talents cooperatively."

My worry was real, if not overwhelming. Everyone has their own boating style and their own way of crossing hurdles. But on an expedition there must be some unity of styles, best agreed on in advance. We had all agreed on a style of caution and conservatism. We would look at tough mazes before we thrashed into them and portage when the passage was unsafe. The adventure would lie in the mysterious wealth of the canyon, not in needlessly pushing our small group to the edge of disaster in a remote land.

My colleagues were, by nature, less conservative than I. My kayaking skills were, I believe, as good as the best there, but I liked to be in control of the rapids I ran. Jim, Gerry, and I had recently boated together on the Salmon River, the Clearwater South Fork, and the Lochsa, in Idaho. We got along famously, but they would hesitate at nothing, where I would occasionally draw up for a closer look, then usually go on to navigate the same rapids they did.

I had not boated with Dee or Chuck. Dee had done some wild runs, but now claimed to be conservative. Chuck, too, had boated very tough rapids, but he agreed to the expedition terms without comment. That was assurance enough for me.

We crawled in our sleeping bags and gazed awhile at the brilliant display of the southern sky. The night was chilly, but not locked in bitter iciness like the nights in the highlands. The river had by now carved its way down to 9,300 feet in elevation, and the cutting edge of the cold was gone.

A few dim lights flickered across the river from Pillpinto, a sleepy Andean village, the largest on the shores of the upper Apurímac. Rarely, except here, is the Apurímac valley wide enough to allow the building of real pueblos. *Pillpinto* means butterfly in Quechua, the language of the highland Indians.

A year ago, I had come to Pillpinto with my sons to reconnoiter the river. We had walked up the main street, typically full of chickens, pigs, ducks, donkeys, and waterholes. Then school let out. A horde of restless youngsters burst out the door, spied us, and sped en masse down the street toward us. They engulfed my boys with embraces, handshakes, backslaps, smiles, gesticulations, joviality—all the expressions that youth can imagine. All I saw were two blond heads bobbing up and down in the crush of dark-haired friendliness. Steve, then twelve, loved it, but Mike, five years younger, found it a bit overwhelming. Our grand entourage then traipsed down to the bridge, where I photographed the spontaneous, smiling faces.

Now we had the opportunity to visit Pillpinto again. The next morning Dee and I walked across the bridge and up the narrow dirt street of the village. We passed between adobe buildings, walking around and among the kids, pigs, dogs, and chickens. I started again to photograph the crowd of children following us, but now they went rigid, concrete smiles on their faces. A portrait photographer, perhaps, had passed this way since my visit of a year ago, because the frozen pose was religiously

Chuck Carpenter gives a child of Pillpinto a ride on the back of his kayak. ≈

struck by all the people anywhere in the field of my lens. How could I get spontaneous pictures?

Dee engaged the children in a soccer game with a tin can. This favorite pastime of Peru diverted their attention from the camera, but as I focused in, they saw me and set up like instant plaster. The sight was hilarious, but the photography was devastated.

We went on, the pack following us, Dee joking. They called us gringos and Dee turned on them, tugging at his newly bought Indian cap, and announced, "I am Inca gringo." The kids were in an uproar.

When we returned, a great crowd of adults and children were milling around our boats. The throng had begun as a trickle early that morning, when the first spears of sunlight had grazed our beach. Now the whole village was there. But the kids were the problem. The first day of stowing gear inside the boat is always tough, deciding where to put things at varying levels of accessibility. With two hundred mischievous youngsters thrashing around, playing, kicking sand in our gear, thumping our boats, asking endless questions, it was almost impossible.

Dee drew a line in the sand and told them not to cross. Then at 9:30, the adults shooed them off to school. There must, I fear, have been a strong undertone of disorder in the school—perhaps a little difficulty in getting the students to concentrate on civics and history—for soon the teachers brought them back, this time three hundred strong. To our deep relief, they maintained a stranglehold of discipline.

We entered our boats and cavorted in the nearby water awhile, beneath the amused gaze of the villagers. Chuck pretended to be tipping over. Gasps of excitement from the audience! Then he capsized. Moans! Finally he burst out of the water, paddling upright by means of an eskimo roll. Cheers and accolades! It was, I am sure, the finest circus ever to come to Pillpinto.

At 11 A.M. on that first day of September 1975, Apurímac Expedition II was launched from a trampled beach across the river from Pillpinto. Our adventure had at last begun.

We passed through some small rapids in an open canyon, soon reaching Ccapa, a small, picturesque village perched high on a ridge overlooking the river. We pulled up at the narrow beach there and gave several youngsters a ride on the back of our kayaks. A distraught father raced up, apparently believing that his son had been seized by kidnappers—or lunatics. His agitation disappeared as soon as we brought his son back to shore.

Other adults hurried to the beach. "Come up and drink chicha," they urged, almost demanded. We suspected that their perpetual habits of hospitality, added to insatiable curiosity about so strange a procession as ours, would make our escape difficult, once we were up there drinking chicha, the homemade beer of the Andes. We declined, extricated ourselves awkwardly, and paddled onward.

We ran through more small rapids, and gradually the canyon deepened. Walls of broken rock and brush ascended vertically to peaks 5,000 feet above. A while later a deep gorge loomed ahead, and we passed cautiously into its shadowed depths. It became dark, as if night were falling, although it was only 3 P.M. The rock walls had been buffed clean to a height of 30 feet by the monstrous floods of the rainy season. Above the high-water line, long, wispy veils of dried moss hung from the walls. Damp side alcoves were filled with moss-covered trees, ferns, and flowers.

We camped early, at 3:30, as everyone had been drained by our hectic preparations and exhausting travels. We were still in the deep shaded canyon, and our small sandbar was without sunlight.

"I'm going to try out this fishing gear," Jim announced, pulling out the light-weight rod that made up part of our survival gear. He would use a small golden spinner as a lure. Soon he ambled back to the tents with a string of a half dozen rainbow trout. The light-weight grill was set up over a fire, salt and margarine were applied, and we were soon feasting on the succulent fish.

Darkness fell at 6:00, and we talked to pass the long night, reliving adventures a continent away. I recalled my descent of the lower canyons of the South Fork of the Salmon with J. Dewell, Jim Byrne, and Roger Turnes, the first successful navigation of this turbulent tributary of "The River of No Return." Dee described his own subsequent descent of that river, running solo in cold, stormy spring weather, the water running high. "I thought that was the end," he said several times, describing turbulent passages where he could neither continue on nor climb out, his hands virtually frozen by the icy water. I shuddered at his approach to adventure, which impressed me as altogether too risky to provide any sense of enjoyment. But according to what Dee had told me over the telephone, when I had first called him about the Apurímac expedition, the South Fork experience had changed his approach to boating. "I'm a conservative boater now," he had said.

O ur attention now turned to a rare spectacle. That afternoon a brush fire had raged high above us on the right-hand canyon wall, pouring columns of gray smoke into blue Andean skies. Mile after mile of mountainside was ablaze. Now, in the darkness of night, the great fire was behind a ridge, but its bursts of flame would cast a flickering red glow on the opposite canyon wall. The beauty was indescribable. Buried in the womb of this narrow defile, beneath dark cliffs looming above the gently rolling water, bathed in the warm glow of pulsing firelight, I felt that I had truly been transported out of this world. On this unforgettable scene, we drew down the curtain of sleep to close the day.

The fire burned all night, and luminous clouds of smoke were pierced by darting tongues of flame, as the conflagration moved around the ridge toward us in the dim light of dawn. Whatever its origins, the fire was transforming essential plant nutrients from vegetation to fragile ash. The heavy rains of February would wash the ashes down these precipitous slopes into the river; thence on a long course to the Atlantic Ocean. The land would be impoverished by a substantial amount of its life-sustaining fertility.

W e left our camp in the gorge at 10 A.M. and paddled an hour longer between the upthrust walls. Only minor rapids marked our path. The river then splashed through some turbulent drops, and we busied ourselves avoiding exposed boulders.

We soon approached Colcha, the village, according to the news report, that was to be moved to a site downstream because of flooding on the Apurímac. The great, gravelly bank below Colcha was indeed eroding away, as the Apurímac, like other rivers, thrashed in slow motion across the width of its valley. But there seemed to be no threat to Colcha in less than geological times. However, some steep, eroded slopes above Colcha showed evidence of sliding. This threat must certainly have been the one driving Colchans to a new townsite; it must, even now, be one that keeps the town's citizens awake on dark rainy nights, listening for a dull roar, yearning for a new village on flatter land downstream.

As we drifted through the valley of Colcha, all the interesting facets of human life in the Andes were displayed. A farmer tilled the soil behind a team of oxen. An old woman washed her feet in the river, chewing coca, oblivious of reality. Another woman, with a giant water pot slung on her back, skulked off as we approached.

Then we came across some young boys, maybe seven years old, wading naked at the river's edge. I paddled near and asked innocently, "Could I take your picture?" The boys, already suspicious, dashed for their clothes when they saw the camera, while their older brothers split with laughter.

Below Colcha, the rapids intensified. Two short portages were needed to get past some turbulent chutes. In the worst of the two, four of us worked in coordination, helping each other down the left side. Dee went alone down the other side. I hoped that our teamwork would continue.

In the late afternoon we passed under an awesome suspension bridge called *Puente Huarancalle*. Then we paddled beneath the beautiful little pueblo of Cusibamba Alto, lying like a dream from a stage prop on a sloping embankment above the Apurímac. Soon afterwards we passed the adobe buildings and corrals of an hacienda on the opposite bank. We camped below it, on a livestock-trodden beach bordering a patchwork of fields. Back past the fields, less than 2 miles up the wide valley we had just descended, the fascinating bridge of Huarancalle awaited the birth of another day.

One certainly cannot accuse Andean peasants of idling away the morning. They stir with the crow of the cock and have herded their livestock to pasture before the sun bursts over the hills. I was anxious to return upcanyon to the crossroads at the great suspension bridge to watch the morning pageant of the Andes. In the gray light of dawn we were stirred from sleep by some young people coming up the trail from a nearby hacienda. They found us still strung out in sleeping bags, looking and feeling like crumpled sacks of flour. They began their visit by inspecting our gear with determined curiosity. When finished, they issued an invitation.

"Please visit us," they implored; "you can eat breakfast at our house. It's on the way to the bridge."

"Who wants to go?" I asked. Soon Gerry, Chuck, and I were following them up through the fertile fields bordering the river.

"Welcome to my house," were the words of greeting extended along with the hand of Señor Salmánez in the front yard of the hacienda. "Please sit down; breakfast will be prepared in a short while."

Señor Salmánez was well-dressed and courteous, even aristocratic. He wore a brimmed felt hat, a white shirt beneath a black sweater, a threadbare suit of gray, and leather dress shoes with the cracks of age worn into them. He came from a prominent family; his uncle in fact owned the fine new Hotel Wiracocha in Cuzco, where we had stayed the previous year. He himself taught in a nearby school, and he had a certificate of accreditation hanging in proud display on an otherwise bare wall.

His wife, dressed in a gray skirt, a blue, partly buttoned sweater, and also adorned with a felt hat, slaved away deep in the sunless, smoky kitchen. While we waited, I found in my gear a small mirror for the pretty young mother who had helped bring us up from the beach that morning. "Would you like this?" I offered. She smiled, took the mirror, and glanced quickly at herself, giggling in embarrassment.

We walked around the garden while we waited. We found vegetables grown in scattered clusters around the buildings and between the peach trees. We sampled some small carrots and noted the oncoming crop of watermelons and potatoes. The potato is the staple of the highlands, but it fades from importance and gradually disappears on the descent to the jungle. We wouldn't see many more.

Breakfast was served in waves. First, coffee and bread, then boiled eggs, and later, a delicious potato soup laced with vegetables and flavored with cilantro. (See Plate 3) After breakfast we thanked our gracious hosts; then Gerry and I followed their teenage son, our guide for the morning, back along the trail toward the bridge of Huarancalle.

The bridge was still deeply immersed in the shadow of the mountain. Slung 60 feet above the water, to escape the churning wrath of the river in the rainy season, the bridge links two huge sentinels of rock that form a natural gateway across the canyon. The morning parade of the Andes was already under way. I sat on the beach by the river to watch and photograph the crossings. Gerry and our teenage guide

The bridge of Huarancalle. Puente Huarancalle spans the Apurímac River and connects the populated Cuzco region to the remote highlands. The bridge is used for foot traffic only; many livestock cross the river here.

walked up to inspect the bridge and its foot traffic and to see its users close at hand.

From my rocky lookout on the bank of the Apurímac, the shadowed mass of the bridge was silhouetted against the bright morning sky and sunny hills. Colorful figures flowed across it with herds of livestock. I imagined that it must have been this way in the days of the Incas, when great rope bridges had been engineered across the river canyons. It is possible that one crossed at this very spot, that this was truly the enactment of a very ancient scene.

Women, men, and children trekked across the walkway in the sky, as they had always done. But the llama—the only beast of burden in Inca days—was now replaced by the horse and the mule. A few of the horses were ridden across the bridge, while the strings of pack mules were led across. The staccato hammering of their hooves on the wooden planks drove echoes deep into the hills.

My thoughts took fanciful leave, following the echoes across the canyon into the distant hills to the southwest, into the land from whence these travelers had come. Here the high, cold hills were dotted with small hamlets and haciendas with wonderful Spanish-Andean names: San Lorenzo, Yauripata, Bellavista. I imagined work-bent campesinos tilling their fields, herding their livestock, plodding toward their colorful pueblos, where my maps showed only brown contour lines on white paper.

My maps did convey one sharp message, however. That land is remote and rugged, full of Apurímac tributaries slicing down between 13,000-foot peaks. Life there is hard and austere. The trail on my side of the river led into a land of shattering contrast. It wound 6 miles north, up through a broad side canyon to the village of Paruro. Here a road twists down the canyon to meet the trail. Buses rumble in from Cuzco, little more than 20 miles distant.

Here, via the bridge, the trail, and the bus, the hill people can transport themselves into a land of screaming jets, precision tourist cameras, and flush toilets—into an opulent civilization with a wealth beyond their dreams and a technology beyond their comprehension.

Two contrasting lands, then, have been forged together by the thread of cable and wood slung across the canyon above my head. Because of the bridge, the people of the hills are connected to the spirit and the reality of the great city, connected by a two-way street to its markets. These profound links of culture and goods, flowing across the narrow bridge, have gripped everyone. It has given them material gains and a vague glimpse of the great world beyond; it has dazzled them with splendid, unreachable dreams; and it has thereby brought to focus the harsh reality of their own land and meager livelihood.

My thoughts were interrupted by a cloud of dust descending the trail from the hills. Two herdsmen were bringing a flock of sheep to market. The procession halted abruptly at the precipitous landing to the bridge, where the sheep would not budge. Stones, sticks, and waving arms created only a confusion of dust among the circling, dodging animals. A herdsman seized a reluctant sheep by the ears and dragged it onto the bridge. The sheep braced its legs and bucked as it was pulled slowly over the abyss. After 20 yards of bridge had slid beneath its resistant feet, the sheep broke free and raced back like unbridled lightning to solid earth. It seemed somehow to sense its destiny in those distant markets of Cuzco.

After an hour of struggle, no sheep had passed. The herd still milled around the platform on the end of the bridge next to the hills. We could stay no longer and would never know how this matter was resolved. Our first great challenge lay below us on the river, and we wanted to confront it before the day aged any more.

The river called. The call is the thundering rumble of distant rapids, the intimate roar of white water . . . a primeval summons to primordial values."

John J. Craighead

If we send no ships out,
Then no ships will come in,
And unless there's a contest held
Nobody can win.
For games can't be won
Unless they are played,
And prayers can't be answered
Unless they are prayed.

Helen Steiner Rice

≈ PACPERO

M Y MAPS AND AERIAL photographs had identified the challenge ahead. The main map for this region, which would guide us a few more days, was fairly detailed, scaled at 1:100,000. It showed a steep canyon ahead, which I called the Canyon of Pacpero ("pock-peár-o") after a major side canyon, Quebrada Pacpero.

The 50-meter contour intervals on my map periodically crossed the thin blue line labeled "Apurímac." Ahead of us, in the canyon, the contour lines drew closer together, promising a steep gradient in the river. The map's scale offered us few details, but its gradient appeared to be about 120 feet per mile for 3 or 4 miles into the canyon. A gradient this steep could mean intense rapids or possibly even unrunnable cataracts, depending on the nature of the riverbed. If it was evened out in many small drops, we would be able to run the rapids in our kayaks. If the river bottom was broken coarsely by gigantic rocks into big and ugly cataracts, we would have to portage around them. We might even have to carry our boats up and across the hills, because the map showed that the river ahead was confined in a narrow walled canyon, whose shoreline might be too constricted to walk along.

Aerial photographs confirmed the maps. This was reassuring, because they had not always been accurate, as we had discovered to our dismay in the Gorge of Pichigua the previous year. But the aerials, like the maps, offered too little detail to confirm the possibility of passing along the shoreline. Details from any source, in fact, were so obscure that we simply had no idea of how we would get through the rapids or how long it might take.

The evening before, Gerry and I had tried to find answers to some of these puzzles. Below our camp, the canyon walls closed in on the river. A footpath threaded along the high embankment at the foot of the converging hills. We had hurried down the trail, hoping to catch a glimpse of the rapids and the canyon before dark. The trail divided several times, then simply fizzled into criss-crossing animal paths. "Which way?" I called to Gerry, eyeing some steep cliffs blocking us.

"Let's try to climb up the hill to the ridge," he replied. "Maybe we can see the river from there."

We began to work our way up the dusty hillside along the faint tracks. Some goats scrambled off to one side to avoid us. The underbrush thickened and started to tear at our clothing and skin. Every other plant had an armament of spines or stickers. Cactus plants and thorn bushes grew in profusion. "You know," Gerry said, "this would be hell to have to portage up through these hills off the main trail."

We had finally reached a point where more than thorns and spikes rose to bedevil our progress; a jagged ledge capped the hillside, making the prospect of getting up to the ridge difficult.

"I think we could work up along that steep break," Gerry said, pointing to a short, steep gully cutting up through the ledge, "but it would take quite a while."

"Let's get back down," I suggested. "It's getting dark—too late to see the river anyhow."

We returned to camp, sobered by our experience. The possibility of going up over the hills had been a safety valve for the expedition; now it no longer appeared to be a viable alternative. Our options had been whittled back by what we had seen.

After the trek to the bridge in the morning, Gerry and I arrived in camp to find clusters of highlanders surrounding the boats. Our three comrades were anxious to get under way.

"We'll go down a ways to scout out the river," one of them called over a shoulder, as they launched from the shore of the Apurímac. Their early departure made our preparation more difficult.

With three boats gone, the clusters of people collected around the two remaining camp areas. They seemed especially attracted to mine, perhaps because I could speak some Spanish. As I tried methodically to pack my gear away, the curious bystanders would casually pick up various objects lying at my side, inspect them, then pass them on to the next outstretched hands.

"What is this for?" "What is that for?" "How does it work?" They asked an endless series of questions. At one time, four irreplaceable objects were circulating in the crowd: a paddle was over on one side; a closure device for a waterproof storage bag was on the other side; and

The author explains map reading to children living near the Paruro crossing. ≈

a fuel tank and nylon stuff bag circulated somewhere between. I was forced to keep track of these to see that they didn't leave camp, while simultaneously answering questions and packing gear. My progress was slow and frustrating.

"Do you need some help?" Gerry said, walking up from his boat after having finished stowing away his gear.

"I sure do!" I exclaimed. "Help me watch this stuff; I'll pack and answer their questions, then we'll try to get out of here." Although Gerry was not at that time conversant with Spanish, his presence took the pressure off me, and we moved speedily to completion. At 11:00, we entered the river.

Soon the water was twisting through rocks—a nice rapid to warm up for the task ahead. We joined the others at the corner below and pushed on into the intensifying fury. Dee always forged ahead. This was annoying and frustrating—and became a source of dissension. For most people, it is a special thrill to be first to find a route through mazes of rock. I tried to see that everyone who wanted to had an opportunity to lead through the rapids, an impossible task until Dee somewhat controlled his headlong rush forward.

The valley now became deeper and narrower. After a mile of exciting rapids, we were suddenly halted by a monstrous cataract. I disembarked on the left bank. "Jim, will you and Chuck scout the right bank while Gerry and I check the left?" Both, we found, could be portaged; the left-side shore ended in a spectacular ledge, over which the boats would have to be lowered by ropes. The right shoreline was shorter and less complicated, so we chose that route. The three of us paddled across above the cataract to a landing on the right.

We began our first strenuous portage of the trip. It was a hard battle to get our heavily loaded boats over and through the maze of rocks on the shoreline. Each foot of our passage was agonizing.

Near the end of our portage, while each of us labored at some minute part of the onerous task, the abrasive clatter of tumbling rocks echoed down the canyon wall. Rockfall! Stones and pebbles came flinging past us from the cliffs above, and we each dove for the shelter of the closest boulder. A pebble, "like a rock from a slingshot," hit Jim's helmet before he could protect himself. He was unhurt, but we were all shaken up by this sudden, unexplained threat.

"Do you see anyone up there?" I called out. No one did, but a banded ledge 100 feet up could easily conceal a man. We hurried to complete the portage, one eye on the threatening cliff, one on our demanding work.

"Look!" Jim said, "a native fish trap!" There, in a deep recess in the rugged shoreline, lay a beautiful structure of reeds, intricately woven into the shape of two attached consecutive funnels. This trap, carefully placed in a natural sluiceway at the edge of a rapid, would force its finny prey to be washed down its wide mouth and through its narrow throat—into a terminal cage from which there would be no escape. Fish for dinner!

"Someone may want to keep us away from the fish trap," ventured Gerry. The thought of hidden eyes watching from above and precarious rocks rolling down the cliff with a mere touch hastened our final leg of the portage. Once in our boats, we raced out into the middle of the river, away from the ominous cliff, and breathed deep sighs of relief.

Had someone been up there, tumbling rocks at us? No, I don't believe so. We found that many Apurímac walls were shedding streams
of rocks—sometimes in remote canyons where, perhaps, no one had
ever walked before. It is sobering and a little bit scary, but such is the
nature of this wild canyon cutting its swath through the Andes.

We paddled downstream but were very soon forced to stop again.
The cataracts had begun in earnest. It became, now, a tedious
battle with the fury of the river.

We stopped for lunch at 2:30. Nuts, dried fruit, and a candy bar,
washed down with water. Then we scouted a short way downstream.
The river continued wild and unrelenting. We began again, portaging
and lining down the left side, finding our way among the boxcar-size
boulders.

Working around the cataracts in the middle canyons of the Apurímac was backbreaking torture that would be repeated again and again
on our way down to the Cunyac road crossing. Below Cunyac, we
proceeded differently.

Those who remember descriptions of portages in the north woods
along sylvan forest trails, a canoe slung across the shoulders, must now
imagine a different terrain and a different problem. The shoreline of
the Apurímac—in places where one is lucky enough to find a shoreline—is smothered by giant rocks. They extend from the canyon walls
out into the shallows, then on to the center of the river, where they
create the twisting, foaming rapids. There are no paths. Beaches of sand
are few and usually small. Whether one is lucky enough to be able to
progress by boat, or unlucky enough to be forced to go on foot, it is
always across and between these ageless behemoths that have tumbled
down from the canyon walls and tributary ravines into the canyon.

Our loads were heavy; at this point we were each shepherding about
100 pounds of food and gear through the canyon, including the weight
of our boat. On the leg below the Cunyac crossing it would be even
more. The heavy weight of our loads, while uncomfortable, was secondary to their awkward form, shape, and dimensions. The river kayak
has exquisite lines, streamlined, fast, maneuverable, stable, responsive.
But it was designed for running rapids, not for carrying like a backpack.
Off the river it becomes as awkward as a fish out of water.

When the rapids and cataracts blocked our passage in the river, we would go to shore and look for a way past. Wherever we could, we took advantage of shallow eddies and channels near shore to line our boats, letting the water carry their weight. The paddler needs only to guide it and urge it on—or sometimes restrain it—by hand or with an attached rope, in passing from one pool to the next. The difficulty with this is that the boats frequently drag on unseen rocks or hang up in channels that twist and dive so sharply that the boats cannot follow. Walking in these shallows in order to keep the boats on course can also be treacherous. The rocks are moss-covered and slippery, and there is the constant risk of breaking a limb. After a few days of this, everyone's ankles and lower legs are bruised and scraped.

Progress down these broken, rock-filled shallows was slow and torturous. But there were worse things than this. A stretch of lining would usually end in a blockade of giant boulders, and then we would face the infinitely more difficult task of lifting and dragging our heavy boats up over the rocks, farther along the jagged shoreline, and finally lowering them over rocks or steep ledges into the next pool of water.

We worked cooperatively on the portages. Wherever we could walk over the rocks, two of us would seize opposite ends of a boat and stumble down the shore with it. Problems here arose in the awkward gait forced on us by the randomly spaced and sometimes unstable boulders. In order to carry a rigid boat between two porters, there must be two equal paces. A long step taken by one to span a void between rocks pulls suddenly on the other; his counterpull will sometimes drag on the first porter just enough to force him to miss his step and to stumble. It is an awkward business at best.

In some places we could not walk at all. The rocks would simply block our path. One or two of us would then climb the rocks, finding a position from which we could seize and pull the loads to some intermediate platform. The boats were offered up by those still below. Then those below would scramble ahead to the next rock or the next ledge to receive, in turn, the slowly transmitted burden.

There were other ways to get down these punishing shores. Jim, for example, had his own special technique. He had built a special yoke, designed to lodge firmly in the cockpit, then over the shoulders. One man, theoretically, could use this to carry a boat slung upside down across his head and shoulders. Jim would occasionally struggle down over the rocks with his loaded boat affixed to the yoke swaying above his head. It frightened me to watch it. If he lost footing, the whole mass of body, boat, and gear would surely topple onto the rocks in a broken pile. Fortunately he was sure-footed, and this fate never overtook him.

When we could, of course, we would get in our boats and paddle. Some of these paddling intervals were only a few short boat lengths between plunging cataracts. Even a short distance of paddling was relished, because it spared us from an equal distance of hideous portaging.

S o the afternoon of the third day was consumed in laborious struggle, changing from one minute to the next in form but not in intensity. We stopped at 5:00, an hour before dark. In that whole day we had gone only 2 miles.

Exhausted, we camped for the night on a small spit of sand on the left bank, the roar of the rapids booming at us; those below promised to torment us the next day. The biggest question mark for the upcoming day lay half a mile ahead, down at the left bend in the canyon where the large side canyon, Quebrada Pacpero, broke in from the right. There my maps and photographs showed that the canyon narrowed again, and the river became solid white.

We lit a fire with driftwood and relaxed while the water was coming to a boil. Then, inexplicably, Dee started climbing up the steep bank immediately behind our camp. He was stopped by a vertical, eroded layer of earth and rocks, held together by roots from the brush above. Incredibly, instead of calling it off, he battled his way up this unstable face, with no apparent object in mind except the challenge of it. I thought to myself that this was a senseless way to risk our expedition, but I decided to say nothing, for fear that it would multiply the tensions brought to focus earlier in the day.

W e arose early the next morning, anxious to get through this hostile canyon. We heated water on our small kerosene stove, prepared tea, and ate breakfast, then broke camp in preparation for departure. Dee had plotted a course immediately downstream. We would first cross to the right bank, because the shoreline there was less broken by boulders. We would then portage and line several hundred yards past the next rapids.

Dee and I started first. As we struggled along the shore, I looked up in amazement to see Chuck running down through the rapid. He had apparently decided he would rather confront its considerable hazards than face another long portage. Spinning and turning, broadsiding against rocks and washing out backwards, flushed through lunging chutes, he provided an incredible display of survival.

Chuck was a good boater, everyone agreed. He had forewarned us: "You haven't seen anything yet; wait 'til I really get into gear."

"Oh my God," I thought, "I am really mixed in with a band of lunatics!"

As we had first left camp that morning, the thatched roofs of a small homestead had come into view downriver, perched on a small, flat indentation partway up the canyon wall. Soon the owner appeared, up on the right bank. He seemed without fear of us, which was atypical for the lonely men in the hills and canyons beyond the pueblos. Soon the reason was apparent: his cheek was stuffed full of a wad of coca. This colorful man, half toothless, with black stubble whiskers, tattered felt hat, and sandals, brimmed with hospitality. "Come to my house," he begged, "drink chicha with me."

"It is not possible now," I said. "We must get down this canyon." He followed us as we worked, insisting on our visit. "Perhaps we will walk back up to visit you this evening," I said, thinking that at this rate of progress, we would not have far to walk.

The small, numbed man of the hills followed us a while longer, watching every strange move, amused at our absurd efforts.

And our efforts that fourth day did indeed seem absurd. It was a long day chopped into small bits by endless variations and combinations of lining, portaging, and paddling. We worked down past the dreaded Quebrada Pacpero, past truly enormous, unrelenting cataracts. Nevertheless the canyon was just wide enough to allow us a strand of shoreline, so that we always had a refuge and a pathway when the rapids roared us off the river.

Past Pacpero, a few blocks past the great central bend to the left, the canyon eased ever so slightly. Here we stopped at noon for lunch, already exhausted, less than a mile beyond our last camp. We tried to organize ourselves again, to streamline our difficult passage. We agreed to rotate leads, to have someone follow the leader within sight, within helping distance, but not close enough to crowd him out of eddies. The others would follow, each keeping track of those closest.

W e commenced again at 1 P.M. More and more we were running the harder rapids now, closer to the limits of navigability. No logic, no sane reasoning, could justify this; we were too far from help now to take such chances. But we had lost our willpower; we seemed unable to resist the primrose path down the river, beyond the reach of the brutal portage routes ashore. And we had several close calls. "The toughest rapids ever run with loaded boats," Dee ventured.

A typical rapid is described in my diary:

We run for a block or so in rocky, technically difficult water, scouting each drop from the eddy above. The gradient increases and I get out of my boat to look, as I am now in the lead. Very rocky, but we can run the top part. It is easier on the right hand side, so I signal the others to start over there. Dee and Chuck find a channel and proceed 50 yards. I have to cut diagonally right through a complicated channel, as I must start from my left shoreline position. Three out of five of us hit a large protruding rock on the right beneath a turbulent chute. Below that, we get out and line 30 yards through a rocky stretch edged by a giant boulder. The channel below us now is turbulent, but difficult to line. I run it, but hit the wall at the bottom, which is deflecting water back to the main channel of the river. I emerge unscathed.

Dee follows, gets off to a bad start, tries to compensate for my wall collision by slicing from right to left, but washes up on a boulder to the right of the channel from where he hoped to start his diagonal plunge.

Immediately his boat broaches: the stern washes around, and bow and stern become pinned by the current to rocks on opposite sides of the channel. He begins tipping upstream, into the water. The water begins flowing into his boat, and we are threatened with its breakage. I try to paddle back up to him, to give him a handhold on the bow of my boat, because he has nothing solid downstream to pull him back in that direction. I get within four feet, but the strong current lets me no closer. Gerry rushes down the shore, steps out on the rock, and lifts the bow off its anchor. The boat capsizes and washes down. Dee swims with it, past the wall, out into a pool in the river, and then to shore. No harm done, except for shattered nerves.

By the end of that afternoon, the cataracts had expended much of their power, and we delighted in a few blocks of tension-free whitewater before making camp. The worst of the canyon was behind us.

We had gone only 2 or so miles that day, but it is hard to analyze precisely the passage of that grueling bout with the Apurímac. Probably 90 percent of our distance was paddled. The 10 percent portaged or lined constituted an arduous 1,000–1,200 feet over monstrous rocks and through the slippery shallows. The process of scouting rapids, and just the sheer complication of running some of the rock mazes, had also consumed a big chunk of our day.

We stopped on the left bank at 4:30, exhausted. We established camp on a large beach laced with house-size rocks and occupied by a small herd of horses. We drove them off and cleaned up after them, though the beach continued to smell like a barnyard.

"Look!" Jim exclaimed, "a giant bird!" He pointed left above the nearby hills, where a monster of a bird soared in lazy circles across the blue sky. Its body twisted in flight, and suddenly on the back of its outstretched wings we saw a distinctive pattern of white bars on black. It was an Andean condor! With my sons the year before, I had seen two of these remarkable birds floating majestically down the Urubamba Canyon past Machu Picchu. These are true giants among flying birds, sometimes achieving an unequalled weight of 30 pounds and a wingspan of 11 feet. They are acknowledged masters of soaring; they can glide for hours with no more than imperceptible changes in wing angle. Their numbers are now diminishing under the pressure of human encroachments; seeing one of these remarkable birds is a rare, exciting privilege. We watched from our beach until this giant of the skies drifted off with the clouds to distant mountains. How I wished I could follow this condor's flight; to see at a glimpse a million square yards of this fabled land; to drift over timeless canyons and pueblos in the quiet back eddies of this raucous world.

We finished dinner after dark, the only practical course with such short days. Chuck and Gerry went to sleep immediately, depleted by the exertions of the day. I sat in my sleeping bag, propped against a rock, writing in my diary. Little gnats were drawn magnetically to my headlamp, swarming about my face. On a previous night, small moths were the main nuisance. I gave up and turned off my light. The annoying bugs melted into the darkness of the night, their illuminated flight across the beam of my light replaced now by the methodical march of stars across the clear southern sky.

The fifth day of our voyage arrived with the chilly air of a steel-clear dawn. I woke up optimistic. We were almost through this absurd canyon and should frolic down the river today! I called over to Jim, who was stirring but still prone on a nearby sand spit. "How many miles today, Jim?" I asked.

Jim sat half-way up, blinking away the night, and said, "Maybe fifteen. Where's breakfast?"

"Ughh, don't talk about food!" came a weak voice from a nearby heap of camp gear. Chuck had awakened sick—a case of intestinal upset. We had, it seemed, sampled too much Andean hospitality along the way! We would delay our departure until Chuck felt better.

By 10:30 Chuck had become impatient with waiting and felt that he might as well suffer on the river as in camp. We pushed off. Immediately we hit a big drop in the river. Gerry, unable to catch the eddy above, dropped in backwards, overturned, and was pulled out of his boat by the thrashing current. Moments later Chuck came through and was capsized at the bottom. He managed an eskimo roll to right himself and came up looking startlingly refreshed by his brief dip.

We had only half a mile left of the great rapids. We boated most of this, but were forced to line a few short drops. We finally escaped the canyon at 11:30. Calm water lay ahead—or so we thought!

The average gradient in the river had now decreased to 20 feet per mile. Seasoned river runners will tell you that this hints strongly at a leisurely run. Unfortunately the great Apurímac had never heard of this rule of thumb and resorted to a different strategy. Its rapids, instead of becoming smaller, simply moved farther apart, separated by deep, quiet pools of green water. We had to paddle hard in the quiet pools to make up our lagging mileage, then at the end of each calm pool, we faced the same sort of monstrous rapids and cataracts that had plagued our de-

≈   Gerry Plummer descending an Apurímac rapid beneath cultivated fields on the hillside.

scent for the past two days. This mischievous, flaunting river, I thought to myself, has not reformed one bit since we encountered the Gorge of Pichigua the previous year.

With our progress still hindered, I began to wonder if we would make the Cunyac Bridge before our food ran out. But my attention was soon diverted from this troubling prospect to a more pleasing element of our journey: the incredible scenery of the middle Apurímac.

I had come to these middle canyons with the expectations of a dry landscape and dull scenery. Indeed, I knew the canyon to be deep, but here in the dry season, with few of the dark gorges that always create their own atmosphere of beauty, I expected little more than the terrible rapids to entertain us. We had been unexpectedly surprised with views of the great fire; of the one gorge with walls clothed in dried moss; and of the open vistas near Colcha. Now our excitement grew as waterfalls began tumbling down the high canyon walls, eight of them in less than 2 miles. At noon a cluster of three plunged into a shoreline oasis on the right, inviting us like sirens beckoning ancient mariners to come rest beneath the trees on their misty shore. Without a word—not a single moment of discussion—we all drew ashore.

A silvery stream rolled across a shallow notch on the canyon rim 2,000 feet above, then plunged from ledge to ledge to land at our feet. The other two waterfalls began as springs midway up the wall. These waterfalls had created a shoreline Eden and a mossy film of green on the cliffs, perpetually immune from the withering blight of the dry season. More waterfalls were visible beyond our beach, each of which had created a green plume of moss and ferns streaking down the arid walls.

The high mountain palisades and lofty peaks began to impress us too, growing steadily in height and angle. Giant faces of vertical rock were reminiscent of the Grand Canyon. Ahead loomed the rocky abutments of Cerro Tauja Orjo, at 15,000 feet (4,624 meters) above the sea, 6,500 hundred feet above the winding river. It was a grand and wonderful spectacle.

The people now appeared more primitive, more basic, as we pulled relentlessly away from the influence of civilization. Next to the oasis created by the three waterfalls, on a high embankment hemmed in

69 ≈

between the river and the canyon walls, lived a solitary Indian couple. They walked nervously down to our shaded resting place. We tried to communicate. Alas, their language was incomprehensible Quechua. Their erratic, nervous manner reflected a terror at the unknown purpose of this visit by strangers unlike those ever seen here before. The old man crossed himself repeatedly and muttered some saying again and again, while pointing below. "I think," said Chuck, "that he is giving us a Christian blessing for our passage through the hazards below."

It is hard, indeed, to imagine Christianity reaching this corner of the world. Perhaps he had learned Christian ways as a youth in some village in the hills, then somehow stumbled into this fertile Shangri-la in later life. Whatever his origins, this man was dressed more strangely than anyone I had seen in the highlands. Only his tattered felt hat with its rumpled black hatband was typical. Below this he wore a coarsely woven sweater of faded white, extending just past his elbows and held by a single button where it puckered at his neck. Over this was his formal attire: an ancient pullover vest, machine woven black and shiny as a raven's breast, spotted by the stains of daily life. At the bottom of the "V" at the neck of the vest lay a tilted, gray patch. A brightly colored band of cloth, perhaps a folded bandanna, served as a belt.

His pants looked like faded denim; they were largely smothered beneath gaudy, stiff cowboy chaps, probably cut out of raw cowhide. At the thighs the chaps were covered with a long, rough coat of brown and black hair, speckled with white. Near the knees and on the outside of the leg, the hair was worn away and the gray, crinkled hide beneath looked like the skin of a mummy! The total disharmonious outfit was a rustic bit of color and dazzle.

Soon after the failure of communications, the small, sun-wrinkled couple retired to their grass-thatched hut, hidden behind bushes and trees up on the embankment.

"I sure would like to find out how these people live and work here," I said to Gerry.

"Come on," Gerry said, "let's go up and try to quiet his nervousness." We started slowly up the gentle embankment toward their house. We had barely begun when the small gnarled man walked briskly down the hill to meet us. His friendly demeanor was gone. He carried a formidable

Andean garden tool—half plow, half hoe—which could crack a skull with ease. I extended my hand to renew our greeting; he nervously reciprocated. I hoped that from some distant memory he would sense the meaning of common words of Spanish. I tried to assure him of our peacefulness; tried to seek his permission to see his house; but he only blocked our path and mumbled his reasons in Quechua. He pointed repeatedly downstream, a clear invitation for us to leave. I pursued these delicate negotiations a few minutes more, while Gerry stood to one side and photographed the affair. Alas, the chasm between our worlds was too great! The small determined highlander and his hefty garden tool prevailed. We left his little enclave and paddled on down the river.

Earlier we had seen a billowing cloud erupt from an arboreal shoreline on the right-hand side of the river, half a mile farther along. The beach from which the cloud arose was isolated from the guarded homestead beneath the waterfalls by a line of cliffs thrust down out of the hills directly into the waters of the Apurímac. Now, as we drifted forward, the cloud reached from earth to sky.

It looked like dust, like emanations from a powdered ceremonial ground impacted by countless stomping feet. We wondered who had come down those steep canyon walls to create such a commotion and what strange activity might entangle us in its web. We were definitely apprehensive. Paddling quietly forward, hugging the left bank, we passed through a narrow channel to keep out of view of this strange place. Once alongside a high embankment concealing the origin of the cloud, our way now clear for a quick escape down the river, I called out tentative greetings: "¡Buenos días!" (good day!) An old highland Indian with a smudged face shuffled over to the edge of the embankment to greet us. Unafraid, he waved us up.

This gentle man lived even farther into the back eddies of civilization than his neighbors upstream. One telltale sign: a faded red cap of knit wool was atop his head, rather than the traditional felt hat. His clothes were as strange as his neighbor's but exquisitely different: his ragged vest and pants were of striped gray, like a railroadman's uniform. His long-sleeved shirt of faded blue was so decayed by age and wear that his whole right arm stuck out, and only a fragment of torn cloth held together the shirt's strangely patched shoulder, with the buttoned sleeve around his wrist.

His every characteristic, especially his friendliness, was in total contrast with those of his neighbor. I marveled at finding two such dissimilar enigmas in half a mile of Apurímac shoreline. I wondered if they had ever seen each other, separated as they were by that immense cliff that rose between them.

It was soon apparent that our newfound friend lived alone. He led us across the embankment into his private grove of trees, up to his fire, smoldering in an enormous heap of leaves. The billowing smoke was white and suffused with light, like a cloud of dust, which is exactly what we had mistaken it for earlier. Immersing himself in the swirling smoke, he shaped up the pile and added more leaves.

"He's making charcoal!" Jim exclaimed. "That's why he has the big heap of leaves—to limit the air getting to the fire. You have to cut way down on air to make charcoal."

We couldn't imagine how he got the charcoal out of here, for we couldn't even see a trail breaking the cliffs in back of this green island. Of course there must be some means of passage, else this ancient inhabitant would not be here at all. Perhaps he floated in on a reed raft! But we could probe these secrets no further—our host spoke only in Quechua, the timeless language of the Incas.

He beckoned us on back into the trees, to a mossy patch of jungle nourished by springs. Here he had a small thatched hut, deeply shaded beside a trickling brooklet of clear water. He placed a sheepskin over a log to make us a seat. He emerged from the hut with a plastic jug and poured some of its milky liquid into a clay bowl. He handed it to us. "Chicha!" Chuck said, tasting the brew. We passed it among us, sipping. It was yeasty and lumpy, quite unappetizing. Soon I noticed that each time it came back to me, it was just as full as when it had left; but this was not surprising, since when I passed it on, it was not any emptier than when it arrived! Our distaste for the precious offering of chicha was embarrassing, but we soon solved the problem. The remainder of the chicha watered the nearby squash while our host was looking away. We did not wish to visibly reject this Andean hospitality by turning back an uncleared dish, lest a grave offense be imagined. (*See* Plate 2)

Gerry and I walked around the area and peered into the hut. A few bowls and hides were scattered about, but other than the plastic jug for chicha, few ornaments or utensils of civilization were apparent. There was not even an iron garden hoe. We wondered if he had ever had a wife and children here—and what might have happened to them. Here was a true hermit's enclave, a primitive, self-sufficient world. A grass-thatched hut, bowls carved out of wood and made of clay, animal hides for covers, a garden by the river. What admiration we had for this little, trusting man.

We gave our friend a few small gifts, shook his hand, then left his special world behind.

A few miles farther on we came to the junction of a major tributary, the Río Velille. The union of the waters was an angry one. The Velille roared down from the left over a ramp of polished rocks, swelling the Apurímac's volume by 50 percent. The Apurímac itself also boiled by in fury; the thrashing crosscurrents in one of its narrow channels tossed us about like matchsticks, nearly pinning us on the broken rocks. Below the merger, the power of the river was perceptibly greater. The Apurímac was destined to become the world's greatest river, and here it took a bold step toward fulfilling that destiny.

Later that day, we came to a river crossing where a suspension bridge was under construction. Nearby a small platform, dangling below wheels creaking across a lofty cable, still carried the traffic of the Andes across the river. Attached ropes were used to pull the cargo back and forth. Fascinated, Jim and I lingered behind to watch some of the last crossings ever to be made on the old platform. Just then a man walked down out of the hills to cross. He climbed onto the small platform and sat down, grasping the steel bars from which it was suspended. Then the bridgekeeper pushed him off, paying out rope as the airborne carriage flew down to the other side. The passenger disembarked, and the keeper drew back his rolling platform by hauling in the extended line.

A crossing in the other direction would make the keeper earn his pay, for his side was higher, and any passengers would have to be inched up hand over hand.

We entered another canyon, passed a few more rapids, then joined

≈ A primitive "bridge" utilizing a platform suspended beneath a cable. The platform was pulled by hand across the gulf.

the others on a sandy beach, where we made camp and ate. Afterwards Jim and I talked awhile, dwelling on the marvelous enchanted canyon and our fitful progress through it. By now he would usually stop by for a chat after the evening chores were done. A bond of companionship grew between us.

After our talks, I would pull out my pen and notebook to inscribe the events of the day. The bugs still swarmed to my headlamp. I had reluctantly used my mosquito headnet—an idea of Jim's—to keep the darting creatures away. Although the threads of the headnet would light up and block out the beauty of the night, the solution was functional. I would write this way until 9:30 or 10:00, then lie back and enjoy the glassy brilliance of the night sky, lit by a luminescent Milky Way. Soon I would be lost in profound sleep.

Much later that night, a few drops of rain splashed on my face, putting us on alert that the dry season was coming to an end.

On the morning of the sixth day, just as we were prepared for our dry breakfast fare of peanuts, salami, and dried fruit, we heard Jim ask from behind some rocks, "Is anyone hungry?" He then strolled casually into camp bearing a monster of a fish—a 26-inch rainbow trout that we estimated to weigh 12 pounds. Immediately the peanuts, salami, and dried fruit went back into the pack and the grill and pans came out. We cut the fish in pieces and fried it in margarine. We had a gluttonous, positively disgraceful feast and didn't leave until 10.

We soon reached the end of the short canyon. The valley widened, and two villages appeared, perched on opposite sides of the canyon. We had arrived at Huata and Huaro Bamba. When we stopped, a crowd accumulated and invited us to visit the villages.

Gerry and I went up the left bank to visit Huata, while Chuck and Dee split to the right to see Huaro Bamba. Jim agreed to stay by the river to watch our boats.

We saw some houses just above the river and thought our hike would be short. These, we learned, were just the beginning; fragments of Huata were scattered up and down the hillside like mud flung at a wall. Our path up was lined with giant prickly pear cacti that towered above our heads. The spiny discs, some nearly 2 feet across, leaned over the trail here and there, bidding us to be careful. The area around was also riddled with maguey (sometimes known as the century plant or American aloe), a plant with dusty green spine-covered swords radiating out from its base.

We walked past gray adobe houses, thatched with straw and perched on tiny benchlands breaking the monotony of the upsweeping mountainside. Stake fences and crude barriers made of intertwined thorn branches served as corrals for burros, cattle, and goats.

Our hosts led us to a small house partway up, where we were offered some hard-boiled eggs and chicha. Then we hiked up again, through the town center, up to the school, the largest building in the pueblo. Its walls were a pastel green, and it stood out like a beacon among the small, gray houses. From the edge of its small playground, the Apurímac looked like a pale, blue-green ribbon winding through the valley far below.

"We would like to photograph some people doing their work," I requested. Usually when we entered a village, everyone would stop working, and it was difficult to sense the true rhythm of their lives. But now they took us down to meet a woman whom I shall call "the weaver of Huata" because of the beauty of her work. She was standing in the small town plaza, preparing dark red yarn on a small spindle. She was clothed in a brilliant blue skirt, a pink pastel sweater, and a felt hat with three yellow flowers pinned to the hatband. (*See* Plate 4)

The weaver of Huata beckoned us to her house. In her front yard was a partly woven poncho. She threw aside her shoes, slipped into the belting of the harness loom, and with dexterous fingers showed us how this beautiful creation was made from strands of dyed yarn. We had seen the brilliant dyes in the markets of Cuzco and Urcos. From these markets the dyes are dispersed to the hills to create spectacular splashes of colorful fabric and clothing. The poncho in creation here had a wide strip of brilliant red coursing down its center. Symmetrically placed stripes of yellow-white, black, blue, pink, and orange adorned its sides. No matter how gaudy it may sound, it was actually a masterpiece of blended colors.

"I would like to buy a poncho from you," I told her, "but we can't carry it down the river."

After we left the weaver, a bizarre event took place. We were led to a small, darkened house, where a dead man lay in a coffin. "Would you take his picture?" they asked. We did as requested without asking why, fearing that our questions, distorted by imperfect Spanish, might lead to some profound embarrassment. Later the villagers asked if we would send some of these photographs to them. They would make the long trek to Cuzco to pick them up, because Huata was beyond the mail carrier's reach.

Shipton . . . has taken risks often enough in his adventur-
ous life, but he has taken them only when he had to,
and he has tried to calculate risks carefully. In his view a
narrow escape from danger is not a matter for pride, but
something to be ashamed of—the escape ought not to
have been narrow.

J. R. L. Anderson

This was the day of the new hatch of mosquitoes, and
several thousand of these keen young sap-suckers were
actively on the job, experimenting with human blood
and evidently enjoying it. . . . the illimitable hordes . . .
are in a hurry: they land with all the fury of youth and
where they land they drill, in a second, through the
toughest hide: death means nothing to them—it merely
makes room for more.

R. M. Patterson

≈ NAYHUA

W E MOVED ON DOWN the river in deepening apprehension. Another short, formidable canyon lay ahead. I called it the Upper Canyon of Nayhua ("nyé-wah"), after the village lying at its foot, since it had no name on any of my maps. To the mapmakers, no doubt, it was just another piece of land too rocky to grow corn.

We paddled 2 miles, followed a huge right bend that thrust the Apurímac northward into the mouth of the canyon, then fell prey to its thundering water. Again the river charged over giant boulders in a stretch laced with complicated channels and 10-foot falls. I pondered the scene of absolute fury that must present itself here in the high water of the rainy season.

Some inhabitants from a pueblo called Tircuyachi, lying high up on the hillside above the river, came down a winding trail to the left bank to watch our tribulations. It was Saturday, a day of drink and merriment, and they made the most of this futile attempt by five gringos to descend a canyon obviously never put there for navigation. "Will you stop and drink chicha?" they asked, as we struggled by.

"Maybe later," I replied, in no mood to tarry.

As before, we would paddle down short pools, then disembark to work our boats over the big rocks. It was an absurd, energy-sapping task.

Late in the day, we established camp among some small pockets of sand lying between rocks on the right shore, safely out of reach of the villagers. Certainly unfriendly on our part, but for now we had to concentrate on this canyon. With curious highlanders around, one can neither sleep nor work. The people across the river watched a while longer, then became bored and melted back into the hills.

We were barely half a mile into this canyon, and my concerns with our progress surfaced once more. "We are on the last of the big drops that we know about," I told Jim that night, "but we are barely a quarter of the way to the Cunyac Bridge. We have gone only 25 miles in 6 days;

our food will run out in another 8. We can't buy much in the hills, particularly past Nayhua."

"I'll go fishing again," Jim offered. "Maybe we can last a month!"

There was also the mystery of the last canyon before Cunyac, a 10-mile stretch for which I had no information on terrain or rapids. I had hoped to reach the canyon with a large margin of time and food, but now that goal seemed impossible. But there were two things we agreed we wouldn't sacrifice, even should we risk going hungry a few days because of it: the time to stop and visit these marvelous enclaves of the highlanders, and precious moments to bathe in the wonders of the canyon.

We slept again beneath our starry sky, each night a little warmer than the last, as we advanced in small, hesitating steps toward the jungle.

Everyone except Jim felt weak and drained on the morning of the seventh day from various digestive upsets, colds, and overexertion. It was with such questionable energies that we faced the heart of the Upper Canyon of Nayhua. The day was one of sweat and toil, inching along the rock-strewn banks, over boxcar boulders, lining down narrow chutes. It was a matter of pulling and tugging, sometimes banging and dropping our boats, slipping on moss-covered rocks, and only occasionally paddling the short segments between big drops. (*See* Plate 5)

I estimated this canyon to drop 350 feet in just over 2 miles, an average gradient of about 150 feet per mile. Evenly distributed, this would be only a foot of drop in some 35 feet of river. Ideally the river would rumble through a foot-high vertical chute followed by a 35-foot pool—easily manageable. Here on the Apurímac, however, the scale was 10 times grander. This monstrous river usually crashed over 10-foot falls, then rolled through choppy 350-foot pools. In order to avoid the rocks at the upper lip of the plunging cataracts and to find a path back to the pool below, we were often forced into a tortured detour by land that consumed over half of the distance between falls.

On the bright side, we worked together exceptionally well. We helped each other constantly, as the success of our venture was at stake at each of these powerful cataracts. At one point I was simply too drained to carry my boat another inch. Gerry and Chuck then took over. And Jim was always helpful. I reciprocated whenever possible. At one point near shore, Dee broached sideways on a rock, and I waded and swam out to pull him off; and I helped Jim recover the boat he swamped when he went to aid Gerry in freeing himself from rocks. With such mutual concern, I grew more confident that we could make it all the way.

And so our day passed, in agonizing exertion. Then, toward evening, we encountered a few beautiful, navigable rapids. Finally we camped, exhausted, near the end of the canyon, not far from the village of Nayhua.

The bugs now attacked in earnest. Only a few biting flies and gnats had bothered us by day, and while the little gnats were thickest at dawn and dusk, they hadn't been bad until now. But suddenly they attacked like vultures. I had learned about these troublesome gnats a year before, when hiking near Curahuasi. They had attacked me almost unnoticed, but each devilish bite had itched for two weeks. I tried various insect repellents on them later that year and found that the common ingredient DEET worked admirably. The problem is, the gnats are so small that they come and go like tiny stealth bombers—they bite, draw blood, and retreat to safety before the itching begins. To avoid them one must stay soaked in repellent, an impractical solution on the river.

Jim's face soon became lumpy with bites. We all turned into scratching machines, rasping our skin with fingernails whenever our hands were free. Gerry hated them most. "I can't stand these *** bugs," he cursed. His florid language should have scared many of them away!

Our scratching was interrupted by the arrival of a friendly delegation from Nayhua. We chatted with them awhile and promised to visit their village the next day. Chuck prepared some tea in an empty aluminum food container. They gave us some pieces of bread. A starchy food such as bread is enticing after days of concentrated fare. I bit at my small crusted piece, which resembled a shrunken hamburger bun, with real anticipation, but absolutely no part of it yielded—hard, hard bread, but good when soaked in soup!

Across a gorge alongside Nayhua—a short distance below us on the river—a strand of silvery cable gleamed high above a roaring rapid. This was Nayhua's bridge, a simple *aroya*. There were no frills here, no suspension bridge, no tiny platform hanging from creaky wheels. Just

≈ A child of Nayhua practicing at the end of the cable for the day he can cross the river in this upside-down position.

the bare cable—and lots of raw courage—were used to get across the frothing river. We watched several men cross the chasm that evening. They slithered across upside down, clinging like giant spiders to the underside of the cable, attached to it by a crude rope harness attached to a wooden slider called a *palilla*, shaped like a boomerang. One passenger employed a second harness and a length of rope to tow a bundle of his belongings behind. Another had a packet slung beneath him. The great cable sagged in the center, and each rider would shoot down the first half like a plummeting hawk. I missed several photographs of this because my camera was not to my eye, ready. Beyond the center of the cable, the laborious hand-over-hand ascent to the opposite side began.

Up near the base of the cable, before it left its rocky platform to fly across the river, some young boys climbed and jostled on its strands. They scrambled to and fro upside down, like fledgling birds beating their wings in practice for that magic day when they would first soar across the Apurímac.

"How old must a child be to cross on the cable?" I asked a village elder the next day.

"A boy must be eight."

"And the girls?"

"They cannot cross."

"Why?"

"They are not strong enough," was his firm reply.

So the great river roars down these canyons and cleaves the land in two. It separates livestock from pasture, cropland from market. It makes schools inaccessible and useless to children just across the river. It hinders communication and deadens the flow of friendship and ideas. It creates two contiguous worlds that, in some respects, might as well be on different continents.

For hundreds of miles up and down the river, it is the same. A few can cross, most cannot. The desperate and brave measures taken by the inhabitants to find any possible way to bridge the chasm is testimony to their indomitable spirit in the face of this immense natural barrier.

The difficulties involved are almost incomprehensible to those of us whose paths are cut by steel blades and dynamite. For us a river can be bridged with impunity and crossed almost instantly in the luxury of our automobiles. Such bridges are rare in the Andes and nonexistent in the Apurímac backwaters. Even more primitive bridges are scarce. Few are the major crossroads where a family and its livestock can cross on walking bridges. Here and there in between are the hanging cables, where only unencumbered men can pass. But even a length of cable is a luxury in the canyon, and ropes are sometimes woven out of native plants to span the restless waters. Occasionally there are primitive rafts made of reeds, but these must usually follow a strand of rope across the river, lest they be flushed into the rapids below.

Such desperate crossings are rare, bright threads of success. Between them lies mile after mile of threatening water, cutting off human communication as effectively now as it has for thousands of years.

The following morning we trudged up to Nayhua, as we had promised the villagers. This would be our last visit to a highland pueblo, since below the settlement the canyon narrows and proceeds into a land of increasing isolation. There are no more villages of substance on

83

≈   The pueblo of Nayhua.

these shores for 200 miles—far away, beyond the mountain barriers, in the jungle.

Nayhua lies on gently sloping benchlands cut by a tumbling mountain brook, whose water flows along ditches to fertile fields for dry-season irrigation. The abundant food produced has helped make Nayhua a village of relative prosperity and contentment. Where the path to Nayhua cuts across the fields, it becomes a formidable corridor, lined with trees and bushes, interwoven with thorny branches and interspersed with living cactus plants. With these prickly barriers, the burros don't stray into the corn, and predators don't get into the chickens.

Beyond the fields the trail opens into the village center. As we approached, the picturesque narrow streets were dotted with children, animals, and fowl. The houses were large old adobe buildings with roofs of straw. Behind a wall was a public shower with metal plumbing, a rare luxury in these mountains.

"Would you like to see the school?" asked the young *gobernador* (mayor), who was our personal guide. The townspeople now crowded around us, and we became a parade marching up the trail to school (the schools here, for reasons I don't understand, are always found in the highest reaches of the pueblos). We toured the small schoolhouse, whose rooms seemed almost bare of educational materials. When we reassembled in the playground, we found people preparing for a group photograph—one shot of all the assorted inhabitants who had managed to follow us. Most of the townspeople, perhaps three dozen adults, must have been there.

"No!" said the gobernador, suddenly changing his mood. "We will have two photographs: first we men, then the women and children!" The women said nothing as the proud men of Nayhua segregated themselves into a beaming pack of chauvinists, ready to be photographed. (*See* Plate 9)

The women of the Andes generally stand in the background when anything of importance is decided on, although there are exceptions. We had seen a beautiful school teacher at Pillpinto in the thick of organizing the school kids during our visit there. But the spark of initiative has so far not reached the women of these pueblos. The haughty men would not appreciate my saying this, but of the two groups photographed that day, the women were by far the more interesting.

Highland women are, generally speaking, quiet and industrious.

They cook and carry and weave things of beauty. They, alone, are splashed in color, and they lend a remarkable vibrancy to this mountain land. The women of Nayhua, grouped together, looked like a topsy-turvy rainbow. Many of their skirts were brightly dyed, but the colors of their sweaters and caps were dazzling pinks, reds, yellows, greens, and blues, in plain and checkered designs. Highland women all wear rather plain felt hats, but occasionally a dash of color sparkles from a hatband. They do not all wear shoes; bare feet are as common as sandals.

As we left the school ground, a festive mood broke out. The women sprinkled flower petals in our hair and gave us oranges and eggs. We were treated like kings, at the center of attention. The villagers marched us down to see their new bread oven, freshly made of clay and still unfired and untried. I hoped that with this oven they could make a more pliable bread than the rock-hard disks given us the night before!

Before leaving, we visited a barefoot artisan engaged in the ancient Inca pursuit of weaving a rope of bark and plant fibers to hang across the Apurímac. We were told that this was for a bridge down below, and our hopes jumped at the prospect of seeing an all-rope bridge in the style of the Incas, since they are now exceedingly rare in the Andes. Alas, we found later that the rope bridge was no more than a single cable spanning the river—a far cry from the magnificent suspension bridges of the Incas. There would be no Bridge of San Luis Rey in this canyon.

We picked a few dozen oranges, paid the woman who owned the trees, though she didn't expect payment, then hiked back down to the river. We were ready to resume the odyssey.

We were glad to be at the bottom of the canyon. All night long we had listened to the roar of its last great rapid. This was a common sound now, since we often camped by unrunnable cataracts so that we could carry our boats, emptied of camp gear, down the shore at their lightest. We also camped in these places sometimes because we were simply too tired to face another portage at the end of the day.

"How is the river below?" I had asked the village elders.

"Muy suave" (very soft, or gentle), one replied. This prospect glad-

A rope maker of Nayhua. ≈

dened our hearts, as fresh as the memories of the tortures above still were.

We started again at 11 A.M. "With luck and easy water we should reach another big tributary today," I said, "the Río Santo Tomás."

The first rapid below Nayhua had two large drops. Dee went ahead on foot to scout them. He signaled back uncertainty, strongly hinting at caution. All of us except Chuck walked down the shore to look. Suddenly Chuck appeared from above already in his kayak, on the river, with full momentum. He dropped over the first lip, capsized in a giant hole, washed onto a large rock, and was pulled from his boat by the heavy turbulence. Body and boat flushed separately through the next big drop. We watched helplessly from shore, since none of us was near our boats. Fortunately, Chuck recovered by himself; he swam to his boat and dragged it back to shore, where he could empty out the water to prepare to launch anew.

This solo run seemed careless to me. We had talked about safety over and over, and had all agreed on certain rules of safe conduct so far from help. One rule was that a lead boat should not go through a hazardous rapid without a companion boat prepared to follow and help. I thought of saying something, but that proved unnecessary. Chuck was reluctant to run big drops all the rest of the day, and even lined several drops that everyone else ran.

The next drop was another giant cataract, which again we portaged. "When do you suppose that 'soft' water promised in Nayhua will begin?" Gerry asked, grunting at the end of a heavy boat. Paradise arrived immediately thereafter! For an hour and a half we boated down superb, technical rapids—narrow channels twisting downward amid enormous rocks—without a single portage. They were perhaps not "soft," but they were all decently runnable. On second thought, that is soft by the standards of the demonic river known as Apurímac!

At one point in the rapids, we were accosted by hail. The popping on our helmets sounded like machine-gun fire and was highly disconcerting in the midst of intense rapids! After fifteen minutes the hailstorm vanished, leaving only a thin residue of white and a renewed doubt about the longevity of the dry season.

Somewhere in that stretch of runnable rapids, we crossed the imaginary line that was coincident with the margin of my last 1:100,000-scale map. Beyond, the coverage was no longer so detailed. There were only cruder maps, scaled at 1:200,000, on which the contour lines no longer reached the river. We would have no further information on the gradient of the river in any canyon. A few sketchy clues from my aerial photographs were all that remained.

We ate lunch, then pushed on into the deepening canyon, marveling again at the great height of the canyon walls. Big peaks loomed far above us, and several waterfalls came cascading down their steep flanks.

The rapids worsened, and we were forced to portage and line several drops. We began to push ourselves again to take on rapids that were altogether too difficult. Turbulent chutes and frothing rock gardens followed one another in close sequence. Twice we faced almost impossible right turns in turbulent chutes between house-sized boulders. We collided frequently with the great rocks. Twice I was thrown on my side, but righted myself with a quick paddle brace. (*See* Plate 6)

Again I turn to my diary to describe a brief moment of our travail:

Dee goes through one drop and waves us down a turbulent chute having powerful crosscurrents. I paddle into the maelstrom and am nearly thrown end over end by a giant, frothing hole at the bottom. Gerry passes okay, then Chuck is capsized and rolls back up.

Jim is thrown against a nearby rock sideways, and the bow of his boat soars five feet into the air. He makes a difficult brace on his right—upstream—and pulls himself around backwards. He catapults through the adjacent chute upright, unhurt, but in reverse! A close call!

I wondered how long we could keep up that frenetic pace, with such a narrow margin of safety. We were courting disaster by running those great drops, but we would have faced hunger if we had taken the time to portage them all. We faced tough decisions with each major rapid.

We camped late, at 5:30, beneath a cloudy sky. Through a large break in the white canopy above us, a shaft of sunlight poured onto the summit of a great mountain. The ageless giant of the sky, ablaze in the orange light of the heavens, seemed immutable, eternal. But this demon river will cut it down, wait and see!

≈ Jim Sindelar runs an Apurímac rapid near Nayhua.

The ninth day arrived, a day, finally, of progress.

Our start was rather late, past 10:00. We were delayed by repairs Chuck needed to make on his boat, following the upset and violent collision with the rock the day before. He started late and proceeded leisurely with his work. I fumed at the unnecessarily long delay, knowing that we were still behind schedule. "Would you please try to get started earlier when lengthy repair work is needed?" I asked Chuck. My voice must have unintentionally reflected my irritation, because at the end of the repairs, Chuck rushed to load his gear and left by himself.

The four of us followed down the river, but soon Dee had surged ahead once more. We saw neither Dee nor Chuck again until well into the afternoon. I disliked seeing the party split this way for so long; the canyon seemed friendly enough, but experienced expeditioners know that accidents often strike at the most unexpected times. It is precisely then that part of the strength and expertise of the group should not be out of sight and out of reach downriver.

Despite the late start, we moved swiftly down the canyon and through intermittent long but runnable rapids. At 11:30 we passed beneath the footbridge Puente Huacachaca ("woka-chá-ka"). Nearby the foundation of a much older bridge had plunged into the river, blocking the shallows like an ancient sunken barge. Across the river the opposite abutment stood in crumbled ruins, covered with cactus plants and tropical bromeliads.

We stopped to watch a family pass overhead. A pack horse carried their supplies. Once across, they scrambled down toward us on a spur from the main trail. The woman was striking. Her strong brown face was lit with burning black eyes. She was dressed well, but in the tradition of the hills. Her social approach proved to be as unusual as her beauty. She walked briskly up to the shore, where we were parked in our boats in an eddy. While her husband stood in the background, she asked us all the usual questions: "Where are you going?" "What are your motives?" "Where are you from?" We talked awhile and found out that they were from a little village, Capi, up in the hills, eight trail miles distant and high above us.

Then arose a new twist on mountain hospitality. Suddenly the woman lit three fresh cigarettes and held them out to us. This was a kind gesture, for cigarettes are treasured in these hills. It was an awkward moment—we were all nonsmokers, but cognizant of the possible feelings of insult should we reject her gift. Our personal, perhaps unkind, decision was to decline. "No, gracias," I told her. "You are very kind, but we do not smoke." She extinguished the cigarettes, perhaps to save them for another day, or for more appreciative guests! We talked a while longer, then the family left. I hope she understood.

The deep gorge of the morning was now breaking down into a wider canyon. Bird life became increasingly abundant. We had seen occasional flocks of iridescent green parakeets ever since we passed the great suspension bridge of Huarancalle, on the second day. Now they became more numerous and more quarrelsome. They raced up and down the canyon in groups of ten or fifteen, darting and scolding. Closer to the water, diving birds skimmed up and down across the river, sometimes plunging like bullets into the swirling currents after some unknown morsel. These birds were joined by ducks, swallows, and large, black cormorants.

People as well as birds fished in this valley. No villages or haciendas bordered the river, but people had found it worth trekking in for the prospect of fish. They had established reed fish traps every mile or two in the swift shallows of the river.

Barely past noon, we arrived at the mouth of the Río Santo Tomás, which discharged another large volume of water into the Apurímac. The current was swollen again, and the river gained another increment of speed and power; greater care would be required in the rapids. "It raises the ante," explained Jim. "Mistakes will be more serious from now on."

The Río Santo Tomás had been our objective for camp the night before, so we were half a day late. But since 10 A.M. the Apurímac shoreline had glided past our boats with unprecedented swiftness. Despite interruptions, we had gone 8 miles in two hours—farther than we had gone on all three of our worst days above.

Dee and Chuck rejoined the expedition, and we sped on until 2:30. Then three large rapids broke the euphoria. The first was short but turbulent, with a choice of three plunging chutes at the bottom. We scouted it thoroughly, then ran it. Only Chuck capsized in one of the chutes, but he rolled up instantly. The second rapid was passed uneventfully, and then we faced the third. It was a long, turbulent rock garden, full of boiling holes. No route was evident to those who scouted from the left. I had landed on the right bank and thought I saw a route between rocks down my side. Making sure that I was covered by those behind, I launched. What a ride I had!

I misjudged the current near the top, was swept toward the center into a giant hole, turned backwards, and plunged in reverse toward shore. I was then catapulted down a narrow channel backward. I fought desperately to maintain balance and keep my boat from broadsiding on the teeth-shaped rocks. Wiggling and maneuvering backwards, I reentered the main channel, then turned and completed the rock-strewn run. There was no better route, so the others followed. Jim and Dee fell into problems just like my own, but Chuck and Gerry came through clean.

Our pace picked up again. We passed under two broken and twisted suspension bridges, Puente Churoc and Puente Cotuctay. These were more primitive than the suspension bridges above. The only steel wire was in their high longitudinal cables; the floors were woven from reeds and branches, tied in places by rope. Some natives told us that the bridges were much used despite their twisted form and obvious disrepair. Crossing must be hazardous.

Below, a waterfall more magnificent than any we had seen previously glided over the high left wall, plummeting from ledge to ledge toward the distant valley floor. Gusty winds whistled across the great stone face. Each large gust would seize the silvery ribbon of plunging water, shatter it, and whip it across the bare rock in a million shining droplets. Only a bare trickle survived the winds and arrived below at the river's edge.

Late that afternoon, Jim announced: "I'm tired of nuts and salami; we're going to eat fish tonight!" He pulled out the fishing gear and cast from his boat. Several two-pounders succumbed to his fishing wiles. I drifted with him as he fished, but Dee and Chuck paddled on. Later, Gerry paddled ahead too. We fished and paddled intermittently, as the sun dropped over the mountains.

"If we don't find the others soon, we'll have to camp without them," I remarked.

"Too bad," Jim said, "we would have to eat all these fish ourselves!"

In the grayness of dusk, after having agreed to paddle only one more bend, we found our comrades camped on the right bank near a cliff-bound pool of deep, quiet water. "Perfect for fish," Jim said, casting out one last time. A finny monster nailed his lure; it raced back and forth beneath his kayak, as he struggled to keep it on the line. I thought he would capsize.

"How can I help so you don't join that fish?" I asked.

"Give me a tow; we've got to get to shore." I towed Jim, and Jim towed the fish. Near land, Chuck waded out to pull a 10-pound rainbow trout from the shallows.

We didn't eat nuts and salami that night, nor the next morning, either!

There is something ominous about a swift river, and something thrilling about a river of any kind. The nearest upstream bend is a gate out of mystery, and the nearest downstream bend a door to further mystery.

Wallace Stegner

And see the rivers how they run,
Through wood and mead, in shade and sun,
Sometimes swift, sometimes slow,
Wave succeeding wave, they go,
A various journey to the deep.
Like human life to endless sleep.

John Diver

≈ THE GREAT GRANITE GORGE

W E HAD TRAVELED something like 25 miles in the relentless pace of the ninth day, virtually halving the distance to the Cunyac Bridge. This was the first solid progress of the trip, and in one fell swoop it eliminated the annoying lag in our schedule.

We had now dropped to 7,140 feet elevation, as shown by Gerry's altimeter. This too marked our advancement; it was a point partway down a descending scale of progress that would reach its end only when we had completed our grinding plunge to the jungle, at about 1,800 feet. We had already lost over 2,000 feet from our start at 9,300; ahead we would have to descend a full vertical mile before we could breathe easily again.

With the slow fall of the altimeter's needle, the temperature crept upward. The days were now warm, the nights pleasant. The water in the river was still cold from its birth in the snowfields. Enough chill remained there for a trout fishery, but the warmth of the days was nibbling it away. Unknown to us that night, no more trout, in fact, no more fish of any kind, would broil over our fire for the rest of the trip.

That evening I brought up the subject of resupply. When we reached the Cunyac Bridge, until today a distant goal, three of us would go to Cuzco for fresh supplies, while two would remain behind with the boats. "Who will volunteer to stay?" I asked, hating myself for requesting anyone to sit on a hot shore all day, fighting bugs. Jim volunteered, and Chuck was conscripted.

"You need to make a list of the things we should bring back with us," I told Jim and Chuck.

"Six quarts of beer," Chuck said nonchalantly, sprawled on the sand.

We discussed the details a while longer, then turned in as the campfire flickered into oblivion.

T he night that ensued was so strange and eerie that the mere thought of it sends shivers coursing up and down my spine.

The high rimrock was perfused with moonlight, while the canyon below remained gripped in blackness. The air was filled with strange songs and whirring noises. Occasionally one voice drove all others beyond consciousness. It came from some unknown bird of the night, whose call was one of wild, intoxicating beauty. I have never seen this bird, so the reader must fly with my imagination to visit him, clinging with white claws to raw, dark rock just below the brilliant flood of moonlight on the canyon rim. Piercing eyes search the night, then he charges the darkness below on furious wings. An electrifying sound fills the canyon, and immediately all life goes silent—time stands still, and the mother of the Amazon pauses in her perpetual flow.

That is how the electrifying mood of the night embraced me, how those magnificent sounds tugged deep at my soul. The bird was probably a member of the remarkable order *Caprimulgiformes*, an order that includes whippoorwills, nightjars, and nighthawks. Its call was patterned like those of a common nighthawk, but ten times more raucous and powerful—utterly primordial.

Soon I fell asleep as the moonlight crept down the canyon wall. But the night was not yet done with me. I awoke to the sound of a nearby voice, and it was filled with consternation. "What's that?" Jim asked, pointing to a heavenly light, looking brighter than any star, thinly covered by a small disc of cloud in a transparent sky. The swirling disc would ebb and flow, but always at its center was the brilliant light, whose remarkable luminescence shone through the strange patch of white.

Jim, whom I have never known to be intimidated by anything, sounded distraught at the sight. I didn't know what strange thing it was either; it seemed difficult to fathom in the stupor of half-sleep, when everything is part magic anyway. "I think it's just a star," I tried to reassure him.

"But the cloud hasn't moved," he said, "and the light is way too bright for a star."

The night bird renewed its primordial call, and I shivered in the excitement of this wonderful mysterious night. I felt no threat or uneasiness at this singular sight; my only concern was the distress I perceived, perhaps exaggerated, in a comrade. I continued to persuade him with arguments that there was really nothing unusual in the night. Now, much later, I don't know. I cannot explain the brilliant light and the slavery of its loyal cloud. I only know that I have never seen a night so beautiful and rich in the mysterious throbbings of the universe as that night spent deep in the canyon of the demon river.

Someday, I thought to myself, this expedition will grind to its inevitable end, and I will go back to civilization, where people sleep in houses with roofs that lock out the stars, the moon, and the planets, in a place the ancient birds have fled. Then nighttime will be for sleeping, and its true beauty will fade to the mere wisp of a memory.

On day ten we were off early, at 8:30. Soon we came upon two Indians pushing into the current a raft made of clumps of long reeds, cinched together by ropes. It was large, maybe 5 by 20 feet, and heavily soaked with water. Its barefoot *balseros* (raftsmen) were clad in cutoffs, T-shirts, and—least of surprises—felt hats. The older man, perhaps the father of the younger, had a small bundle slung around his shoulders. A black plastic jug of chicha was lashed firmly to the deck. The balseros wielded two long poles, with which they pushed the boat when in the shallows, while they paddled when in the deeps.

We clustered around to photograph this transient crossing. Soon we were shocked to find that they weren't crossing at all; they were going down the river! Intrigued, we followed closely. They arrived at the head of a rapid, where they grounded their raft on a reef of large rocks. After much pushing and prying, they dislodged and shot on through the rocky channel. I was so utterly fascinated with this bizarre adventure that I followed on their heels without scouting first.

"Where are you going?" I asked in the quiet pool below.

"Five kilometers down," the older man told me. I asked more questions, but got incoherent answers. Both men seemed ill at ease speaking Spanish; it was clearly not their native tongue.

In another rapid they struck a rock and swung sideways, becoming pinned by the strong current rushing in from above. The two men struggled long and valiantly to free their water-soaked craft, but without success. After a while, Dee and Gerry swam down to help. It was tough, heavy work, even with the four of them. Then they were pinned yet again, near the bottom of the following rapid. This time Jim kayaked up from an eddy below and clambered onto their boat, pushing his empty craft to Gerry for escort to shore. Then he pushed and strained with the balseros to finally work the raft free.

≈ Two highlanders attempt to run a reed raft through an Apurímac rapid.

"At this rate, the lunatics will kill themselves," Jim shouted, riding the freed raft to shore. The balseros stopped to rest, offering us a drink of chicha from their black gallon jug.

We could wait for them no longer. As we left, our minds were filled with questions about what they were doing and what might happen to them next. Theirs was certainly not a freight run; they had no freight. It was not a regular run of any kind, because the waterlogged reed heap could never be towed upstream. One could imagine that they made rafts above for some use below, and that these men were in charge of seeing the rafts to their destination. But that idea didn't make sense either, in part because the raft was water-soaked and worn instead of new. Besides, the laws of probability make almost impossible the prospect of their running a raft down the river very many times. Consider the most optimistic odds: on an average trip the balseros run aground only twice; once aground they have a 50 percent probability of breaking free; failing that, they swim the turbulent rapids, with no more than a fifty-fifty chance of making it to shore without drowning. Grim odds, indeed, but judging by their performance while in our company, these odds are generous beyond anything deserved.

In retrospect, I think they stole the boat. Perhaps they were fishing along the shore well away from their usual haunts, found the raft, and simply took it on impulse. Maybe they pulled it off successfully, in the end, with our unknowing help. But I'll wager very few other rafts are ever stolen on the Apurímac. At least there would be very few repeat offenders.

We moved on, passing beneath another battered suspension bridge, Puente Mulpachacha. Its twisted floor and broken strands belonged here, in the bosom of this land of desolation. But then, soon afterwards, an object loomed ahead that did not belong in this ancient canyon, an object as misplaced as some ghost from another world. It was a bridge of white concrete, shiny with steel, spanning the void of the canyon. It stood in silence, as if early for an appointment with destiny, waiting for the inevitable flow of civilization across the mountain. Then a quantum of civilization advanced down the hill, riding on four wheels. It was a pickup truck descending the steep switchbacks toward the bridge, leaving a banner of white dust and thin smoke to drift in the clear canyon air.

None of my maps showed the bridge, but I remembered then a map I had seen the year before, with the red lines of a highway cutting across the Apurímac wilderness aimed for Cotabambas, a pueblo in the hills. Most maps are so inaccurate and inconsistent on road crossings that I had dismissed, and then forgotten, the possibility of the bridge altogether.

Only an hour beyond the anachronism of the modern bridge, we plunged into a magnificent granite gorge. Citadel walls of mottled white thrust skyward, reflecting the brilliance of the noonday sun. The gateway of the canyon was scattered with enormous boulders, polished white by millennia of rushing currents. Green curtains of water sped past them, forming rapids of beauty and simplicity. The grandeur of white walls and rounded rocks, broken with sparkling ribbons of clear water, was so artistically and so massively composed that no cathedral on earth could begin to be its equal.

The benevolence of the waters recalled an old dream of mine, of finding an easy run on the Apurímac down which many people could safely go, enjoying the wonders of Peru's greatest river. Perhaps their trips could start at the highway bridge that had surprised us above and end 20 miles below, at the Cunyac Bridge. That way all those who wished could see the marvels of the Apurímac Gorge while floating on the mother of the Amazon, and the Peruvian government could be made aware of some use and benefit from the free-flowing river, aside from water diversion and hydroelectric projects.

But my dream was short-lived. The rocks grew large, looming above us like whitewashed schoolhouses. The water began to crash between them in vertical torrents, then to split and foam over other rocks below. We marveled again at the sights and sounds this gorge must create in high water, with these great white blocks throwing the water into vast holes, creating whirlpools of unimaginable fury.

Suddenly we came upon a giant drop of thundering water. Here we were forced out of the river, onto massive blocks on the left bank. We discovered a route back to the river—a 15-foot near-vertical, water-filled trough. Pushing our boats ahead of us, we shot down the trough like it was an amusement-park slide, plunging deep into a frothy pool in the river below. We then swam our boats around a rocky corner and into a narrow alcove, where we could once more enter our crafts.

Dee began to pull ahead of everyone else. He would make instant decisions on what he would run and how he would run it, whereas most kayakers in remote canyons study a complicated rapid for long minutes before committing themselves to a passage (some, like Jim, will simply stand there and look, "because I like rapids"!). He paddled some technically difficult mazes without being close to a support boat, which left him without aid in case of trouble. He often disappeared behind the giant white rocks, and we had no way of knowing if he was safe. At one point, after a worrisome disappearance, we came around a corner to find him sitting on a rock, eating lunch. Jim called over in exasperation: "Crouch, you son-of-a-bitch, I thought you were dead!"

My own troubles began in earnest in these turbulent waters. Perhaps I had gotten too cocky and overconfident as a consequence of having so far avoided any serious problem. I had neither capsized nor broadsided on rocks in ten days of paddling these furious waters. But then I dropped through a small chute and swung into a narrow channel, behind a large overhanging rock to the right. The current inched me farther to the right, under the jutting granitic shelf. My paddle, up vertical in a drawstroke position, caught on the overthrust wall, unable to follow me into the shadow beneath the roof of rock.

I could not—must not—let go of my paddle, on which all my hopes for the expedition rested. I tilted outward toward my immobile paddle, then let go with one hand, as I was drawn farther under the rock. As I approached the point of instability, unprotected by the leveraged brace of the paddle, the jumpy water seized me and tipped me over.

I thrashed around underwater for a few moments, trying to grip and orient the paddle. Soon I had it under control and rolled back up, happy that nothing more than a thorough wetting had occurred. It was my first dunking in fourteen days on the Apurímac, ten days on this expedition and four days the previous year. I should have expected it, knowing this mischievous river, but still the effect was upsetting.

Somewhat later, after scouting from shore, I led the others down a maze with three major drops. The first two went smoothly. I pulled left into slow water near shore, so the others could catch up and see my route. When I started again, I was closer to the rocks and eddies of the shore than I had planned. I was forced to follow the lowermost edge of the current, as it doubled back into the riverbed. Halfway out it curled left and dropped abruptly around a rock that looked like a mammoth fallen on its side, glistening wet and white from spray on its flanks. I was too far left, pointed at its backbone, accelerating forward on water that was beginning to lurch with excitement at the prospect of another drop. "Damn," I thought, "I can't cut to the left straight down the river for the blockade of rocks running out from shore to the mammoth rock. I have to swing upstream and go right of the mammoth, down where all that current's going." I dug vigorously into the water, pulling right with a series of hard strokes, and appeared to gain clearance. I would miss the big rock now by a good five yards, and I began to relax.

Just above the mammoth now, I crested a wave that signaled the start of the fall. I looked down and gasped. Below me a thick dark sheet of water raced across my path, headed left, and smashed into spray against the granite mass. I couldn't stop; my momentum swept me onto the liquid sheet, barely with time to make a desperate stroke to try to pull right across the glassy surface to safety, only four yards out past the rock. But the sheet of Apurímac water racing sideways under my boat pulled the bottom of the craft out from under me in an instant. I splashed into the water on my right and was whipped under my boat, head down in the raging water.

I wrestled with the paddle against the blows of the current smashing and twisting its blades; I tried to bring it around into position for an eskimo roll. Little bubbles began welling up around my face, and I thought how beautiful they were, twinkling softly and dancing around in the sunlight that penetrated the water. At the same time, I was scared to death. The bubbles meant that I had hit the turbulence where the mammoth rock broke the sheet into foam. I sensed going into the shadow of the monster. All this happened in an instant, but it was long enough for me to think about the horrible rapid below and how I must absolutely not fail to eskimo roll, or else I would end up swimming down there at the demon's mercy.

The surges of current still pushed me left, so I got the paddle into position for a roll to the left, where I wouldn't have to fight the current. Clink! Clink, clink! Now, full in the monster's shadow, I was racing down the granite underside, my paddle striking the folds of water-worn rock. The noise rang through the water like someone chiseling stone. The impact shook my arm to the bone. My head stayed down and clear, down in dark water where I wanted it now, down away from the racetrack of granite flying by. My breath grew short, and my heart pounded.

I knew I must wait a few more moments. If there were no complications, I should wash past my tormentor soon. If the rock stayed smooth, and if no teeth of granite stretched out to block me, I should soon be free. I waited. Time stood nearly still. Impressions of shadow and depth alternated with spears of light and sparkles of foam. I sensed a dull roar and the chiseling noise. I sensed the interior of my body, my heartbeat, my lungs burning for air. I sensed my determination and my fear. I swore soundlessly. Then, at the last moment of my remaining breath, I washed free of the rock and rolled upright, sputtering in relief.

"Dammit!" I said to the others, still perched in a quiet pool above the drop, "that's tougher than it looks. Maybe you should portage it." They did, and we continued on our difficult descent. But I was shaken by the realization that the river was gaining control, while I was losing it, as ever-increasing volumes of water flooded the rock-laced river.

We camped in a small sand enclave, beneath a towering rock of polished granite. Tortured water swept by and burst down two frenzied chutes—deep cracks in the solid granite of the riverbed—to a tranquil pool below. The roar of the struggling water echoed back and forth between the cliffs above. (*See* Plate 7) After chores were done and the black curtain of night had descended, I lay back against a rock to relax and scribble in my journal. I sat upright again, as an incredible chirping noise thrust itself into the air above the thundering of the rapids; it sounded like hundreds of birds locked in some unfathomable torment. Their shrill plaintive voices ebbed and flowed across the canyon in half-coordinated unison, continuing on into the night. The effect was heightened by our lack of all sense of their origin, since the muting effect of the roaring rapids stole our ability to perceive the direction from whence the sounds came. It was like a bodiless lament echoing from the very soul of the canyon.

In the sobering light of morning, we traced the pervasive sounds to a rookery of swallows on the opposite canyon wall, directly above the rushing river. They were big, beautiful swallows—large, black birds with granite-white heads. I marveled at the strength and grace of their flight over the river, and the way in which they could turn the night into mystery.

It was the eleventh of September, the eleventh day of this expedition, and we sensed the imminent conclusion of this leg of the trip. I had allowed two weeks, and it now appeared probable that we would arrive at the Cunyac Crossing ahead of schedule. The only question mark was our almost total ignorance of the canyon directly ahead, between us and the bridge.

In the granite canyon of the Apurímac Gerry Plummer lowers his boat down a chute to flat water below.

To start the day, we portaged over jagged granite to the pool below the rapid. Around the corner another large tributary, the Río Vilcabamba, entered through a narrow gorge. Swollen again, the Apurímac raced on toward its most reckless adventure, sweeping our five small boats on a collision course with the snow-capped Vilcabamba Mountains, down in the canyons below the Cunyac Bridge. Our spectacular granite gorge disappeared at the junction with the Vilcabamba. We continued now in a wide granite canyon. Several waterfalls tumbled down white walls to compensate for the loss of the gorge. We saw no one all day; more amazingly still, we had seen no one since the highway bridge the morning before. Above the bridge, fishing was common, and a few herders and farmers ventured into the canyon. Below, the land seemed utterly abandoned, like a cursed wilderness.

With the canyon gripped all day in the profound silence of human resignation, we passed beneath a footbridge and were startled by a billowing cloud of smoke rushing suddenly from the nearby hills into the afternoon sky. That night, once again, we saw a canyon fire ablaze. But not a single person stepped forth to break the deep spell of solitude.

The flat pools between rapids were longer that day than they had been in the granite gorge. But their tranquillity was broken by ferocious rapids very little diminished from those of the day before. In the late afternoon, we were forced to line several big drops.

The day went badly for me; I felt weak and lethargic. My boat seemed possessed by a will of its own, and in collusion with the demon river, it went where it and the river wanted, despite my attempts to guide it. In one long, turbulent rapid, I was behind Gerry when he began to backpaddle. I was forced to backpaddle as well, to avoid colliding with him. This negative velocity of the boat in the water, created whenever the water rushes ahead faster than the boat, makes a kayak susceptible to entrapment in foaming holes. Sure enough, I fell into a particularly vicious one. My bow kicked out to the left, and I leaned far out to the right to compensate. I braced right on my paddle, leaning heavily on the stream of water emerging downriver from the bottom of the thrashing trough of water that constituted the hole. I pulled right until my arm ached, but couldn't seem to pull myself over the lip of the hole. I tried pulling forward, but nothing happened. I continued to whip up and down like a yo-yo, and my dislocation-weakened right arm began to tire. Suddenly, after several minutes of violent bobbing, the diving currents sucked my stern deep into the water, leaving my bow pointed high in the air, but aimed downriver. I pulled frantically on my paddle in vigorous strokes and extricated myself slowly from the quagmire of churning water.

My day seemed filled with such marginal events. Various aggravations stalked others in the group as well. After scouting one long rapid, just past noon, Gerry slipped on his paddle and broke it in two. We had allowed for such accidents, but a delay was inevitable. We would join together spare blades with epoxy, then wait while it cured. Dee and Chuck had paddled ahead, but had luckily beached below the rapid for lunch. Another long split in the expedition was thus averted.

"I'll help line your boat down to the beach," I told Gerry. "You can't make it with the broken paddle."

"Here, trade me," said Jim, offering his paddle in exchange for a broken half. He slid into his kayak and swung out into the current in confidence, working through the channels with deft strokes of the single blade. He was perfectly at home with one blade and a partial shaft; his whitewater skills had been learned in a canoe, where a single-bladed paddle was standard equipment.

We landed below and hurried to mix the epoxy. Gerry glued his paddle, and I used the excess to patch a cracked seam in my boat. The epoxy didn't harden enough to be used until 3 P.M.—the day was almost gone as we continued onward.

At 4:30, in the midst of a difficult lining, Jim spotted a nice sandbar. "It's getting late; let's camp here," he suggested.

Dee's reaction to this proposal was sudden and violent. "We are behind schedule," he fumed. "This is serious work, and we've got to go from dawn to nightfall. If it was easy enough to get through these canyons that we can act like we're on vacation, this river would've been explored twenty years ago." He alluded to pushing on alone, if need be, to complete the expedition.

We stopped shortly thereafter and discussed the matter. Dee proposed that we paddle steadily through all the long pools, that we spend less time looking at the rapids when we scouted them, and that we start every morning at 7:00. The others, I'm afraid, had a basic disagreement with Dee, wishing to savor this unique canyon to its fullest. "I like looking at challenging rapids," Jim exclaimed. "It's part of the reason I came here." I tried working out some compromises.

Jim was enormously patient through this, which perhaps saved the expedition from breakup. But he was not without irritation. Later that night he talked to me about the possibility of quitting the river and simply walking out over the hills to the closest road if pushed too hard. "I came down here to enjoy the canyon, not to race through it," he said.

"There is a chance I will hike out, too," I said. "This water is too high; it's twice the volume I expected. I'm not here to court disaster. I'll enjoy the canyon as long as I can, but if I feel that it's becoming too dangerous, I'll leave." Jim and I agreed to walk out over the mountain together, should circumstances and feelings compel either one of us to leave the river.

But it was hard to dwell longer on the remote future, when the todays and tomorrows of our lives were so vibrant with memories and anticipations. Thus our attention returned to the immediacy of our existence. "With any luck, we should reach the Cunyac Bridge tomorrow," I said. "It shouldn't be more than 5 or 10 miles ahead."

"The altimeter reads 6,300 feet; that means we're getting close," Gerry confirmed. He based this conclusion on our somewhat shaky evidence that the Cunyac Bridge was near 6,000 feet in elevation, a mere 300 feet below us.

Late that night, we fell asleep again to the sound of water and strange birds.

D ifficult rapids, several requiring lining, continued to occupy us the next morning. But less than two hours down, a large side canyon ruptured the high right-hand wall of the river valley. Down this canyon, alongside the plunging Río Colorado, the ancient Incas had marched on an ancient road to their magnificent Bridge of San Luis Rey, and from there they conquered the vast northern empire that extended to Colombia.

So it was that on the twelfth day of this journey, two days ahead of my schedule, we arrived at the valley of the Cunyac Crossing. Here trucks rumbled down out of the hills to cross the valley of the Apurímac. They had followed, partway, the royal road of the Incas from Cuzco. That road now lies in decay, and in its place is a potholed dirt road winding in monotonous dusty bends down past village and farm, finally to cross the Apurímac and ascend in twisting, jolting weariness to the highlands of Abancay. This dusty ribbon brings a brief and artificial intermission to the unrelenting savagery of the Apurímac River. It brought an intermission in our schedule too, for here we had to hasten to Cuzco for the exchange and renewal of our supplies.

West of the Vilcabamba, the Río Apurímac runs in one of the deepest canyons of the hemisphere.

Encyclopaedia Britannica

The Apurímac had been the Rubicon of the Incas. For centuries it held their northward movement in check; but once their technology advanced to the point where they could bridge it, they hung a suspension bridge, the greatest in all Peru, across it. At once they pushed their empire northward at a fearful pace.

Victor W. von Hagen

≈ PREPARING FOR VILCABAMBA

FOLLOWING OUR ARRIVAL at the Cunyac crossing on September 12, our thoughts and energies turned to the great challenge ahead: navigation of the deep canyons of the Vilcabamba Range. The first step was to shed unnecessary weight, to make room for enough food to outlast the Vilcabamba. My plan was to return to Cuzco to resupply our food and fine-tune our gear.

We quickly repacked our goods upon pulling in to shore. We left behind, in the custody of Jim and Chuck, the supplies that would continue down the river with us. We were ruthless in plucking unnecessary items from our ongoing loads. Even our sleeping bags were packed up to return to Cuzco; they were sacrificed because the nights were getting warmer. It was important to strip away any excess weight, because we would soon carry a month's worth of food and supplies in our boats for our attack on the Vilcabamba canyons. This is an almost unbearable burden for a kayak, which should be light and nimble for running difficult rapids.

After seeing that Jim and Chuck were comfortably established across the river, away from the main path and free of possible annoyances by curious travelers, the rest of us walked along a dusty spur road toward the highway. We hitchhiked a few miles up the road in the back of a small truck, then waited to hear the rumble of a much larger truck, one of the workhorses of the Andes. Enormous cargo trucks are the backbone of Andean transportation and commerce. They pack goods and people together, without regard for load limits or numbers.

The truck we caught bore a load, as best we could count its squirming multitude, of ninety highlanders and a great pile of cowhides. Men, women, and infants were packed in so closely that movement was virtually impossible. There was no place to sit and barely space to breathe. I climbed up on the swaying sideboard, to perch half over the truck, half over the motion-blurred road. The wind whipped me; several brambles just missed. The others, luckily, found small niches below.

At a lunch stop, we moved into a temporarily abandoned front corner of the truck, not understanding the ethics of territoriality in this unfamiliar situation. The throng returned, and the former occupants pushed and crowded us—they wanted to get back the space they had previously occupied. A wrinkled woman half my size tugged on my shirt and scolded me in Quechua. We accommodated them as best we could. Gerry and I came to equilibrium in a standing position at the front, with no room to move our feet and gain circulation. There we remained frozen, for four long and bumpy hours to Cuzco.

Deposited on a dirty back street in Cuzco, with our circulation now regained, we got on with our errands. Gerry spotted a *ferretería* (a hardware store), at which we stopped and bought three machetes. These were for emergencies, in case we could no longer navigate the river and should find it necessary to hack our way out of the verdant canyons. Back at the Hotel Virrey, we organized food and equipment. We exchanged highland gear for jungle gear: warm clothes and sleeping bags for mosquito netting and large additions of insect repellent.

We did interrupt our chores long enough to walk across the cobbled plaza to visit Carlos Zegarra in the tourism office. I explained our success to date. I also told him, "The villagers have always been startled to see us, but when they regain composure, they ask us our motives. Some are quite suspicious. It would help to have a letter of introduction from you to carry into the more remote canyons."

"No problem," the accommodating chief of tourism said. "We will get your letter at once."

A while later Graciela, a bright young assistant, handed me three copies of a very official-looking letter that urged cooperation from anyone whom we might meet. Such letters go far in Peru, and we needed every advantage we could get.

Finally, and very late it was, we broke our frantic pace to enjoy a civilized meal at a restaurant on the main plaza. It felt good to sit again—and to relax. After a long delay, our food was served. A small piece of chile pepper floated on our thick soup. Gerry unthinkingly gobbled the morsel down. His face suddenly grew tense, as a deep inner glow of red heat suddenly hit him. "There's no such thing as a bland pepper south of Texas," I told him too late.

"Aghh!" he cried, "it's destroyed my mouth! Do you have any extra water?" I couldn't help but laugh. I'm afraid Gerry didn't have a very pleasant respite from our two weeks of camp fare.

We arose early the next morning to make final preparations for our gear. We locked items to be left behind in a special storage room in the hotel kindly made available by my friend Raul, the manager. We also restudied my aerial photographs, which had been left in Cuzco. I arranged them across the floor of the hotel room. We clustered around, taking turns peering through the portable stereoscope, a binocular device that provides a three-dimensional image. We compared the canyons ahead to those behind and found them much deeper—and in some places narrower. Portages from here on would be more difficult. They might, in places, be impossible.

"Look," I said, swinging my finger in a gentle arc across 20 miles of the broken gray shades of the canyon, "here is the first big question mark of the expedition." My finger landed on a distant mountain into which the gleaming thread of the river had melted, utterly disappearing. "That chasm is unbelievably narrow." Scores of times, on dozens of sleepless nights , I had peered down on those hypnotic gray photographs, trying to fathom the secret of remote vertical walls from the flattened, featureless sheets. But the secret could not be pried from the mountain under my finger.

"That chasm is so thin you can't see down inside it in any of these photographs, even though each looks down from a different angle. There's no way to tell what's at the bottom. All we know is that it's very turbulent going into the mouth of the chasm." My finger moved back an inch, to an elf's chain of silver river, frothing thin and white into the mountain.

I had decided to call this gorge the Chasm of Acobamba, after several features in the region that bear the name: a ravine, the Quebrada Acobamba, that leads a stream of Vilcabamba water from the high glaciers into the Apurímac, just above the chasm; a massive 15,000-foot block, Cerro Acobamba, that looms high above the Apurímac on the right side; and rather high up on its flanks, the Hacienda Acobamba. Since the name was indigenous and had a good Andean ring to it, it seemed a most fitting designation for the mysterious chasm.

The real mystery, for us, lay in the haunting question of whether there was any way we could pass through the chasm. The evidence I had was starkly mute. We would not know, it seemed, until the moment of confrontation. If we could not get through, we would have to try going around the chasm, over the thorny mountain—or abandon the expedition altogether. I explained to my companions the strategy I had evolved, on those sleepless nights of study, to deal with the Chasm of Acobamba. "First we pass under a footbridge," I said, pointing to a place where an almost invisible thread crossed the river. "We'll stop below, at this wide point, about 3 miles from the chasm. Way up on the left is the Hacienda Poyonco. The map shows two major trails coming through the hills to the hacienda. There are probably others nearby—hopefully one down to the river. By stopping below the hacienda, we can try to get information on the gorge. We can send out two hiking parties, one as far as possible down the canyon, the other to look for trails over the hills, maybe to an overview above the gorge. This way we can scout both eventualities at once. That should save a lot of time if we run into problems and hold back our commitment until we have all the facts."

The plan met with no objection, and nothing different was suggested. I assumed, then, that it was agreeable as a blueprint for attacking our first major Vilcabamba challenge.

The microbus hauled us and our immense piles of supplies again to the Apurímac. The final stage of the odyssey was at hand.

Once again I stood on the bank of the great river, watching the blue-green waters surge past on an ageless journey to the sea. My thoughts dwelled now on the untamed land ahead—on the remote and towering Vilcabamba Range, at whose rocky foundations this demon river now charged with contempt. Here lay gorges buried deep in majestic canyons. Warnings of the immensity ahead reechoed from my past. "One of the deepest canyons in the hemisphere," flickered through my mind from distant white pages of the *Encyclopaedia Britannica.* "Perhaps the deepest cut in South America," I seemed to hear again from *National Geographic* writer and explorer Loren McIntyre. And in the bottom of that awesome cut, the Apurímac rumbled in fury toward the jungle.

A year before I had peered down into those canyons from the heights above Curahuasi. I had looked 4,000 feet down to a distant ribbon of water and had seen it snaking through a narrow defile toward the rocky ramparts of the Vilcabamba Range. I had hoped to go through this canyon shortly thereafter, but when I discovered the mad temper of the Apurímac, I was no longer sure that I ever wanted to step into its jaws. However, time and a gnawing curiosity about the nature of things in one of the darkest, angriest corners of the world, where no one before had ever felt thick Amazon spray, had crowded back my doubts and brought me here once more.

Now, as I stood by the river again, the old doubts returned, those aching uncertainties of a year ago, when two of us alone had faced the upper Apurímac, lacking information on its canyons, knowing only the rumors of its ferocity. We knew more now, but there were still gaping holes in our knowledge. Photo gaps. Inadequate maps. Questions about the depths of the gorges, the difficulty of the rapids.

The mad rush of the unexpectedly high water we had encountered in the canyons above amplified the threat of the river. As its strength grew, ours weakened in comparison. Its power would increasingly erode our control over the passage below. I couldn't understand why the water flow was so vigorous, with the land still parched in the grip of the dry season. But several times more water was flowing than I had expected, more than I had seen here the year before and too much, in my opinion, to explore safely. Yet there were no records or data, no way to have known of the problem in advance. Such are the risks of challenging so primitive a land.

I approached this challenge with a great deal of internal conflict. I looked forward to the profound experience of exploring such a great river, an experience that few people of this generation will ever know. Yet it was not a sacred mission to me, not worth the sacrifice of life. Just what was it worth? Who can ever judge?

My family was constantly on my mind now. They needed me, and there was no question of that. I am not entirely unselfish, but for reasons I don't understand, their needs overwhelmed my own self-concern. I would think of little else when I faced the stark reality of the challenge later, down in the canyon.

Our preparations on the riverbank began at 1 P.M. We signaled Jim and Chuck on the opposite shore to start shuttling boats across. They dragged ours over the water behind theirs, bobbling on tow lines.

We broke the seals on the three-gallon plastic buckets of prepared food and funneled mountains of edibles into our bulging waterproof bags. We left behind, for some weary foot traveler, a mound of margarine in plastic containers. We still had plenty with us, but the high calories provided by margarine are only useful if people will eat it. "I never want to see another drop of margarine in my life," Jim said. Chuck was similarly inclined, but I still relished it mixed thick in dehydrated dinners.

We finally launched at 4:30, with incredible loads. We each had over 125 pounds, including our boats and paddling equipment. Portages would be pure torture. Our maneuverability was deadened; the once nimble kayaks were reduced to half-sunken cargo boats that crashed through waves like water-logged stumps. Food was the biggest single burden—there didn't seem to be room for it all. Some even went in bulging bags strapped on the deck, because the space inside the kayaks was used up. We had over 50 pounds, enough to last for a month. Enough, we hoped, to sustain our snail-like pace over the roots of the Vilcabamba, buried in deep-cut gorges 3 miles below the ice-clad summits.

We began where we had stopped the day before—where the Río Colorado pours its waters into the mainstream of the Apurímac. From here the road runs along the right bank of the river for half a mile before crossing at the Cunyac Bridge and thrusting up into the dry hills, leaving the Apurímac in its customary solitude.

I paddled ahead of the others to the bridge, alone with my thoughts. This place had a very special and personal meaning for me. Just over a year before, I had made my first contact with the Apurímac from the nearby road. I remembered how tranquil the river had seemed at this spot, how reassuring. Now it flowed faster, meaner, seemingly less patient with the frailties of humans. The tumultuous events of my struggle with the Apurímac since that first meeting sped through my mind, and the uncertainties ahead weighed heavily on me. My diary expresses the depth of my inner turmoil:

My thoughts are with my family and my children, who need a father. . . . I am so anxious to be back with them after thirteen grueling days. I paddle hard. This is one little step, the first on this leg, toward reunion—or eternity. Loneliness and regret fill my heart as I paddle under the Cunyac

Bridge. On to step two, as we paddle beyond the bridge—beyond the last egress from this great canyon for almost 200 miles. Little Michael, I will do everything I can to get back to you. If I have to abandon my boat and my equipment and walk out over these spiny hills, I will do that. Whatever is within the limits of my power.

A short distance below the Cunyac Crossing, we passed the abutments of an abandoned colonial bridge. The two gray-white structures loomed high over the river, where they were turned a warm pink color by the rays of the setting sun. The nearby hills were pink, too, and a few mountains on our path ahead thrust pink crowns through colored clouds. Owing to the late start, we paddled only a few miles. We camped at 5:30 on a wide beach. I put up a tent to ward off a slight chill in the air, to which we were now more susceptible, since abandoning our sleeping bags to save weight.

I felt reassured about the trip now that it was under way, my confidence bolstered by the strength of the group. I hoped our differences could be healed so that we could work together cohesively, as we had the first few days.

The beautifully eerie sound of night birds wafted into my tent on a cool breeze. There is no sound on earth I would rather go to sleep to.

S till dark, 5:30, but a murmuring of voices down by the river. Gray figures milled around our boats. "Who is it?" someone shouted; "is anything wrong?" Chuck, nearest the water, warily made his way over. Several men of the highlands had stumbled onto our boats; we didn't know if they intended any harm. As Chuck drew closer, he found them absorbed in speculation as to where the kayaks had come from. Our visitors in fact posed no problem; this was simply the advance group of a workforce mining salt on the other side of the river. Soon others joined them. A balsero carried them across, three by three, on a flimsy reed raft.

We watched them over there, hammering at huge rocks. The ringing of their blows swept across the canyon to intrude abruptly on our breakfast. I preferred the sounds of birds and water. Soon the canyon would narrow, however, the road would abandon the valley, and no human figure would break the spell of the wilderness for days on end.

We left the workers to their salt and launched in search of the remains of the Bridge of San Luis Rey. Our clues as to its whereabouts were few. I had seen a photograph of the site in Victor von Hagen's book, *Highway of the Sun*. I had also studied the remarkable sketch of George Squier, which had inspired many stories about the bridge, including Thornton Wilder's. Squier had crossed and measured the bridge in 1864. He found it to be 148 feet long, listing sideways, and, though sagging in the center, still 118 feet above the river. "It was a memorable incident in my traveling experience," he wrote. "I shall never forget it." He went on to note that "the fame of the bridge over the Apurímac is coextensive with Peru, and every one we met who had crossed it was full of frightful reminiscences of his passage: how the frail structure swayed at a dizzy height between gigantic cliffs over a dark abyss, filled with the deep, hoarse roar of the river, and how his eyes grew dim, his heart grew faint, and his feet unsteady as he struggled across it, not daring to cast a look on either hand."

We knew that our search for this bridge must focus on the steep canyons below camp. As Squier described the site a century ago, the bridge crossed "between two enormous cliffs, which rise dizzily on both sides, and from the summits of which the traveler looks down into a dark gulf. At the bottom gleams a white line of water, whence struggles up a dull but heavy roar."

His description was in our minds as we toiled through the canyon that Squier had seen from the heights and fought the big rapids that had roared their contempt to his ears. Alas, the traces of the great platforms, the tunnel, and the precipitous trails had eroded and lost their identity. But somewhere that day, drifting deep in some gorge hemmed in by solid rock abutments, we passed the unmarked grave of the bridge that Thornton Wilder had taken back, in his imagination, to the year 1714. "On Friday noon, July the twentieth, 1714, the finest bridge in all Peru broke and precipitated five travellers into the gulf below."

More importantly, we crossed the shadowed trail of history that day. Across that narrow path in the sky, Incas radiated conquest, commerce, and culture to a vast northern empire, where people today still obey ancient customs and speak the Quechua language, first imposed by the Incas. Then the Spaniards came and crossed the bridge in the other direction, and conquered and reduced to ashes the marvelous Kingdom of the Sun.

The bridge is now gone; the empire that created it is dead. No one talks here anymore, or gasps in fright at the crossing. The temple of Apurímac, close by the bridge abutment, has crumbled, its voice stilled. All that is left is a cliff-encased land of stark desolation, whose only remaining pronouncement is that of the perpetual water.

Now we are facing 'the raging god' for a new combat . . .''
Michel Perrin

Once more the walls close in, and we find ourselves in a narrow gorge, the water again filling the channel, and very swift.''
John Wesley Powell

≈ THE CHASM OF ACOBAMBA

WE LEFT BEHIND THE canyon of the Bridge of San Luis Rey and cut ever more deeply into the Vilcabamba Range. Many large rapids blocked our way that day, the fourteenth of our expedition. We lined a half-dozen big drops that were either too turbulent for passage or so rocky that they threatened to damage our overloaded boats. We drifted into increasingly narrower canyons and soon found ourselves 4,000 feet below the hills of Curahuasi, hills on which I had stood in awe and wonder as I looked down the Apurímac canyon and its ribbon of water the year before.

The canyon walls swept upward relentlessly and were heavily crumbled now. They would be a formidable barrier to our escape, should we be forced to leave the canyon. We stopped for lunch at a hot spring, where some trickles of steaming water oozed out of the canyon wall and coated the bare rocks of the shoreline brown with its exuding minerals. We had paddled four hours that morning, and our progress was most gratifying. Our advance had been so good, in fact, that we would soon approach the challenge of the Chasm of Acobamba.

To Chuck and Jim I described how Gerry, Dee, and I had scrutinized, one final time, my collection of aerial photographs during our resupply mission in Cuzco. At lunch I reiterated the plan to make a strategic stop below Hacienda Poyonco, the hub of the trails that wove through this region. After eating we hurried on, leaving before 1 P.M. Landmarks now became critical; without them we might drift too far into the canyon and miss our stop below the hacienda.

The first and most obvious landmark would be a thin footbridge, slung high across the gorge to avoid washout. But would it still be there? My aerial photographs were twelve years old, and any human handiwork in this region of flood and earthquake is of questionable longevity. Peru had in fact suffered two major earthquakes in those twelve years. Nothing can be assumed to have permanence here in the Apurímac's deep canyons.

Beyond the bridge the canyon would widen momentarily, at our rendezvous below Hacienda Poyonco. Its walls would then converge, like the jaws of a giant nutcracker, to form the Chasm of Acobamba.

Early that afternoon, we rounded a bend of the Apurímac and the canyon perceptibly widened. I thought it might be our rendezvous, with the bridge that we were looking for possibly destroyed by the annual floods or by tumbling rocks. "This might be our stopping place," I called over to Jim and Dee. Gerry and I pulled over close to the shore to look at the maps. The others continued paddling. I assumed they would stop and wait for us before the next bend in the river.

I frequently sought Gerry's advice when trying to make sense of the cryptic maps. His mind was quick and perceptive, and he had a knack for recognizing and remembering the endless loops in the snake-like windings of the canyon.

"We're up here, above Poyonco," Gerry said, pointing to a gentle right bend. "It looks like the next right-hand bend is the one we want, down below a ways." I folded my map and tucked it away, deep in a waterproof bag tied behind my seat. When I looked up again, the canyon was empty. Our comrades had gone around the sharp right bend ahead, and were out of sight.

We followed their path around the bend, through a deep gorge, then under the suspension bridge, still very much intact. Nowhere before had we seen a bridge hung at such an inhospitable site. Taking the trail down those walls to the bridge must be a nerve-wracking experience, reminiscent of the passage down the precipitous trail that once led to the Bridge of San Luis Rey. A while later we rounded a corner and were able to view, high on the left-hand side, Hacienda Poyonco, lying amid its steep fields and pastures. This was the planned rendezvous. But still no one was in sight; the others had vanished as if swallowed by the demon river itself. There remained only the rippling of waves and the profound emptiness of the canyon.

I became angry and frustrated. The plan to stop here had been made known and reiterated. The landmark on the hill was clearly visible. Did our three companions take the river and this expedition so lightly that they would simply plunge ahead into the great chasm? We had no way of finding out. It seemed a travesty for them to go on—to leave behind no message, no sign, at this critical crossroads. I simply couldn't understand what they hoped to achieve. We had been no more than five or ten minutes behind them. Was their haste so great that they would unthinkingly put the expedition at risk for a few minutes of time?

I was overwhelmed by a sense of remorse as I thought about how the challenge ahead had been magnified by their senseless haste, especially since the problems of this dangerous canyon had already been intensified by a river too full of water. At that moment I wanted no more of the expedition. What else might this anarchic group barge into below, I wondered, should we be lucky enough to escape the Chasm of Acobamba?

I thought seriously of leaving the river, then and there, on foot—of simply abandoning my boat and packing back to the distant road. I told Gerry of my considerations and concern: "My number one priority, far above running this river—above anything else—is that my children have a father. I will compromise nothing to that priority." In truth, I now felt that I had already compromised that priority too much.

For the moment we paddled on, for I wanted to know if they had indeed passed the point of no return, the place at which the converging walls swallowed the last trace of a path back. At the head of a big rapid, we landed on a strip of rocky rubble on the left shore. We saw them a few blocks below and approached them on foot. They were just in the process of running a big rapid with a row of monstrous, rocky teeth awaiting them at the bottom. The spectacle and the risk were frightening. My apprehension was borne out by their near misses. Chuck was caught and held for a time in the churning hole at the bottom; Jim was caught sideways for long, scary moments across two of the great teeth; and Dee capsized and only with some difficulty swam to shore with his boat and paddle. This is safety? I thought to myself in growing anger.

We walked up along the shore below the rapid, and I vented my frustration: "What the hell are you doing down here?" I demanded. I reminded them of the plan we had agreed upon to stop below Poyonco.

"We saw the left bank to be passable all the way, so we decided to reconnoiter by river as far as possible" someone explained innocently.

"You decided," I said sarcastically. "Why couldn't you wait a few minutes so we could all decide? It would be damned hard to get back to the Poyonco crossing now. You had days to object to my plan and said nothing, yet you closed out one of its main options on the spur of the moment, without even consulting Gerry and me. You made a pretty stupid decision." Jim and Chuck, to their credit, remained calm, but I was disappointed in Jim, of whom I had expected better; also in Dee, who had been around during all discussions of the plan; and finally in myself, for an outburst of temper that promised to achieve nothing.

Dee said that he had never agreed with my plan; I had apparently just mistaken his silence for concurrence. Furthermore, the signed agreements had not been broken, because the point of commitment had not been passed. He seemed to have forgotten that part of the agreement where I wrote: "I reserve the right to make trip decisions, particularly where they relate to safety and scheduling." The language is explicit, the violation, in my mind, indisputable.

After a period of reflection, I decided that nothing would be lost by joining the advance party. The Poyonco plan was dead by default, irrecoverable, because of the enormous labor it would require to go back upstream. Later, then, Gerry and I worked down the river, portaging the big tooth-filled rapid. We camped with our comrades on the left, in small pockets of sand between hulking boulders that had sloughed off an unconsolidated wall of dried mud and rock that bordered our camp.

In the calmness of the night, I gathered together my scattered feelings, assessing my now shattered hopes for a cooperative effort. It would be tougher than I had thought. Impatience and a failure to work together were more likely to destroy the expedition than this demon river. For the moment, though, things had been patched up.

Below are the final words scribbled in my journal on that dark, worrisome night of September 14:

Now, in fact, their decision was probably as good as mine: their proximity plan versus mine of using information and trails from the hacienda. Only time will tell; either one is a gamble. But I cannot reconcile myself to that important decision being made without the leader—without the whole group present—and to the rush forward without word of intent.

Will I leave the river? I don't know. I may. I resolve to determine what our scouting turns up tomorrow. Gerry and Jim, with whom I confide, encourage me to stay. Thoughts of my children dominate my mind, and I wonder why I am different than Dee and Jim, whose children also have a stake in this venture.

There was no room among the boulders for a tent, so that night was my first spent outside completely in the open. Luckily I was warm enough. I seemed to have plenty of clothes, including regular pants, wind pants, wool socks, two shirts, a light down vest, and a waterproof parka. These were supplemented by a light sleeping sack I had taped together out of a cotton sheet bought in Cuzco.

Snuggled in these assorted layers, I finally succumbed to the peacefulness of sleep.

Rockfall! Colossal pieces of rock and earth came tumbling down the unconsolidated wall behind us in the dark of night. The clattering rumble echoed back from a million stony facades that time and the river had cut out of Vilcabamba grandeur. It was an eerie effect in the dark of the canyon.

Chuck, sleeping closest to the cascade of rocks, ambled out on the beach, grumbling. "These cheap hotels don't hold up very well," he complained. He found a new pocket of sand, closer to the river, and we all dozed off again. But our sleep was broken at frequent intervals. All night, new pieces would break loose, and the repeated echoes would start again. The cliff was set back far enough from the river and from our camp to leave us unmolested, but in the wavering mirages and uncanny apparitions of half-sleep, the terrace seemed to tiptoe closer and unloose its arsenal of rock above our very heads.

We awoke still on edge from the falling rocks, but our attention soon focused on the challenge ahead. Below us, the canyon turned gently right. Half a mile below, it broke sharply left on its final approach to the Chasm of Acobamba. We would catch no glimpse of the chasm until we reached that abrupt left bend.

But even getting to it might be difficult. The canyon deepened ahead, while the walls slowly converged, until at the chasm they practically came together. The unconsolidated terrace, which continued downriver from our camp, also converged slowly toward the river, broken only by scattered cliffs. The terrace loomed larger and larger in my mind as a hazard. For one thing, it shed its rocks like tears to splatter on all below. Worse, it was utterly unclimbable; we would not be able to escape directly over its crumbling face, no matter how severe our emergency. Far better were the vertical walls of solid rock nearby, which would at least stay firmly in place if we tried to climb them.

The heightened uncertainty of the canyon below, on its final approach to the Chasm of Acobamba, made reconnaissance advisable.

Someone would have to go down to check it out. Jim and Chuck volunteered. They would have to go by kayak, because each shoreline was cut by impassable cliffs running out into the river. The plan was that the kayaks would be emptied of gear so they would be nimble and light for working back up through the current, past the rapids, and along the fading strands of shoreline. Jim and Chuck would have to have perfect judgment, or they could become trapped down there.

Going down a river is always easier than coming back up. The difficulty of every obstacle they encountered going downstream would be multiplied coming back. If they erred by thinking they could get back past a cliff-bound section of river when they could not, the trap would slam shut above them, snaring them between giant walls and loose terraces to the sides and the Chasm of Acobamba below. They would then face the chasm, alone and unequipped, as the only way out of the canyon.

I shuddered at the risks as I watched them pick their way downstream, finally to disappear behind a cliff. I suddenly realized that in our haste we had not developed a contingency plan in case they should not return that day—or the next. Would it be best to seek help in an effort to get them out; to rush into the trap after them; or to look for them from the thorny mountains above? I didn't know, and I prayed that a decision would never be necessary.

The canyon grew hot as we waited. The stillness of the day was broken only by the rippling current of the river, the buzzing of insects, and an occasional word exchanged between those of us remaining. I was buried in thought, trying to imagine what I would do, given various possible reports from those downstream. Uncertainty and confidence alternately took control of me. How can one judge risks objectively for such an uncommon venture? Where is the level path between foolhardiness and equally foolish fear? These were unanswerable questions, buried in the depths of subjectivity and emotion, but I turned them over and over in my mind. On the positive side, I told myself that I had explored and survived many other canyons and gorges before, although none quite so formidable as this. I could probably navigate what I could not portage or line. I could probably swim whatever I failed to navigate. Probably.

I thought of ending the worrisome monotony by hiking up through a break in the canyon wall and terrace on the left side of the river. It might be possible to find a route to the scarred mountain, around which the river turned in its giant left bend as it approached and then plunged through the unexplored chasm. Somewhere up there in the thorny foothills would be a few trails radiating from Hacienda Poyonco. If we had to go over the mountain, that would be the way.

With the lengthening absence of our comrades, I became convinced that I should start scouting the lower part of the route, in the eventuality that the gorge proved to be impassable. The longer their delay, the more likely it was that serious difficulties lay ahead in the chasm and that an alternative would be needed.

We cast our eyes downstream with increasing anxiety as the hours ticked by. I wished we could know how they were doing and what they saw down there. I had decided to begin my hike up the mountain, in part to reduce the tension of waiting, when two figures suddenly appeared on the left shore. We rushed down the shore and greeted them with an intensity more befitting friends lost a year at sea than those scouting half a mile of river. "What did you see?" we chorused. "Can you tell what's in the gorge?"

They told us that after disappearing from our sight, they had continued down the increasingly narrow canyon. They pulled over to a rocky shoreline on the left side, pulled their kayaks up among the rocks, and proceeded to work downriver along the broken embankment. After a quarter of a mile, their route was blocked by steep cliffs. They had two choices: they could scramble back to the boats, cross the river, then try the other side, or one of them could swim across the river from where they stood, where the cliffs had stopped them. After a moment of disagreement, they decided that Chuck would swim across the river, to save time. After swimming over to the right side, Chuck then worked down the rapid along the shore, swam 50 yards through a deep pool alongside a sheer cliff, climbed out on the right side at a break, then climbed up along the cliff for a better view. He was now at the great left bend, still half a mile from the gorge, and his view was still only fragmentary.

Jim, meanwhile, had prepared for Chuck's return. He swam out to a boulder above the rapid, ready to intercept Chuck if his attempt to swim back across the river was overpowered by the currents sweeping down into the rapid. Jim took with him a makeshift throw line—20 feet of nylon rope tied to 30 feet of webbing. As he waited for Chuck's reappearance, he practiced throwing the line out into the river where Chuck might need help.

A while later Chuck swam into view below the rapid, climbed up over the rocks bordering the frothy drop, then swam as far as possible up along a cliff, before challenging the current. He struck out across the river, swimming hard, and outraced the current to the rock where Jim was waiting. From there they retraced their path back to shore and up the river.

Chuck had made it down to the big left corner. He told us the rapids were impassable for almost half a mile below, clear to the gorge. We could portage these on the left. He could see partway down the gorge. Although it had some big rocks, it looked calm farther down. The trouble was, the river swung right again before the end of the gorge, and he couldn't see what was at the bottom. He thought that if we continued down the boulders on the left, clear to the gorge, we could tell if it was passable.

I was cautious, questioning, after the events of the day before. "Can we get back up here if we find the gorge impassable?" I asked.

"It would be tough," Chuck said, "but we could get back, working from one side of the river to the other, past the cliffs."

We loaded our gear and pushed on toward the unknown.

The river sped through several steep, turbulent drops, before it thrust left toward the gorge. Here we landed, dragging our boats high on the rocky shore to the left. It was now 3:00. Below us lay the roaring cataracts leading into the mouth of the gorge. I thought I knew them well by now, but I gasped at the sight. Many times before I had imagined myself in the sky above them, kneeling above my aerial photographs, and I had traced the frothing waters down to the great chasm, hoping each time to penetrate just a bit more the shadow and cliff that blotted them out at the head of the gorge. But that photographed river had looked different from the river I saw now. It had been softened into a silent white ribbon, running as thin as a pencil line into the ephemeral shadow of a dollar-sized mountain. The river now in front of me was big and starkly real; it was laced with rocks that smashed the water with the fury and sound of a hurricane.

We scrambled along the left shoreline toward the gorge, past the frothing water. Our route was up and down over mammoth rocks. Immediately to the side—much closer now—was the unconsolidated terrace that had crumbled toward us the night before. Room-size boulders were stuck up there in the dried clay like a giant's marbles stuck in putty. Broken stones were scattered all over, mute testament to the erosion of this treacherous material. At the farthest point of shoreline, we climbed atop a 20-foot-high rock. Below us, now, was the Chasm of Acobamba.

At our feet, Apurímac water roared into a 50-foot-wide slit in the mountain. There it churned down between walls of solid rock. I lifted my eyes upward and saw the walls lumber toward the sky, tilting here and there as if cut by a drunk, sometimes overhanging the river, sometimes leaning back. After rising for 600 feet, the walls broke into the steep slopes of thorns and broken cliffs beneath the mountain summits. Streaks and patches of white were scattered here and there on the shadowed gray walls, and I imagined that the god of the Vilcabamba had once started to whitewash and brighten his darkest castle but was driven off by gloom.

As my eyes fell again toward the river, I saw the walls grow darker, as if the sun and the light of the bright blue sky were forever locked out of the chasm. At the bottom the river surged through the somber shadows.

"My God, what a marvel!" Gerry gasped, after long minutes of contemplation. "I've never seen such a gorge. And look how the water smashes into the entrance up here. We might have a tough time trying to get past that."

Indeed the river dropped in foaming cascades beneath our rocky perch and continued on past us for another 50 feet before it calmed—50 feet beyond the last shred of our rocky shoreline. Launching our kayaks here would be suicidal.

"Look over there, on the other side," Jim said. "If we could work our way across between the cataracts, then up that rock outcropping, I think we could drop down past the big rapids. Maybe we could get into that small alcove in the wall at the head of the gorge to get started."

Then our eyes followed the route we would have to take through the gorge; followed the course of the water as it swirled angrily between the imprisoning walls; followed the river surging forward in broken steps. A quarter of a mile below us, we saw the swift current pile up in the center of the river on a pyramid-shaped rock, an ancient derelict that had plunged into the chasm in the lost ages before human memory. The current split around the rock and plunged by; we couldn't tell the size of the drop behind the rock. The twisting channels of water looked passable from our vantage point, but we knew that distance and our low angle of vision might conceal great turbulence. If we should fail down there, no landing place would present itself for recovery. We would simply flush through to the end of the chasm, wherever that might be, to whatever fate it might hold. There would be no way back.

The question of the ultimate nature of the gorge now seized our attention. "We may have troubles with it on the other end," Gerry noted. "Look, it bends out of sight down there."

The river indeed disappeared from view, as the gorge turned gently to the right. The crest of the right wall began to lose elevation rapidly at the bend, and then it too was lost from view as it swung out of sight. "It looks like the gorge ends right down below the bend," Jim observed.

"It looks good," I added. "The river is getting calm down there and it must be almost through the gorge." But we had no way to tell—no way to find out for sure that there wasn't an impassable cataract or waterfall right at the end. And yet we were tempted by the brazen invitation of that final bend. It was probably within two minutes of sunshine and sandbars at the end of the gorge. That temptation was heightened by the grimness of any alternative. Going directly over the mountains from here was impossible. Going back to Hacienda Poyonco would be a two-day struggle the wrong way, against the current of the river and over the rocks of the shore, and even from there we might fail to get over the mountain to the river at the bottom of the gorge. We could scout the gully I had eyed earlier that day, but it, too, was back upstream, hard to reach, and perhaps no more than a hollow promise.

Scouting the gorge past the invisible bend was no simple matter either. We were surrounded by a barrier of cliffs and unconsolidated rock faces that barred our way to a high vantage point for observation. Suddenly we thought we saw a weakness in the barrier. A cleft appeared above us on the left wall, a short distance back up the canyon. Gerry and Dee rushed back to get climbing gear so that they could reach the rim of the chasm for a look. They struggled with a band of unconsolidated rock at the beginning of the pitch and downward sloping handholds immediately above. I admired their efforts, but it was unclimbable—the weakness in the canyon wall was pure illusion.

We milled around glumly, coiling the rope, putting away the gear. We wondered if we could hike back up to the bend, cross the river above the cataracts, scale the cliffs, and reach a vantage point on the other side of the river. No one knew. The temptation to gamble—to run that siren bend in the river without scouting—increased. The group was divided on how to proceed. I felt, difficult as it was, that we should follow the rule I had written down to govern this expedition: "We will enter *no* gorge without positive knowledge that an exit of some kind exists." Dee, however, was impatient and wanted to forge ahead. He turned to Jim and asked, "Is this hike really necessary?"

"Well, the chances are 90 percent that the gorge is okay beyond the corner," Jim responded. "Maybe 99 percent. But the question is, who is going to be the one that goes down first and gives the signal? Everyone agrees that we can't boat, swim, or hike back up and that the walls are essentially unclimbable for our purposes. If somebody else wants to go down and check it out, that is okay with me, but if I am the one, I'd rather spend a day climbing up to try to check it out, and I am personally prepared to do that. Do you want me to go?"

Dee replied, "Okay, no, you and Chuck went down this morning, I'll go up."

The matter was settled then. We would try once more to fathom the mystery of the gorge from a vantage point high above.

We hurried back along the rocky rubble on the left side to our boats. Dee and Gerry collected their overnight gear and climbing equipment. They departed at 5:00, with only one hour of daylight left. We watched them paddle across the river, then clamber up the white cliffs on the opposite side. They soon disappeared from view, over the rim of the inner canyon. We knew they would have to spend the night up there. In the morning we would watch for their signal. Upraised arms would mean "go," and we would start to portage. Outstretched arms would mean "danger," and we would begin our retreat.

The three of us turned to making camp, as it was almost dark. We chose a sand spit as far back from the unconsolidated terrace as we could find, but we were still only 50 feet from its crumbly base. This was the end of our tether; we had been pushed right down to the waterline of the Apurímac. The fragile wall loomed hundreds of feet above us. At least it had been quiet up there so far; maybe nothing would come down for years. But as Jim and I tied down our boats near the base of the terrace, a clattering charge of rocks and dirt slid down near our camp. Little pieces fell everywhere—some even hit the boat we were holding. We hurried to finish the task, thankful that the really big rocks had stayed in place, then we rushed out to our small beach, a little farther away from the cliff.

We started a fire of driftwood and ate our meal in darkness. Another rockfall was heard over the noisy rapid, and a small fragment hit Chuck in the elbow. We wore helmets all the time, not knowing when the next attack might come. "Some formal dinner," Chuck mocked, " when you even have to wear a hat. I thought we were roughing it."

"Gotta dress up sometimes," Jim remarked, "even down here."

We each found a large rock near the water's edge to sleep behind. My rock was somewhat too small, and a fraction of my body remained exposed. With each thump in the nearby darkness, I would curl up closer to my protection. The obstacles to this journey had grown enormous: the uncertainty of the chasm, the dissension, the ferocity of the rapids, and the crumbling of the terrace above our heads. Smaller irritants, such as the heat and especially the little yellow gnats, were getting worse, and these further sapped our morale. Yet there was a bright side to it all, one that I expressed at the end of my journal entry for the day: "Oh well, we are still alive and healthy, and that's all that really counts. So we snuggle up to our guardian rocks, and go to sleep to the thundering roar of the Apurímac."

I first noticed the rain at 3 a.m. It was a light drizzle, and I consoled myself that it was what the Peruvians called *garúa*, so fine a mist that it scarcely reaches the ground. I thought it would soon disappear. My tent was tucked away in the boat, up by the terrace. My gear was scattered around. Our long series of dry nights had done nothing to discourage this casual camp style. But this rain did not go away. Its intensity increased ever so subtly, and soon it began to soak my gear and my sleeping sack. I struggled into my waterproof clothing, itself now drenched by the rain. I began digging frantically for a light space blanket stowed away somewhere in my scattered gear. I finally got under it, cramped behind my rock, wet and miserable to the core.

Three hours later, a gray flush of light grew in the clouded sky to signal the morning. I rose to see Jim sitting there by his rock, water dripping off his nose and eyebrows, down his face. "The best of the morning to you," I said with feigned cheer. "Isn't it a nice view—the waterfall over there, the white cliffs?"

"I would trade it all for a burned-out tank shell to protect against the falling rocks to sleep in," Jim replied. He noted that his sleeping rock had been too small also, and he dubbed the miserable place "the bombshell campsite." "No matter how hard we try," he said straight-faced, "we could never find another campsite with all the uniform bad qualities of this one."

Jim and I fought to bring forth fire from the surrounding sogginess, while Chuck slept on peacefully. We got a flicker, then lapping flames. Fire warmed us on the outside, hot tea on the inside, and the rain went away as gradually as it had come. Our outlook brightened. Once the wet misery had stopped, we discussed the possibility of the rain slowing down our scouting party. Another consideration was that, although the terrace had been quiet that morning, the rain-softened clay holding the rocks together might let loose some really big boulders later on. Perhaps, also, this had been a hint of an accelerated rainy season.

For myself, I wasn't worried much about dangers anymore, unless they were immediate. I had made my decision to go on, and I would do so as safely as possible. If anything radically different arose, I would reassess that decision. Until then, I would plod on; I would face my obstacles one at a time as I encountered them; and I would be thankful for each one I got past. I no longer had the energy or the will to worry in advance. Plan for—and hope for—yes, but worry, no.

We turned our eyes increasingly to the cliffs and hills across the river, where our companions had spent the night. I had not paid attention to the beauty of the site, but now, as the clouds lifted out of the valley and were burned away by the sun, I was taken aback by its splendor. For a very brief interval the valley was wider here, at the great left bend, and we could see the sweeping Vilcabamba hills. A stream from the nearby mountains rippled down the Quebrada Acobamba opposite us and poured over stark white cliffs to become a magnificent waterfall. It was near the top of the waterfall that our scouting party had disappeared in the gathering dusk of the previous night.

I wondered how they had fared up there, soaked in rain, struggling

≈   A waterfall tumbling down from the Quebrada de Acobamba.

among the thorns and relentless slopes of the canyon. We thought it might take a long time to climb high enough to see the far end of the chasm. We were surprised, then, to hear faint shouts above the noisy water of the river at 8:00 that morning. We glanced up and saw them, tiny figures on the canyon rim where the waterfall first tumbled into sight. How strange, I thought, to return so soon. They must have been turned back by a band of cliffs or some other hazard that blocked them from seeing the gorge.

A second glance caught a perplexing message: their arms were upright above their heads, the signal we had agreed to for "the gorge will go." How could they possibly know anything about the gorge this early?

We had anticipated that, to see the gorge, Gerry and Dee would have to climb the steep hill beyond the waterfall, surmount a steep ledge of rock, then work across a thorny slope to the rim of the chasm. It should have taken hours. Nonetheless, when I saw the signal, I assumed that they had somehow viewed the gorge. I had no idea what they had seen, nor how debatable their judgment might be in assessing the dangers from so high and so far away. I had reservations, but I would go.

I thought I was the only one with doubts about tackling the gorge, but Jim told me that he was dumbfounded when they gave the "all clear" signal so early. It didn't seem possible to Jim that they could have gone up, hiked all the way down to the gorge's edge, checked it out, and returned by 8:00. "When they come down, then what?" he said. "I don't know if I can believe them—wish I had gone myself."

Chuck thought about it and said, "Well, I guess we just hang back and let them go first! I bet they didn't see any more than we saw yesterday from the entry to the gorge. If they say it's okay, they should be willing to go first."

We finished our breakfast and packed our gear. Ahead of us was the portage down the rough, boulder-strewn left bank. Despite our doubts, we thought we had better get started.

A while later, Gerry told us the story of their adventure. After shuttling across the river, Gerry and Dee attacked the cliffs near the waterfall.

> We climb alongside [the waterfall] for a while—very slippery—and we come to an impasse after a couple hundred feet.

Climbing out on a spur to the left is more fruitful, but still difficult going as it is either loose rotten rock or scree, liberally sprinkled with cactus and thorny brush. We can make consistent progress though and climb almost two thousand feet before it gets too dark. The moon is full, but clouds have moved in to shield it from us, forcing us to stop on a very steep slope.

Dee and I dig out a tiny bivouac site on the precipitous mountainside, and sleep half-reclining, half-sitting, he wrapped in the tent fly and myself in the floor. There is no room anywhere to erect the tent. Indeed, we even consider tying in [to the mountain] to keep from rolling down the steep mountainside but there is no anchor anyway. It is cold up here with no sleeping bags and the ever-present wind, but we do manage to sleep.

In the middle of the night it begins to rain, slow drizzle, never-ending rain. Of all the nights for such luck! Dee and I huddle together for the rest of the night under the tent fly . . . unable to fall asleep.

As soon as it's light enough, we begin climbing higher. It soon becomes apparent to both of us that we won't have to go more than 500 feet higher before we can see into the parts of the gorge now hidden. At first we can hardly distinguish between canyon wall and river, but soon we can make out a tiny fragment of the Apurímac as it exits the gorge, and it's foamy white!

"Jesus, there's a rapid in there," Dee swore.

"You're right! I hope it's runnable!" Looking around me, I can only think out loud, "Hell, if we can't paddle through this gorge, I don't know what we'll do. There's no way we can carry our gear up this!" Across the canyon the walls are near vertical, and of loose, rotten conglomerate—totally unclimbable. "Let's keep going until we can see it all," as I again start uphill.

The climbing becomes more difficult again, with ledges of the broken rock to be overcome in many places. But as we progress upward, the gorge begins to reveal more of its secret nature.

"It doesn't look as bad from here," Dee broke in. ' "It's short, with green water above and a good pool below."

"And it looks like it has a tongue of smooth water down the middle. It's easy!" I'm nearly shouting. The gorge can be run safely. We'd seen it all now and it's all easy water, apparent even from this altitude. Dee is going crazy whooping and shouting, and I am too, unable to control myself after all the doubt we'd harbored for so long.

Now we had to descend 2,500 feet. . . . Rounding the ridge we are suddenly confronted with one of the most stunning sights I've ever beheld—the head of the valley is dominated by a snow-capped, glacier-clad mountain that must be almost 20,000 feet high. Our map, of questionable accuracy, shows it as Nevado Quishuar [18,947 feet]. Below us it is almost tropical, yet the icy summit is only a few miles distant. The entire upper valley is dusted with new-fallen snow from last night.

Turning to look across the canyon of the Apurímac, we can see the enormous mountain around which the river bends, the first pinnacle thrusting some 4,000 feet immediately above the river before merging with the higher massif behind it. The narrow slit through which Río Apurímac is forced begins almost directly below us. A fantastic viewpoint, from which I cannot easily move.

But Dee has already started down into the narrow valley [of Quebrada Acobamba], and steeply down at that—down goat tracks that fall away between our feet to the valley floor. . . . Unbelievable, but at one time somebody farmed this tiny hanging valley. All around us are ruins of irrigation ditches, terrace walls, and abandoned corn patches. No huts, though, or signs of previous ones. How did they get in here? I wish I could follow the old path upstream. Instead, we let it lead us down to the brink of the waterfall, across the canyon from the other boaters of our party.

Shouting and gesticulating wildly we finally attract the attention of Jim, Chuck, and Cal. Hands up over our heads for the 'all clear' sign. We then slide down more loose scree toward the canyon bottom. We are repeatedly stopped by steep bluffs of dried mud, ledges of rotten rock, impossible cliffs. Several times we have to climb back a hundred feet or more only to try again. I have the distinct impression of trying to hold the mountain together as we descend—every handhold wants to break off in our hands as we grab for balance and security.

Our last move is a classic: stopped by a short cliff as we neared the bottom, we decided to lower ourselves hand over hand on our short (80-foot) length of nylon webbing. It must be doubled around a tree, the only one nearby and a small one at that. This is to make retrieval possible. Dee . . . ties a knot into the loose ends of the sling, then lowers himself over the edge, feet braced against the rock wall.

"It's too short," he shouts up from below.

"How much?"

"About ten feet," as he hangs there by his hands.

"Jump!" I shout back to him, and suddenly the length of webbing at my feet goes slack. Pull it in, untie the knot, lower the packs. Retie the knot, then I begin to lower myself. The knot is a mistake—once at the end of the rope I'm stuck there, unable to reach bottom and unable to retrieve the valuable webbing if I jump. In a desperate effort, I release one hand and try to pick the knot holding on for dear life with the other. It's not easy to untie a knot in webbing, dangling webbing at that, but finally, after several agonizing tries, I manage to get it loose. Then I have to grab one end with my free hand and drop to the ground, pulling it down with me. A spectacular end to an interesting and beautiful hike.

Jim, Chuck, and I started our long portage toward the entrance of the Chasm of Acobamba. Gerry and Dee caught up with us partway down the rugged shoreline. We were soon convinced, as their account of the morning unfolded, that they had indeed looked into the gorge.

The portage we faced was by far the most difficult we had seen on the Apurímac. Since our boats were much heavier than before, they would be almost impossible to carry intact over the Paul Bunyon rubble, as we had done in the canyons above. We were forced to develop a new strategy. We broke our gear down into parts and hauled one part at a time. For example, I divided my load into three parts: the empty kayak with paddle; the large rear storage bag; and the front storage bag plus a backpack stripped off the deck and stuffed with camera gear and

A strenuous portage along the shoreline above the Chasm of Acobamba. ≈

other miscellaneous items. The loads were awkward, tough to grasp and hold, hard to keep from damaging by banging against rocks.

I would carry one of my loads a ways, up and down over the sharp rocks, until exhausted. Then I would go back for another. Three times, thus loaded, I would stagger ahead. Twice, between loads, back—500 yards of stumbling for 100 yards of progress. We gained ground like snails.

Gerry described our path in his journal:

> Over these enormous rocks . . . up and down, jumping across gaping holes between boulders. Up and down again, now sliding down the sides of monoliths larger than most houses I've ever lived in, now crawling on hands and knees beneath these rocks. . . .
>
> At one point we must climb over 50 feet above the river, and immediately descend back to the water on the other side, only to begin to tackle another boulder again. . . . It is every torture imaginable. . . .

We cursed our heavy loads. We dreamed of how they would shrink as the days went by. We would eat much of the food; we would use our toothpaste and our mosquito repellent and our matches and our suntan lotion. Ounce by ounce we would cut them down. But the harsh reality of this day—filled with the torture of transporting our bulging, nearly fresh loads along that broken Acobamba shore—was not much assuaged by that distant promise.

Our constant companion in that struggle was the unconsolidated wall. It stood above us like some ancient warrior, guarding the canyon. Fragments of stone were scattered around, proclaiming its wrath. Other stones and boulders were exposed and would soon come down; they bulged like cyclopean fish eyes from the mud wall. Each rain, like the one last night, would wash away a few more grains of support. As I looked at the rocks, I thought of the sword of Damocles hanging above us by a thread, a thread of caked mud. We kept our helmets on.

The irritations of the day compounded themselves. The sun came out burning hot. Biting insects dogged our path. And near the end of the portage, I found a deadly scorpion clinging to the life jacket, near my neck.

The torture of the portage ended just past 1:00. We were now just above the entrance to the Chasm of Acobamba, on the left side. We could go no farther down this side. To continue, we must cross the river, portage the outcropping on the other side, and hope to reach the calm alcove spotted earlier by Jim in the mouth of the gorge. We were still not sure that this could be done.

Jim and Dee crossed first. There would be no return for them now. I watched their boats bobbing on the water, cutting through rolling waves above the cataract at the entrance to the gorge. A mistake here would plunge them onto the rocks of the cataract, beyond anyone's aid. But their crossing was faultless. They clambered out on the broken rock wall of the opposite shoreline. They checked out the route to the alcove and found it passable.

I was shaking when my turn came. The rolling waves above the cataract, the finality of the commitment to the gorge, were strong medicine for someone whose life had always been cushioned by civilization. But I was committed and so I went; soon I, too, gained the rocky shore across the river. After the crossing Dee expressed to me similar feelings of trepidation in launching across that throat of water. I was surprised. I had not until then had the impression that fear was an emotion that Dee had to contend with.

As I sat catching my breath, I looked around. The rock walls above were gleaming solid now, the mud-glued conglomerate having been left behind. Our perch was solid rock too, a 40-yard-long strip of cliff thrust bluntly out into the river—just enough of a platform to get us to the alcove. I marveled that this stubborn old canyon, this demon Apurímac, gnarled and twisted by millions of years of geological madness, would, in the end, accommodate us so perfectly. First it laid a portage path down the left side of the cataracts; then it overlapped it with a shorter one on the right, where we now gathered; and finally it smoothed the water in a short corridor to connect them and then provided an alcove for our launch. If the portage had stopped 30 feet sooner, or had been anywhere 30 feet out of kilter, we would have been forced over the mountain. That is what I would have expected of this demon. I wondered to myself if we were being tricked by this sage old master of the Andes! We would soon see.

The four of us on the rock outcropping soon began the short but difficult portage to the alcove. Gerry, who had gone too far down the left side to come across with us, was struggling with his boat near the shoreline, in the very teeth of the cataract. Suddenly it looked like he

≈   The Chasm of Acobamba.

was going to try to kayak through the massive drop! "Come on across," I shouted, but my voice was lost in the thundering noise of the river. He shouted back, but we heard only the roar of the water. I kept motioning; I was frankly worried, because he looked irritated that he had started badly. But he worked his way back up the shore. He then crossed the river lower than any of the rest of us had, practically on the edge of the first cascade.

All together again, we hurried through the portage. Finally, our five boats were parked in the protected water of the alcove, a six-yard-deep dimple in the chasm wall. We were ready for the final test.

With Gerry and Jim in the lead, we burst into the chasm! Out into the narrow slit in the Andes, onto Amazon waters crashing down from the high and frigid mountains! Down the dark slot, hidden from the sun, barely illuminated by a thread of sky! The walls flew by; rocks boiled past; rapids churned beneath us! It was the most exhilarating experience of my life.

I tried to stop to take pictures. Everywhere between the walls the water was surging and pulsing, allowing neither a straight aim nor a steady hand for photography. I turned around and quickly shot the entrance of the gorge, then noticed everyone but Gerry moving ahead. The two of us drifted on together, wishing to prolong the beauty and awesomeness of this unexplored crevice, but finding no place to stop. We plunged through the rapid by the colossal pyramid rock, then around the bend that had so deeply perplexed us. Here, the water was calm, and we drifted slowly toward the exit.

Soon we emerged to sun and warmth. The gorge passage had taken maybe ten minutes. Our time in the chasm seemed like nothing against the days and months spent thinking about it, studying it, preparing for it. The tensions were now, quite suddenly, broken. It was a relief of unimaginable proportions.

We had made it through the Chasm of Acobamba! One more small riddle of our universe had fallen; one more dark corner was now explored.

Have you gazed on naked grandeur where there's nothing
    else to gaze on,
  Set pieces and drop-curtain scenes galore,
  Big mountains heaved to heaven, which the blinding
    sunsets blazon,
  Black canyons where the rapids rip and roar?
  Have you swept the visioned valley with the green
    stream streaking through it,
  Searched the Vastness for a something you have lost?
  Have you strung your soul to silence? Then for God's
    sake go and do it;
  Hear the challenge, learn the lesson, pay the cost.

Robert Service

Although it is worthwhile to know *how* to run difficult rapids, it is essential to know *when not* to.

Dave Harrison

≈ TO THE ROOTS OF VILCABAMBA

THE HIGH CRESTLINE OF the Cordillera Vilcabamba trends east-west across the scarred face of Peru. The Apurímac, struggling northwest to escape the cold grip of the altiplano, knifes deep into the south-facing flank of this awesome barrier of stone. The river now deflects west, as if taking aim to pour into the Pacific. Only later does it circle back out of the mountains to cross the continent going east, out across the wide flat of the jungle, across endless green plains, out to the far, far coast of the Atlantic, to die in its tropical waters.

Just past the Chasm of Acobamba, the river makes its most daring thrust at the roots of the Vilcabamba. It strikes 2.5 miles in a bold line north, a liquid arrow aimed at Nevado Quishuar (5,775 meters, 18,947 feet), Yanococha (5,425 meters, 17,800 feet), and Sacsaroyac (5,994 meters, 19,665 feet). It is deflected only after it has sliced through the ramparts of Quishuar and Yanacocha to within 5 miles of their icy pinnacles and within 12 miles of giant Sacsaroyac. It then spurts west, gnawing at the roots of other Vilcabamba kings as it roars to shake itself free of the cordillera.

Soon our path would run into the mountains along that northern arrow of water, then west as it gnawed at the roots. Everywhere we would have to fight our way over fallen pieces of mountain—the chips left from the cutting of the canyon.

A few blocks past the Chasm of Acobamba, we found some small sand enclaves on a shelf of barren, angled rock above the river. We stopped to camp, exhausted. Clouds threatened, and we protected our gear from rain. There was no room for tents.

I awoke surprised not to be drenched, staring at a brightening sky with a luster like cold steel. I yawned and slowly got up. I strolled down the crescents of sand curving between folds of rock to a terrain of cliffs and a jumble of rockfall downriver. I picked my way between the cliffs, over the rocks, my eyes searching ahead. I burned with curiosity as to what we faced for our seventeenth day.

My aerial photos had shown another gorge lying below our camp.

The thought of it was a little frightening now, after the Chasm of Acobamba, but I was optimistic that the gorge ahead might be an improvement. The shutter of the camera in the sky, on that high-flying plane that passed above here twelve years ago, had clicked right over the canyon. I could see on one photo a gray ribbon of water snake through the gorge, hidden briefly by cliffs. The flecks of white—rapids—looked short. The indications were reassuring, but the interpretation needed care, for the evidence was gathered from so high that the whole width of the Apurímac was no more than a half millimeter—thin as a split dime—on the photographic print. I preferred to look into the gorge and see it life-size. I pushed on downstream toward that goal, beneath a bluing sky.

As I clambered past rocks along the shore, low cliffs rose before me and barred my way to the deeper sanctums of the canyon; I could go no farther. I prepared to turn back, dissatisfied.

Just then a big fox with hair afluff and eyes full of life trotted down the embankment in front of me. Somewhere he had eaten well and was fat and content—and a trifle careless of my presence. There were not many people down here to bother a fox, I guess. He wove ahead among the stones, as if to cut off my path. He was sometimes on top of rocks, sometimes behind; I would see a black-tipped tail follow a gray back around a corner, then a black nose and sharp ears lead a light cinnamon chest and belly out the other side.

Then he stopped, not 50 feet away, suddenly alert to my presence. He swung around to gaze at me with contemptuous dark eyes, then trotted briskly away. I reprimanded myself for leaving my camera in camp.

Opposite our shore, a cliff rose from the water like the walls of a castle. Up high a rounded white roof sat firmly on the cliff, curving back toward the hills. It was textured with creases and channels, and hundreds of streamlets of water trickled down through them, glistening like strings of diamonds in the hot morning sun. The strands ran together one by one and fell over the wall in a prismatic veil. In this way the waters of the tiny Río Pacobamba joined the torrent that would labor to the sea.

We started the morning by paddling beneath the descending curtain of the waterfall, craning our necks to see it spinning through space. We took some pictures and then one by one, except for Chuck, we peeled out into the current to start our descent. While Chuck lingered behind to enjoy the splash of water, the rest of us paddled downriver. We maneuvered through some tight chutes of water rushing through a maze of large rocks. A ways below we pulled in to wait, scattered along the left shore, Dee well ahead.

Our concern for Chuck grew as the minutes ticked by. I don't know how long we waited—maybe half an hour. Then we saw him round the bend dripping with water, badly shaken, and clearly unhappy. He had paddled off route in the rocks below the waterfall and had capsized in a narrow chute. He swam for some time in the turbulent current before getting to shore and getting back in his boat. This had happened out of sight, out of earshot, beyond reach, beyond help. Chuck is a wilderness boater of extraordinary skill and strength. His mishap was a shocking reminder of the sovereignty of the river, even in its most ordinary rapids. It seemed to strike fair warning that we had better work together in the dominion of her waters.

The capsize upset us and brought us together again to patch up our careless descent of the river. As leader I felt the sting of our failure most sharply. A sound expeditionary party, as I have always viewed things, should look out for all of its members all the time they are on the river. It is almost an axiom of nature that some of her ugliest surprises are saved for places where they are least expected—such as the rock maze above. We had organized procedures for mutual support earlier, but they kept falling apart except in the worst throes of the river. Dee would often start ahead; others would then follow randomly. Soon the party would be spread in disarray up and down the Apurímac. My words to Dee had been of no avail. I am not a leader who bellows commands like an army sergeant. I was not there to order subordinates around or threaten sanctions; I was there to coordinate an expedition among friends and equals. Only Jim, Gerry, and I worked consistently together down most of the river. I was eventually forced to give up trying to convince the others to keep our party together. Repeated failures had discouraged me. Now a more insidious element intervened to threaten our accord: the accumulation of strain from the hard battle with the river.

I was becoming deeply fatigued by the relentless drive of the river

145 ≈

and our unremitting pace. It was a bone-deep weariness, born in the herculean physical challenges, fear, conflicts, and uncertainties that ceaselessly rose to confront us. It was clear to me now that I had not conditioned rigorously enough for these demon canyons. But in this I had had no choice: the immensity of the task of planning and organizing the expedition, along with the concurrent demands of my work, left not enough hours for sleep, let alone time for running up mountains, bicycling, or swimming.

Fatigue, I should add, is a common element of difficult expeditions, no matter how toughened the participants. It becomes hard to solve problems beyond immediate survival. Communications become difficult. One avoids talking out problems, particularly when they have proved refractory in previous encounters. As John Ridgeway, in his book *Amazon Journey*, observes: "a little more open discussion . . . would have helped, but usually we were too tired in the evenings to do anything except eat and get to sleep. . . . As always when in a situation of prolonged tiredness, each of us was engaged in a personal battle with the worst points of our own natures."

Thus dissension was not surprising. I knew misunderstandings could crop up, which is why I wrote the rules of the trip in advance, so that we would have a mutual basis of understanding and a common approach. If everyone had followed those rules—as each person had promised in signing up for the expedition—our difficulties would have been minor, totally resolvable. But we failed. The large part of the blame in my view was Dee's: he ignored—even flaunted—the rules, and in so doing shattered the morale of the expedition.

While Dee was often beyond reach ahead of us, Chuck might be alone anywhere: ahead, behind, on the shore. He would usually tell no one of his intentions in advance. Such had been the case today. He, too, must share the blame for his unaccompanied accident. But, in fact, we tried to correct the situation. Jim volunteered to run sweep. This meant that he would wait at every significant rapid until everyone got safely through. It was clear now that Jim was the most reliable boater, and he felt no compulsion to race to the head of the party.

Thus we anchored one end of the loose chain of our descent. The other end still ran free, still tore us apart, and continued to threaten the safety of the expedition as we approached the challenge of the core of the Vilcabamba.

Our bearing changed inexorably from south to north, as we circled wide around a towering spur of rock that jutted out of the flanks of the cordillera. At the end of the circle we found ourselves on the liquid arrow catapulting toward the Vilcabamba's heart. In its first bold thrust north, the arrow of water sliced a gorge, the one I had tried to reach that morning, out of the ramparts of the range.

We were swallowed by walls as we entered the gorge. The river grew narrow; it compressed and deepened as it entered a slot barely 50 feet from one wall to the other. It was incredible to see such a constriction of rock holding a river so big. The levees that confined the river were gray rock abutments that rose hundreds of meters in search of the sky, leaving us buried in shadows. The water beneath us surged darkly and powerfully into the depths of the sanctuary.

High on the left wall a waterfall tumbled in the sun, over ledges mottled green and brown with moss, before plunging down into the black obscurity of the river. Gerry and I lingered to admire the spray, the rock, and the dark beauty of the canyon, and shot up our film. Now, hoping not to take empty cameras through the rest of the gorge, we looked for a place ashore to stop and reload film, but nothing broke the immutable walls rising from the water—no crevice, no ledge, no strand of beach. We drifted past the convolutions of rock all in shadow, helpless to stop against the sweep of the current. Then, ahead on the left, we saw a dark entrance in the wall, barely above the level of water; it looked like the mouth of a cave.

"Let's try it," Gerry said, and we rushed forward, caught up more in the adventure of the dark formation than in the prospects of loading film. We landed on sand at its mouth and stared back into the darkness. Our eyes discerned the outline of a grotto, carved from the solid rock of the gorge. We entered beneath a low ceiling that dripped everywhere onto a sandy floor. We explored its mysterious recesses, leaving footprints where no human had trod before. Then we remembered to change film. We had to bend full over our cameras to protect them from the dripping water. In a few minutes we finished the task and prepared to go.

We left the grotto and paddled to the end of the gorge. We emerged to sunlight, the water still calm, still headed north. A few small rapids broke the tranquillity, then a larger one. Jim waited in the pool below. This was our new plan for safety, but Jim would have waited in any event.

I was unsure of the best route through the rapid and went ashore to check it from the vantage point of higher ground. Gerry pulled ashore ahead of me. As was customary, we pulled our boats up on the bank to avoid having them washed away by waves. But as Gerry started walking down the shore, his boat, resting on inclined rocks, suddenly slipped back into the river. I saw it wobble out in the current, some 50 feet ahead of me.

"Watch out, your boat's going!" I shouted at him. Gerry turned to see his kayak—his food, clothes, and only means of survival—soloing out across the water toward the abrupt drop of the rapid.

"Oh my God," he growled, and lunged after the boat. He was soon up to his chest in the rapids—but too late. The boat was out of reach, accelerating toward the rocks and foam.

I rushed back to my boat, having had no time to scout the drop. The elements of a stark dilemma raced through my mind. If I chose wrong, the expedition could end in this noisy, uncaring rapid. The following factors ran quickly through my mind in deciding what to do. Gerry, freed of his boat and bound to shore, was out of the picture now, unable to help. Neither would any aid come from Chuck and Dee, who were an unknown distance down the river, out of sight. This left Jim and me alone to bring in Gerry's boat and gear and to cover each other in case of mishap. Yet before I could help, I would have to get through the rapid. There would be no time to scout out a passage, for the recovery had to be made quickly, in the pool below the rapid, before the errant boat and its contents were lost to other rapids down the river.

It was entirely possible that Gerry's boat would smash open on the rocks, scattering his gear, requiring every sinew of our efforts to recover enough to make continuation on the river possible, or at a minimum, to make evacuation from the canyon feasible. But even if the boat washed through clean and unbroken, it would fill with water and be hard to work to shore. The paddle would probably wash free of the boat, and we could ill afford to lose it.

All of these prospects were compelling in their message: Jim would need my help down there, and I should hurry on to offer it.

But as I came up to my boat I also weighed the risks of going on down. I had not seen the drop of the rapid. The edge was wide and rocky, like a prehistoric jawbone set with broken teeth. Tongues of water raced here and there, twisting between the rocks. Nowhere did it look deep and clear, and the invisible ramp of the drop might hold serious hazards. If I should capsize and be pulled away from my boat, I would add to the problem, not to the solution. Jim would be alone with an impossible task. We would lose at least one boat, and maybe two.

I looked down at the waves and rocks once more, and in an instant decided that the risk was worth taking, that I should try to get down to help Jim. I pushed my boat out in the shallows and slid inside. My mind filled with dismay at the recurrence of circumstances that made such risks necessary, when they shouldn't exist at all. I wondered how many more times we would needlessly face such hazards, with our party scattered helplessly along the course of the river.

Damn it, I thought, now angry—and I flipped my sprayskirt on and pushed into the river, knowing that this is just the kind of unforeseen emergency that gives you strength in numbers; just the reason I wanted four to six boaters on this trip in the first place. Yet it doesn't mean a thing if they're not around to help. A hundred people here wouldn't do any good if they weren't helping each other. Now that we were in this predicament and needed the others, they were no-damn-where in sight!

I was launched now, scanning the waters for signs of the derelict boat, but it, too, was gone, having disappeared over the big drop in the rapid. It was now my turn. I approached the ledge of rocks across the river, where the ramp of water plunged down out of sight, and searched for a smooth place to start between the scattered teeth. I chose a V-shaped slot, where the water swirled over a lip depressed between two bulging boulders. This route would just have to go—I can't fail now, I told myself. I lurched down the channel, skimmed past big rocks on each side, then plunged into the pool below, upright and safe.

Jim had by now cornered Gerry's boat, which was in good condition, considering its unguided run. He was pushing and nudging it across the choppy pool toward Gerry, who had run down the shoreline to help pull it in.

"The paddle's down there," Jim called as I emerged from the rapid, and he motioned farther downstream. I hurried down, catching the paddle before it drifted into the next waves. In a few minutes we had everything but a missing sponge (used to sop unwanted water out of boats) back to Gerry. We could breathe easily now and take a moment to be thankful that it hadn't ended in tragedy.

The three of us followed the river north in its relentless drive. Soon we caught up with Dee and Chuck, who had stopped at a great rapid. Here the river plunged over two big drops and accelerated toward a cataract. The water whipped to a frenzy as it churned down the last descent and fell upon a mountain of a rock. Foaming and roaring on collision, it dove under, forcing its way through some black cavern to seek the river beyond. Only one channel of water escaped this fate by running past the end of the rock, and it was white with turmoil.

"You could probably make the first two drops," Dee said, "but if you wash into the last one, there's a fifty-fifty chance of being killed."

Like a thousand times before, there was a temptation to run part of the rapid. This way one could bypass over 100 feet of tough portage at the top. The risk was that failure anywhere in the staircase of the two drops would leave a boater helpless, in water accelerating toward the final fury. It was a risk to be weighed by each person in the depths of his conscience. I turned my back on it. So did Dee and Chuck. Jim and Gerry elected to run.

We crossed the river to the left bank and landed at a point just above the first drop. From here the three of us began to portage. The other two studied the channels, the waves, the holes, the rocks. There was no room for error.

As Jim prepared to run, I stationed myself on a projection of shore by the narrowest neck of the river above the final descent. I had at my side, in neat coils, a 50-foot length of rope. If either of them washed by in that range, I could pull him in.

As I waited I estimated that the rope would span well under half of the channel. There would be less than an even chance of reaching a swimmer out there. Those were unpleasant odds, but there was nothing more to be done. A boat sent out for rescue would itself be flushed into the cauldron. I hoped they wouldn't need help, but the immensity of the drops they faced worried me.

Jim's approach was methodical and cool. He circled above the first drop and aligned himself to strike its center. He gained momentum as

Plate 1: The Gorge of Pichigua. This narrow gorge, lying at about 13,000 feet in the southern highlands of Peru, was a difficult obstacle for the 1974 expedition.

Plate 2: A charcoal maker of the Apurímac uses sign language to offer us a glass of chicha. This unusually clothed man lived alone in a small enclave surrounded by river and cliffs.

Plate 3: Gerry Plummer and the author enjoying breakfast at the hacienda.

Plate 4: A weaver of Huata.

Plate 5: A strenuous portage bypasses an Apurímac rapid near Nayhua.

Plate 6: One week into the 1975 expedition Gerry Plummer faces a difficult rapid in the canyon of Nayhua.

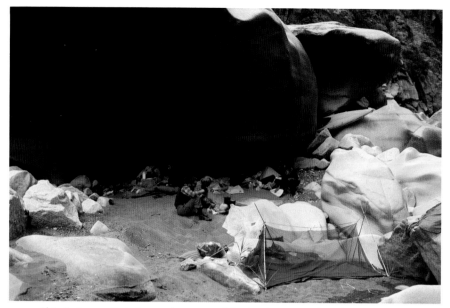

Plate 7: A campsite in the granite canyon of the Apurímac. From the left: Gerry Plummer, Chuck Carpenter, Dee Crouch, and Jim Sindelar.

Plate 8: Jim Sindelar runs a rapid on the Apurímac as its waters race through the Vilcabamba mountain range.

Plate 9: The colorful women of Nayhua.

Plate 10: A woman sharing a meal with her chickens in a smoke-filled hut near the bottom of the trail to Choquequirao.

Plate 11: Gerry Plummer pauses beneath a jungle waterfall.

he was swept to the lip, where the water ahead arched down over rocks like a sheet of clear plastic, and broke into waves below. He plunged down the liquid face and rode through the waves at the bottom. Moments later he went over the second drop. Then he was suddenly safe, and I felt a surge of relief, as if I had made the run myself.

As Gerry prepared to go, a new sense of consternation welled over me. Gerry was not as experienced as Jim, and his eskimo roll was less certain. Therefore I thought that if he capsized here, his roll might fail and he would be flushed toward the fatal rock. I inspected again the coils of the rope, to make sure I could throw them free of tangles.

It was Gerry's turn to circle upstream to align himself above the drop. He approached the edge, then plunged down the face of water. I saw him crash into the back-rolling wave at the bottom, spray flying everywhere. I watched as he tipped, braced upright, tipped again; then I saw his cockpit cover pulled off the boat on one side, as he went over in the waves. Suddenly he disappeared behind a large rock, and for a while I could see no more. I waited in dreadful fear.

I now expected the worst. Gerry must have been pulled loose from his seat for his spray cover to have been torn off; this meant that he had lost his firm position in the boat and that a roll would be difficult. Even if he should roll up, the loosened spray cover would allow wave after wave to pour into the cockpit, making his boat heavy and unmanageable for the rest of the rapid.

I held the rope now, ready to throw, waiting for the pieces to emerge from behind the rock. Gerry, however, was not so easily subdued. He had been spun by waves into an eddy behind the rock and there—hanging upside down in the water—had pulled himself back in his seat. Then he rolled up and refastened his spray cover. He had taken in water, but not too much. Soon he was paddling ashore, as if nothing particular had happened. I went limp with relief.

Later I told Gerry I had been worried about his safety. "Gerry, I don't want to see you dead. I could never forgive myself if you got killed on an expedition of my making. Besides, we need your strength for the rough parts ahead. Please—I'm asking you as a friend—don't take on such risky runs."

I think my words had some small effect. But Gerry would continue to be Gerry, and his adventuresome streak would not quickly abate, as we pushed on toward the most tortured stretches of the canyon.

From this point on the river went mad. It became almost solid white as it foamed down the last half-mile of its northward plunge. The cataracts crowded together, and the interludes between them carried racing water. The passages around them on shore were truly horrible.

We labored over two hours going down the broken shore on the first portage. The task was grueling and in places precarious. A segment of our path was a shelf in the canyon wall, narrow and angled down into the river. We carried some of our gear across the treacherous steps of the shelf. We lined some of it past, stuffed in the kayaks. As Jim inched his way along, holding the line to his boat below, he suddenly slipped, plunging into the river. But he managed to swim his boat to a safe landing below.

We worked down the portage surrounded by the grandeur of the canyon. Cracked white walls twisted upward to end in the emptiness of the sky. Clouds formed and broke over the peaks ahead. Now and then the clouds were dismantled, and the great frosted crown of Yanacocha would glisten in sunlight. Beneath it we were mere specks, inching down the rubble and chaos of the canyon. The mountain sat astride our path, daring the river. I hoped the Apurímac would remember to turn aside in time, before we crashed into the massive barrier head-on.

We finished the portage a while after 3 P.M. We bore deeper into the canyon, into the heart of the mountains. The river began to trend left, away from its collision course with Yanacocha. Merciful river! My mood now was anything but flamboyant. I would stop enough above the brink of each new cataract to feel safe. I would portage far enough past to escape its grip. I was resolute in avoiding what I saw as undue risks. My comrades, each to a different degree depending on how each perceived the threats, would shorten the portage by boating closer to the teeth of the rapids. I was often left to work alone along the shore, and this was not to my liking; it was not my style of expedition.

We stopped above a large rapid at the bend where the river broke abruptly left to escape the mountain. We made plans to camp in a spacious alcove cut deep in the right wall, carpeted with sand. I unloaded my camp gear, then lined my boat down the rapid in preparation for the next day. The others decided to run the rapid before unloading. Then, finding sand at its bottom, they made plans to camp down there. It was a sound decision. It made no sense to lug gear up the shoreline, then back again to start the next day. But the change in campsite discouraged me and deepened my sense of solitude in facing the rigors of the canyon.

I worked back through the rocks toward the alcove, my mood slipping into black shadows of regret. At the alcove I would gather together the gear I had laid out and face the aching weariness of hauling it back across the mounds of the rocks, all the time brooding on my added burden, thinking how my gear could have been taken down with my boat at the beginning. The darkness of my mood was increased by the loss of the small iodine container I carried for water purification, misplaced in the shuffle of gear on the shore. I criss-crossed the sand and the rocks in a search of frustration, alone between the roaring river and the silent cliffs.

I gave up, discouraged and weary, and shouldered a load of gear to begin plodding down to camp. Suddenly my emotions broke like ocean surf. Waves of choking sensation welled over me like a narcotic, as I struggled alone among the rocks. I was numbed by a sense of remorse and a deep yearning for the common path of companionship. I felt alone like someone lost at sea, the rest of the world dead, battered by ancient storms that had always before drawn humans together in little knots to face the blackness, but that was blowing now with no one there; alone with the nothingness of a vacant horizon.

At the same time—and strangely contradictory—I was rocked by resolute determination, a sense of stubborn, unbending independence. I could do this canyon, and I would do it, and I would continue to do it the way I chose. If I had to feel alone, so be it. If I had to go alone and find my own path, I would, and I would muster every inner resource I had ever known to get by safely. Nothing would stop me or change my way. And with this I pushed my way downstream toward camp, another step into the challenge of the depths of the canyon.

The experience of those moments immersed in the flood of my soul could only be described as profound, not at all unhappy. They cleansed the cobwebs of doubt and anxiety from my mind like a breath of fresh air, yielding a new perspective on the raw drive of my heritage of human spirit. This, perhaps, is how my forebears came across the plains, and those before them across the ocean. Everyone could have quit or refused, but they clung like bulldogs to their goal.

But now, in this modern age, much of the fire has died. There is so much civilization around that we can't always find a goal to match the limits of our deepest resources. We find conditions that muzzle us on every side and that drag at our inclination to reach and grow. The spirit of humankind, I feel, has withered along the barren course of the freeway.

The pages of my journal touched on my frustration and the start of its resolution:

I feel like waving them on and doing this canyon in total, awesome isolation. I long for a companion to take the route I take; help plan the strategy; work hand in hand at each move. I have never been on an expedition where everyone is so independent and remote, from each other as well as from me. In clutch situations, there is unanimity of action, but in the grueling, daily routine of getting down this awesome canyon, it is done largely man by man.

We talk about this tonight, and I do feel a closeness with Jim and Gerry. Jim, although not having previous expedition experience, is the stalwart of the trip. Astute, wise to whitewater and canyons and boats, he is very sound. Gerry is strong and warm. Dee is isolated, incredibly efficient, . . . Chuck is in another world that I cannot fathom. Strong, quiet, independent.

Such were the impressions that I recorded that night. I would, of course, not go alone. I did have friends in Jim and Gerry, and they were among the best I had ever known. They were struggling with their own problems and following their own inclinations, bent differently than mine. But they would be there, I knew, in any true time of need.

That night, a few fireflies flickered bright messages against black canyon walls. I lay awake and watched them awhile, scribbling occasionally in my journal as I thought of the day now closing. I found it almost unfathomable that the events of that day—of a brief 4-mile span of river—could flood the soul with such a wealth of experiences. I pondered the intensity of our existence and thought about the way it contrasted with that of so many of the people we had left in a world far away, sheltered in the womb of civilization. I imagined travelers and vacationers driving in air-conditioned chariots across 400 miles of freeway in a day, experiencing nothing. In 100 times our distance, they would never touch the rock nor feel the warmth of the sun. They felt no spray, no rain, no breeze of nature's making. They felt no fear, stretched no emotion, had nothing particular to be thankful for.

I shivered at the thought of this plunging canyon and its black demon river—and I thanked God I was here.

The rapids were near, and an uninterrupted, uniform,
headlong, rushing noise filled the mournful stillness . . .

                                        Joseph Conrad

In the year 1555, owing to the great abundance of winter
rains, a piece of the mountain fell into the river, of such
size, and bringing such masses of stones and earth, that
it blocked the stream up from one side to the other,
insomuch that not a single drop of water passed for
three days, until the pent up river rose above the mountain that had fallen across it. Those who lived in the
valley below, seeing that so great a river had dried up
so suddenly, supposed that the world had come to an
end.

                                    Garcilaso de la Vega

≈ DEMON RIVER

W<small>E WERE UP EARLY</small> on the eighteenth day to face a monumental portage. I had studied the obstacles ahead the evening before, clambering down the shoreline and up onto a rock to look, and could barely believe my eyes. Never had I seen such a mass of rocks scattered about in such chaos, extending so far. Blocks of granite 50 feet high lay at all angles, piled on top of one another like a giant's gravel pile. They blanketed the valley floor from the nearby slopes to the shoreline and down into the riverbed. In the river they stood so high they formed barren white islands and spurs mounded above the surface of the flow, baked dry and lifeless by canyon heat. The current swirled around these giants to find a path through, then plunged over stone lips and exploded to foam on more rocks below. It bellowed its anger to echo in the canyon off white, broken walls.

The river was unapproachable. It was out of the question to run it for any distance anywhere in sight. One could if one wanted cross here and there and sneak through a few of the pools near shore, but the sullen growl of the water warned against anything more. The shoreline, as well, was almost unapproachable. To move was to confront pinnacles, corners, and faces that seemed more fit for mountaineering than for the descent of a river.

From the top of my rock I saw a strip of green foliage following the river, back away from the shore. Aha, I thought, there is my portage path, a green carpet through the rocks. I entered the growth to find the best route. There, however, I found a jungle of thorns and bamboo. I pushed on ahead, and it worsened. One thorn tree alone, with its gnarled limbs dipping down to create a hedge of spines across my path, nearly turned me back. And the rocks were not absent here, nor even much diminished in size; they were simply wallpapered in thorns and slippery green stalks. I broke to my right, through bamboo over my head, and escaped the thicket across great, white rocks.

The green carpet would not do. And the river was not runnable. Once again I pondered the shoreline. Here the floods had cleaned out the thorns and the tangle, and the receding water had left the rocks dry. After all, it looked like the best choice. I resolved, then, that I would go down the shoreline.

Once again I prepared my gear for portage. I stripped my backpack off the rear deck of my boat and loaded it with incidentals: cameras, lenses, wet-suit gear, rope, canteen, lunch. As before, I would carry that and the front storage bag as one load; the larger rear storage bag would make a second load; and the boat and paddle would be a third. I would carry each load until aching muscles asked me to put it down. When I returned for the subsequent load, I would always pick up the one I had left farthest back, thus keeping my gear together in one area.

I started alone at 8:30 A.M. The five of us launched on three different routes, all of which would converge some distance downstream, past another cascade in the river. Jim, Dee, and Gerry started across the river, where they would line some distance down the left side. They would cross back below. Chuck began working down the right bank, close to the river, lining the eddies where he could. I started my day on a zigzag path weaving through rocks, a few hundred meters along shore. Then I worked back from the river, up to a place where big blocks had reared into the air like cathedrals and had then toppled on one another in a barrier of broken, angled stone. But where they leaned on each other, they left tilted underground passageways. Here I entered, dragging and carrying my loads beneath stone roofs that had been twisted and broken in the agony of their formation. Through one, then high over a block where I had to tilt my boat on end and drag it up, then through another. Here I emerged into a tiny glen, peaceful and flat among so much rubble. Down its center sparkled a stream of clear mountain water.

The stream tumbled out of Quebrada Huaynacachora, a raw side canyon that spiraled into the sky. Up there, in glacial cold, it eroded the ice and the rock from the flanks of two giants, Nevado Quishuar and Nevado Yanococha.

As I looked up the quebrada, with my head tilted back to see to the top, Quishuar thrust its magnificent white crown through a pillowcase of clouds. It loomed closer than ever now—barely four miles up the twisted canyon. I felt that I had truly reached the roots of the Vilcabamba. And my river out there—it was roaring happily as it ate the mountains away.

I loaded my kayak with stacks of loose gear and boated it a short distance through the glen along the stream from Huaynacachora. I disembarked on the rocks, unloaded, and began to carry again. The day grew hot. My trail continued across a stony flat leading away from the quebrada, back down over the embankment of the Apurímac, and along its rocky shoreline again. At the river's edge, I drenched my shirt in water to fight off the heat.

Some distance down the shore, all our routes converged. We continued through increasingly troublesome terrain. At the worst point, a thicket forest grew over low ridges of granite. Here Chuck developed a route like a maze, leading through passages cleared among the thorns, ascending and descending ramps and faces of granite two stories high. We finished the portage across a rubbled path aimed crookedly toward shore. We were scorched by the midday heat.

In totality the segments of my path were maybe half a mile in length, although I will never be able to say for sure. The distance was multiplied by five for the three carries and two returns needed to advance my load from resting stage to resting stage. It would be multiplied by five again for the agony of my route, with its angled and uneven steps, the tilted rocks that sometimes gave way, the forced detours around slabs, and the confrontation with big blocks, where my gear had to be pushed ahead to free my arms to climb the faces.

It was grueling, and it took the whole morning and more. But it was an adventure and a challenge, and I loved it. I was happy. I worked hard, and I felt good physically; I began to believe I was getting in condition to handle the inhumanities of the Apurímac.

My judgment was premature, however. The demon was wearing me down, not strengthening me. I would never again be able to call up that much strength and endurance. The river had barely begun with me.

The difficult bypass had nearly led to disaster in another quarter that morning. As Gerry described it:

Jim, Dee, and I decide to cross the river and try the left side. We can line the boats down most of the way, and the three of us team up to carry the loaded boats one at a time over the short stretch next to the final big drop. At the end of this carry, though, all we can do is return to the right bank by ferrying, where further lining begins. . . .

Jim and I begin working together using long lines to pass the boats around obstacles, and Chuck has caught up to us and is loading his boat when I suddenly call for silence. Thought I heard a strange sound, but couldn't tell for sure. I did decide to scramble up on the boulders alongside the river to see if I could hear better, and at this point I heard it again. It was Dee!

Motioning to the others to follow, I ran and jumped over boulders as fast as I could. . . . Coming over the top of one giant at river's edge I looked right down on Dee, up to his neck in dangerous waters. He was braced between several boulders, holding on to his boat for all he was worth to prevent the current from tearing it away and carrying it over the next drop. As I lowered myself I could see that he was actually pinned by the boat and current, and although he probably could have extricated himself from his predicament, it would have been at the expense of his boat being carried over the drop.

It took both Chuck and myself to hold the boat while Dee moved into position to lower the kayak over the drop where Jim carefully retrieved it. . . . If Dee had waited a minute or two and worked the long lines with us as a team, he would not have gotten in this dangerous situation, as the rest of us had no problem.

We ended the abysmal portage, had a short lunch, made our shoreline preparations, then launched again at 2:00. The ferocity of the water relented, and we were able to kayak a mile or so, as the canyon broke west toward the sun. Soon we came to a bar covered with sheep-sized white boulders huddled low and flat, back to cliffs on the right. At the top of the bar, a cluster of wires spun high above the river, across to the base of the cliffs. Here was another aroya crossing, where some unknown trail breached the river. From the cliff end of the wires, a path led down the boulders and up an embankment to a hut. Soon we saw a man standing high on the hillside, staring at us. Here was the first native figure to enter our sight in four and one-half days.

After a while the figure descended the hill and came over the aroya like a spider on a silver web. Before us now was a man of Indian descent, a youngish man perhaps twenty-five years old, robust, wearing drab clothing from some faraway store.

"What is the name of this place?" I asked, curious because no habitation had appeared on my map.

"It is called San José," he replied. "We get here on a path branching off from the trail to Hacienda Parcas."

Parcas, I knew, was located on the south slopes of the canyon farther down. It was on the long overland route to the Inca ruins of Choquequirao, which we would soon be approaching by river. Hiram Bingham had come that way when he trekked to the ruins in 1909.

"What do you do here?" I asked.

"Raise bananas, a few papayas, avocados, some corn," was the response. Our mouths began to water at the thought of fresh produce.

"Is there any fruit we could buy?"

"Not ready," was the rather curt answer.

Dee and Chuck had already investigated the orchard. Dee described how he had been up in a banana tree when it broke off at the base, nearly sending him over a cliff.

Beyond the wire aroya we began another long series of rapids. (*See* Plate 8) Soon we were ashore, skirting more unrunnable drops. While lining down the right, the clouds parted above to reveal the full vertical splendor of Nevado Quishuar, still not 5 miles away, towering nearly 3 miles above our heads. It stood frozen in grim indifference above the dashing, playful waters—which would eventually bring it down like a castle of sand. But until then, the mountain would dominate this country with its awesome majesty.

We made a short run and camped at our next portage. Down the canyon the river echoed its madness. More of the same struggle would confront us tomorrow. The light of the setting sun painted the stern, gray walls of the canyon in soft orange. Above the rock the sweeping slopes were turning green and taking on a tropical appearance. We were plodding into the jungle.

Night fell and bathed away the wounds of the day. A calmness and soft beauty descended over the mountains to cloak the meanness of the canyon. In my journal I wrote of the wonder of the night: "A full moon rises over a green Andean ridge. A haze permeates the mountain air, and gives the high peaks and walls, bathed in moonlight, a mysterious illumination. Certainly one of the most beautiful nights I can remember."

The gray light of morning illuminated a 3,000-foot slash of scarred rock coursing down a mountainside between green-clad ramparts ahead. "I'll bet that was a smoking big rock slide!" Chuck offered.

"Yes, and things are apt to be really messed up with rocks down where it hit the river," Jim added.

"I wonder when it happened?" I asked rhetorically. "It's been scoured pretty clean and hasn't grown back much. Of course, rooting again is slow on that steep rock."

"Maybe it came down this century—maybe a thousand years ago," Gerry remarked.

I recalled then the enigmatic passage written four centuries ago about a great slide that came down somewhere in the canyon of the Apurímac, penned by the half-Inca chronicler Garcilaso de la Vega. The only clue as to the whereabouts of the slide was this: "The overflow extended for fourteen leagues [about 50 miles] above the stoppage, as far as the bridge [of San Luis Rey] on the high road from Cuzco to the City of Kings [Lima]."

Could this be Garcilaso's 420-year-old fall of rock? We were only about 25–30 miles down the canyon from the bridge of San Luis Rey, not 50, as hinted by Garcilaso. But this didn't altogether rule it out. Inca scholar John Rowe told me that Garcilaso wrote from memory in his old age; his recall of distances might well have been vague and subject to exaggeration. Or perhaps no one knew then just how far downriver the slide was.

I wondered what other clues might bear on the puzzle. I tried to imagine a lake backing up over us, becoming so deep that in three days it would fill the canyon most of the way back to the Cunyac crossing. It would have to be enormously deep. I remembered from the readings of Gerry's altimeter that from the bridge of San Luis Rey, the river had dropped over 650 feet through rapids to reach this point. This meant that "Lake Garcilaso" would have to have deepened to 650 feet or more at the rockfall to stretch back to the great suspension bridge of the Incas. It was almost too incredible to contemplate. Could the raging, rain-swollen river fill the canyon to that depth in a few days? That would require a flow of about 20,000 cubic meters per second (700,000 cubic feet per second)—Mississippi-size flow. But who knows what the Apurímac does down in the canyons in the darkest hour of the rains? I would not hastily dismiss the possibility, not in this remarkable land.

"Jim's right," I remarked thoughtfully. "We might have some pretty big rapids down at the bottom of the slide."

As we prepared for our departure, the young man from San José came down to watch from across the river. He followed us along some distance, as we battled the rocks and waves. Soon he became bored with our paddling and urged us on with waving arms, at first suggestive but then demanding. Sometimes he motioned us toward frothing slots that only a madman would consider. I think we sorely disappointed him.

Later, when we approached his shore, above another long and impossible drop, I asked him, "Do you want to help us?"

"What do?" he said, looking suspicious and a little bit puzzled.

"Can you help us carry boats down there?" I asked, motioning down along the rocks of the shore.

"How far?"

I didn't know how to answer him, because I didn't know what lay ahead, so I told him the only objective I knew:

"To the cable bridge of Choquequirao."

If I had known the commitment I was asking of that poor Peruvian! But he didn't seem to know what was down there either. "That's okay," he said with a shrug.

"Is there another man?"

"Yes, I will get him. What will you pay us?"

"Fifty soles each," I said, knowing that if they worked well that morning, we would pay them more. Fifty soles was just over a dollar, a lot of money here.

Our friend wound up the embankment toward San José to fetch the other man.

"I wonder who's up there," I mused out loud. "We haven't seen anyone else, either yesterday or today."

All too soon we knew. With our friend was an older man, somewhat shorter, whose face was taut with nerves. His thin weasel eyes burrowed into our gear, searching, worrying. He looked at us distrustfully and gripped tighter the machete he bore. It struck us suddenly that there was nothing on this shore to use a machete on—except us.

The others had started along the shore, so the Peruvians carried just two boats, Jim's and mine, 100 meters or so down across rocks. Here they complained of the difficulty and refused to continue. The older man claimed he didn't know where Choquequirao was, anyway. I thought they were starting an early play for higher wages. I was surprised, then, when they evaporated among the big rocks along the shore. They had failed even to ask for money for the work done. Their actions were strange and disquieting. I imagined them boiling with antagonism: first their banana tree was toppled; now they had labored with our boats and had collected nothing for it. I wondered if they might not plan some frontier justice. The image of the machete hung like a black question mark in the air.

The five of us were together again, facing a 400-meter portage down the right bank. We began to break our boats down into the usual three loads.

"Someone will have to stay up here with the gear as long as the two natives are around," Jim remarked.

The others each packed off a load, so I stayed behind to watch the remaining gear. While I waited, I busied myself fixing a broken strap on a small pack I would use for the trip down. One by one the others returned to pick up loads, and I thought, "Fine, I will wait until someone spells me." Chuck returned and looked suspiciously inside his boat.

"Were the two Indians near this?" he asked.

"No," I said, "I've been watching it. Nothing's been taken."

He trudged off with the boat on his shoulder. Then I noticed that the only gear remaining on the shoreline was my own. I waited awhile, but no one returned to relieve my watch. They had all vanished in the jungle of rocks. I became angry. I had watched the gear for at least half an hour, and no one else had seen fit to help guard this end. And now they were gone.

I had no choice now; I had to begin. And I had to make my carries so short that I always had my gear in sight. I could not go behind or over any tall rock if it broke my line of vision. At each such obstacle I would have to set my load down, on or beside the rock, and return for more. The short hauls were inefficient and slow, but I dared not expose unguarded gear, in case the two Indians came back.

I was apprehensive and watchful as I worked my way along the wasteland of the shore. I remembered how quickly the two had disappeared into the rocks, and knew they could reappear as quickly. I half expected a confrontation, shuddering at the thought of the tense man with weasel eyes and a machete, and I kept my helmet buckled tight.

So I continued my short carries, wary and annoyed, thinking that surely someone would eventually return after completing his own portage. Then I glanced down the river and saw Chuck paddle away from shore, turn into the current, and drift from sight, with never a backward glance. I was exasperated when I remembered that just a short while before he had relied on my surveillance and protection of his gear.

I finally arrived at the launch site without incident. Jim and Gerry were waiting; the other two had departed. Jim apologized; he had utterly forgotten the Indian problem. The incident slid from my mind, becoming a pebble of memory in the rocky stream of the Apurímac.

C huck and Dee continued on ahead, out of sight. We struggled down to the great slide. Here our pace slowed to a crawl, as we scouted and plotted an intricate route to line through the maze. In such places a group working together is better and faster—everyone can share the burden of reconnaissance and the lining of hard passages. Yet we worked now as two groups and were forced to discover twice the route through the slide.

The vast jumble of rocks covered the valley floor and the riverbed for a quarter-mile along the canyon and formed one of the most powerful rapids I had ever seen. Yet by staying off to the right, in the shallows, we eventually worked our boats down on long ropes without having to carry them around. It was tedious work, clambering around and over the big rocks, slipping, sometimes swimming, but it was infinitely better than a portage on shore.

And so it went from the gray light of morning to the deepening shadows of afternoon. My journal touched on the obstacles of that day, noting that "the huge waters of the Apurímac crash over boulder after boulder with little respite." Then the journal entry took up our progress: "And so we plod on like snails. We start by paddling 100 yards; lining 50; carrying 200; paddling 50; carrying 400; paddling 200; lining 500; paddling 100—or something like that. Less than a mile. At the end I am so tired that each step is a traumatic burden."

Dee and Chuck were still not in sight at 5:00. Beaches of sand were now rare among the hulking rocks, and we were growing tired. When we came to a small sandbar, we stopped for the night. By our side was yet another enormous rapid, laced everywhere with the cussedness of the Apurímac as it lashed out at the Vilcabamba rocks. We were in two camps now, huddled around two different fires, two dots of light that no longer touched, each flickering back the darkness of the canyon. If one light grew dim, those camped by the other light wouldn't know, couldn't help. I regretted the deep split in our expedition; the end of cooperation. I regretted the thinning of the margin of safety that comes when one person fails to help another against the canyon.

But these regrets were overshadowed by the joy of evening. We were comfortable here; we could rest tired muscles and sip tea by the camp-fire. And I was with friends—people who cared and helped and tried to make this expedition work, and who loved the canyon for its own sake. I felt very content.

The date was September 19; we were nineteen days now below our start at Pillpinto. The moon had been brimming fuller every night, as it flew in splendor across the face of the Andes, bathing our canyon in a mystical light, reflecting nocturnal beauty. Now on this night the moon grew full, full of light and magic and playful tricks. In its glow the canyon turned falsely gentle. Soft rays played on the rugged walls and made them look like the gates of heaven. They cloaked with gentle shadows the thorns and scars on the faces. The cliffs, the slopes, the jungle above were frozen in ghostly white splendor. Only the ribbon of river danced and played in the night. The light on the water sparkled like diamonds and concealed the demon beneath. It beckoned me over to ride its waves in a gentle flow to the sea.

I admonished myself as I wrote that night not to be seduced by the marvelous flood of light and water: "As I write in the moonlight, the silvery waters of the Apurímac race by. The magic of moonlight makes the water look smooth and wispy, somewhat pillowy, like cotton clouds racing over the hilltop. Gone, the deep holes, the massive turbulence. But listen well, and do not be deceived by moonlight. That drumming roar tells all, conceals nothing, of the crushing power of the mother of the Amazon."

D ay twenty signaled another long fight with the river. We carried
around the rapid the moon had tried to lure me to in the night.
Then we paddled to the beach where Dee and Chuck had camped. No
one brought up the subject of our separate camps and our increasingly
separate paths. We started in earnest the backbreaking task of inching
down the river. Cataracts stretched ahead of us with incredible continu-
ity as far as we could see. Fractured rock lay everywhere. The river
thrashed like a wounded snake down a canyon of low, broken walls.
Where the coil of the water hit a cliff at the side, it pinched off the
shoreline and destroyed the path along the rocks.

As we came down these shores, laboring with the weight of our gear,
we would suddenly find the river and the cliff converging to a wedge
in front of us. At the tip of the wedge we would see the fury of the river
beating on the walls. There we had to stop, to take another path. We
had to cross the river and take the far shore, where again we would
labor among the rocks, up to the next wedge, and begin the cycle anew.

Our boats now served only the function of carrying us over the river
from one portage to the next. As we approached the extremity of each
wedge, following the line of the cataracts that rumbled down the canyon, a strip of calm water would appear, smoothed over from shore to
shore as if by command. There we would load up and cross. I wondered
often that day what would happen if we came to the wedge, the last
rock of the shore, the place we must cross, but couldn't.

The demon Apurímac—it taunted us and tortured us and threw us
around like matchsticks. It scorned us and controlled us and forced us
to march through the eyes of its needles. Yet at our breaking point it
relented; the needle's eye was always there when all other passages were
closed.

So went the day: right, left, right, left. Four different carries, two on
each side of the river. We advanced less than a mile. The last portage, a
monumental carry on the left, followed an embankment of rocks
plunging sharply into the river. Fingers and knuckles of gray cliffs
dropped down from the canyon wall, breaking through the stony
masses like a prairie train scattering buffalo. Our path wove up and
down the embankment as we sought passages through the rocks and
the fingers of the cliffs. At one moment we were wading waist-deep in
the river beneath a roof of stone; at the next we were climbing steeply

to the very top of the embankment to skirt one of the plunging ridges. We trod each segment of the tortured, broken path five times to move our train of gear.

Jim and I began to lag behind. By 3:30 I was exhausted beyond recall, my portage still unfinished. I abandoned my boat to the rocks and plodded along with my gear. Below the last thundering drop of the rapid, an enclave of sand appeared amid the crowns and ridges of rock. It dove deep into the river, whose waters still bubbled from pockets of air pulled down in the turmoil above. I sat down on the sand and stared at the bubbles, unhappy at the break in my struggle. Jim clung to his task and brought his final load down the steep slope of rocks to the beach. There we established our camp.

"Don't be discouraged," Jim told me that night. "There's no sense in this pace. We've forgotten how to enjoy the canyon. We're pushing too hard, to the point of danger, even up on these boulders, or when we're lining the rapids. It would be easy to slip and break a leg when we're so tired. We shouldn't expect to keep pace with the others. They're younger and they're at it all the time, working and conditioning outdoors. Look at them. Gerry's profession is teaching outdoor sports, Chuck's working on the Alaska pipeline. Dee climbs a mountain most mornings. Why worry about imitating what they do?"

"You're right," I replied, "but I don't want to be the one to hold things up, particularly with Dee so impatient. Look, I want to hold this expedition together. I'm its father. If it fails it's my fault. Maybe I picked the wrong people—that's my fault too. So now I'm here I'll do everything I can to keep it going smoothly. But, frankly, this pace is starting to tell on me. I can't even boat safely anymore; the constant portaging has taken too much out of me."

"The portages are getting to our equipment, too," Jim noted, and we talked about this for a while. Our long struggles on shore, so much bumping and sliding on rocks, the constant picking up and setting down in rough places—all this punishment ground and tore at our clothing and gear. Our shoes, nylon-light for the river, grew shredded and thin. We each had one extra pair, but even these might not last if we kept wearing them so hard. And we wouldn't get far in this country without shoes.

Our thin vinyl, waterproof storage bags were critical too. If we wore leaks in them, or split the seams beyond repair, water would soak through to our food and spoil it. We wondered how many more times we could drag them in and out of the boats, as we did at the ends of each portage, without wearing holes in them. How many rocks could we slam them against and drag them across as we carried them down the shore?

This day had brought agony, and its intensity had thrown back all other realities. Yet there was a thin silver lining. Here is how it looked to me as I wrote in my journal that night:

Today we have, essentially, completed the first week of the leg below the Cunyac Bridge. Our schedule calls for four, with a possible stretch-out to five or so. Perhaps one-fourth through, then. Yet it seems we have been in this canyon forever. I seem to remember nothing else than plodding over boulders with gear and boat. Any other activity I have ever done seems remote and far away. Will it relent?

There is some hope. The Apurímac is plunging away madly and has now reached 5,000 feet or below. It can't go on forever. Will we outlast her? I don't know. Nothing is so unpredictable as her arsenal of weapons. One day at a time, we try to cope with her vagaries. It is still a toss-up.

D ay twenty-one dawned clear, and I arose early to go back for my boat. I was refreshed by sleep and invigorated by the morning air, and I moved lightly back over the obstacles of the embankment. Soon I had the boat back to the roof of rock that forced us into the shallows beneath. Instead of wading, I climbed into my boat to paddle across. All at once it felt as light as air, like a magic carpet ready to fly. It was free of its great load and turned at the touch of a paddle. I grew euphoric and spun around gleefully, suddenly feeling that I could do anything in this cloud-light boat! The thundering drop below me would be easy.

Wait! I thought. This river's madness is taking me with it! I'd be destroyed down there! Better get back to shore quickly.

I got back to camp in time for breakfast. We ate, then packed hurriedly. We faced a short run, then a confrontation with the last big rapid before reaching the trail to Choquequirao.

We landed on the left shore to scout. The rapid was big and powerful, strewn with rocks and pitted with holes. A general consensus developed that we should work somewhere down the shallows among the big boulders, away from the power in the center. Then Dee saw a route he liked, going out to the middle of the river. It started from the left bank and churned through a series of chutes of increasing power, to the heavy water rolling down the center.

Dee entered his boat and started alone. No one else was ready to go or ready to cover in case of accident. Partway out he smashed through a hole at the bottom of a chute, lost his momentum, then slid softly over the brink into the next drop, where his boat flipped over like a toy. He struggled to roll, failed, and was soon swimming alongside his overturned boat. The two plunged into the depths of the chutes near the center.

We watched aghast from shore, worried at the length and the power of the rapid. Yet we were completely helpless. We were all out of our boats, and even had we been in them, no one could have reached Dee quickly without following the same perilous route. It was a breach of safety that could lead to the loss of a boat—or a life.

I exchanged words quickly with Jim, who was nearby. Our actions would be simple and direct. Because I was nearest, I would hurry down the shore to see what help was needed. Jim would prepare to follow with ropes, kayak, or whatever I signaled for.

I raced down the shore, across the great rocks, scrambling, jumping, slipping. My breath grew labored. Yet I knew I must keep going, that there would be no moment to waste if trouble had developed. Glimpses of the river showed it empty; Dee had disappeared from sight. I was now quite certain that he was pinned at the bottom of one of the chutes dropping among the boulders. I motioned for Jim to come help me search, and I raced farther down the shore, past the end of the rapid, to see if Dee might have washed onto rocks or the shore down there. Still no sight of him. An oppressive sense of hopelessness fell across me like a shadow.

Farther down I stopped briefly to scan the river. Straight out from where I stood was the shocking sight of Dee drifting by, upright in his boat. He had pulled it ashore below the rapid, behind one of the building-size rocks, and emptied it. He had then launched again while I was searching, out of sight. My body now shook with exhaustion. The sense of renewal I had felt early that morning had dissolved into the deep fatigue of the night before. I stumbled over the rocks, back toward my gear, back to the labor of moving my own boat down through the shallows that edged the rapid.

I was never thanked for the effort I had made to assure someone else's survival.

Choquequirao is a ruin on such a spur, jutting out above the Apurímac on the western side of the Cordillera Vilcabamba. Seen from its terraces, the thunderous river is no more than a silver-grey line creeping along its gorge far below: and looking downstream, the darkly-matted valley walls disappear into a hazy distance like the background of a Leonardo painting.

John Hemming

We . . . stood in complete amazement at the sight of its tumultuous rapids, two hundred and fifty feet across, tearing through the Canyon at a fearful pace, throwing up great waves like the ocean in a north-east storm.

Hiram Bingham

≈ CHOQUEQUIRAO
Cradle of Gold

W E REACHED THE trail leading to Choquequirao ("cho-kaye-key-ráw-o") at noon. We stopped on the left, opposite the trailhead, to make our final decision as to whether to visit the Inca ruins high up on the mountain. We faced, on one hand, a rare opportunity to see a remote ruin, long thought to be the gold-laden last city of the Incas. And the view of the canyon was reputed to be splendid.

But to varying degrees, we were all exhausted. We faced many unknowns ahead and had had great difficulty with our progress in the last few days; any other barriers of that magnitude could cut deeply into our supplies—and our strength. And the hike up was over a vertical mile, no minor feat for travelers wearied by the demon river.

"Do you want to go up?" I asked the group, hoping for an agreeable consensus. Gerry and Dee said they did.

"I'll watch the boats," Jim offered; "the rest of you can go up."

"I think you should go if anyone does," I told him; "one of us will watch the boats." His opportunities to travel and see such marvels had been more limited than ours, and he had already been stuck with more than his share of volunteer work, including boat-sitting.

"I'll stay," Chuck offered; "I don't really care too much to go up."

That settled, we paddled across the river toward the rock embankment at the foot of the mountain of Choquequirao.

After the Spanish betrayed and beheaded the last Inca, Tupac Amaru, in 1572, outposts along the rugged slopes and valleys of the Cordillera Vilcabamba became Spanish possessions. For a few decades silver mining flourished in some areas and sugar plantations were established in the Urubamba Valley. But this land gave its resources grudgingly, and within forty years it was almost abandoned. Tropical growth reclaimed the terrain and covered alike the remnants of Inca splendor and Spanish colonization.

Nearly two centuries afterwards, the world began to wonder what had happened to the last Inca citadel and especially to the untold wealth of gold and silver rumored to be hidden there. There was at that time a tradition of an ancient Inca town north of the Apurímac, known as Choquequirao, or "cradle of gold," in the ancient language of the hills. This town soon became the focus of the search for the last refuge—and the lost gold—of the Incas.

But the approach to Choquequirao was incredibly difficult. It was necessary either to cross the rugged gorge of the Apurímac and surmount the turbulent barrier of the river, or to approach it from the Urubamba River below Machu Picchu and over the high crest of the Vilcabamba Mountains. And once it was reached, jungle vegetation had to be torn aside to uncover the extensive handiwork beneath. But the allure of gold knows no bounds. A party is reported to have crossed the Apurímac on rafts in the mid-1700s and to have found the ruins, but no gold. Later in that century it was again searched for gold by a wealthy landowner of the region.

A Frenchman, the Comte de Sartiges, visited Choquequirao in 1834. He approached the ruins from behind, via the slopes of the Vilcabamba. His journey was one of untold hardships. An attempt to cut a trail was abandoned after three weeks. Then he and his companions pushed on through the tangled growth and mountain steepness for five more days before reaching Choquequirao. Their food was now almost consumed, and they could explore for only a few days. Nevertheless, they saw enough to convince them of its unsuspected size; it was a place where fifteen thousand people might once have dwelled.

With each failure to find gold, the rumors of its amount grew. Ill-prepared parties set out, some reaching the ruins, some being turned back by its defenses. By about 1850 its reputation as the last Inca refuge had become entrenched in the minds of treasure seekers and scholars alike. Attempts were then made to build a trail to Choquequirao so that an entire workforce could be maintained there. A local magistrate, with a company of soldiers and unlimited mountain Indians at his disposal, succeeded only in reaching the crest of the Vilcabamba in back of the town. They could not penetrate the precipices guarding the ancient city.

Another local official, J. J. Núñez, formed a company of treasure seekers to raise money for a massive assault. His party worked down to the Apurímac River and then faced the problem of crossing it. Finally, according to Hiram Bingham's account, an aged Chinese peddler with a string around his waist swam across the river. With the string, other components were pulled across, and soon a suspension bridge, made of six strands of telegraph wire, spanned the river.

I find this story believable. The Apurímac levels out a short distance above the trail to Choquequirao. It could be swum, although I would not volunteer to do it. (There would need to be a lot of gold to get me out there towing a string!)

After the bridge was established, a zigzag trail was constructed up the steep slopes and cliffs to Choquequirao. Again, no gold was found. In February of 1909, at the urging of Señor Núñez, Hiram Bingham, who later discovered the ruins of Machu Picchu, visited Choquequirao. February in the central Andes is the season of rain, and that February was particularly nasty. After slipping on sodden trails, Bingham finally approached the canyon of the Apurímac. "We began to hear the roar of the great river seven thousand feet below us in the canyon," he wrote. They descended on worsening trails and reached the river in darkness. "We . . . could see nothing although the terrific roaring of the 'Great Speaker' made us wonder what lay before us. We were told the river was over a hundred feet deep."

The next morning, Hiram Bingham was shocked at the sight of the river. "We stood in complete amazement at the sight of its tumultuous rapids, 250 feet across, tearing through the canyon at a fearful pace, throwing up waves like the ocean in a northeast storm. An incredible mass of water was dashing past. The river had risen more than fifty feet because of the heavy rains. The bridge swayed in the wind on its six strands of telegraph wire. So close to death did the narrow cat-walk of the bridge appear to be, and so high did the rapids throw the icy spray, our Indian bearers crept across one at a time."

Hiram Bingham crossed too; he ascended the other side, and there was struck by the magnificent view. Finally he stood at the ruins "at the top of the southern and outer precipice, five thousand eight hundred feet immediately above the river. . . . The view from here, both up and down the valley surpasses the possibilities of language for adequate description. Far down the gigantic canyon one catches little glimpses of the Apurímac, a white stream shut in between guardian mountains."

Hiram Bingham was not trained in archeology, nor did he then know anything substantial about the Incas. He had been brought here by Señor Núñez to find gold but found none. Yet his trip was hardly a failure. Choquequirao was the spark that set Hiram Bingham's imagination on fire. It ignited his determination to know more of the lost city. He visited the historian Don Carlos Romero in Lima and was assured that the Spanish chronicles were decisive about Choquequirao: it was not the lost city of the Incas.

Two years later, in 1911, Hiram Bingham returned to discover what is perhaps the most spectacular set of ruins in the Americas—Machu Picchu.

The true identity of the lost city has now been established, according to evidence cited by Hemming, and it is neither Choquequirao nor Machu Picchu. It is the ruins of Espíritu Pampa, less than 50 miles northwest of Choquequirao, in a land buried deep in jungle growth and swirling mists. I hope someday to visit there. But for now our sights were set on the magnificent but somewhat empty cradle of gold above.

We landed on the sloping ledges at the trailhead and dragged our boats up on the rocks. There were no flat places to repack our gear for the hike. Dee occupied the best site, a shallow crevice in the rock where one could pull out gear without having it roll down into the river. Jim and Gerry found lesser sites. No suitable place remained.

While I waited for Dee to pack and vacate his site, I looked around at this historical crossing. Hiram Bingham's suspension bridge was now gone, perhaps washed out by an even greater flood than the one he witnessed here. In its place were a few twisted strands of telegraph wire forming a single cable, an aroya across the river. An Indian later showed Chuck how a horse is taken across: the poor animal is tied to the wires by means of a slider to prevent it from washing into the rapids below, then forced into the current to swim its way across.

After a brief interlude I was able to pack my own gear. I pulled the backpack off my deck and loaded it with camera equipment, clothing, two days' worth of food, and miscellaneous gear. The valuables to be left behind were stuffed deep in the bow and stern, and then the boat was rolled over to block its cockpit and abandoned to Chuck's care.

At 2 P.M. Jim and I started up the dizzying slopes of the canyon. Gerry and Dee were already gone. After a while we found Gerry waiting at a small farm, where an aged Quechua woman busied herself with chores. Her hut was made of bamboo poles and sticks, thatched in straw. We watched in fascination as she lit a cooking fire in a fire pit inside her small hut and blew it to full flame using a short length of reed. Smoke filled the hut and poured out the windows and cracks between the poles. It was a choking, acrid smoke with a peculiar smell that I now identify with that region. The woman sat in the midst of the smoke unperturbed, sharing a meal of cooked corn with the chickens gathered in her house. Our presence did not seem to bother her routine. (*See* Plate 10)

Jim, Gerry, and I pressed on. Dee had long ago disappeared up the trail.

Soon the expected magnificence of the view evolved. The river was indeed a silver ribbon below us, still roaring in its gorge. Mountains rose in splendor across the great canyon. The late afternoon sun tinted them pink and illuminated a faint mist that filled the sky to the distant horizon. As we climbed higher, enormous mountains thrust above the canyon wall downriver. These appeared to be true Vilcabamba peaks—distant, obscure, magnificent. The setting sun was now setting them ablaze in color.

The trail continued its relentless zigzags up the sweeping slopes. The long battle with the river began to tell on me, and I lagged behind. Soon I was forced to stop every fifty paces and catch my breath. Each step became excruciating. Plodding on now required every ounce of strength I had left. Jim and Gerry held back patiently.

I felt bad about this, but cheered myself thinking about the great Hiram Bingham panting up the same trail sixty-six years before. "It seemed like a pretty serious undertaking," he wrote, "to attempt to climb up a slippery little trail for six thousand feet, to an elevation twice as high as the top of Mount Washington." Later he admitted that "the two *Yankis* [he and his companion] had a hard time of it and were obliged to stop and rest nearly every fifty feet."

We stopped to eat at the only flat place on the trail, near a small stream pouring down from the mountains. We made a smoky fire, every bit as ill-smelling as that at the hut below! The foul smoke seemed to emanate from the hollow stems of a brush-like plant. We boiled the water a considerable time now before we could use it to prepare food and tea. We usually bypassed this tedious boiling by the addition of iodine disinfectant to our water, but Dee was somewhere ahead with the only iodine kit on the mountain.

We finished dinner after nightfall and hiked on into darkness. We looked for a campsite, but on that whole mountainside we could not find a square yard of flat ground. The whole world here was tipped on its edge and covered with thick brush. Much later we found a small, sloping meadow just off the trail, imbedded everywhere with rocks. We found the flattest place we could and pitched Jim's tent in the matted grass, directly over the protruding stones. Thick mists began closing in over the mountain.

Suddenly a strange male voice stabbed through the dark. "Where are you going?" it demanded in Spanish.

"To Choquequirao," I responded.

"Come stay at my house," the voice now insisted, "it is just above this place."

Looking out of the tent now, we glimpsed the dark figure of a man standing by several mules over on the trail. His offer was tempting, but we had just settled into the tent, ready for a well-deserved rest. We had not yet had time to realize the agonies of our campsite and couldn't find any enthusiasm to repack and move up the mountain.

"Many thanks, but no, not tonight," I called over. "We will visit you in the morning." It was a decision we soon regretted.

It began raining later and continued all night. We had no sleeping bags to warm or cushion us. Three of us lay crammed in a two-man tent—cold, clammy, lying on rocks. The long equatorial night seemed never to end.

We arose in the weak gray light of morning, hardly rested. We folded the wet tent and plodded on in a light drizzle. Heavy mists hung around us. Occasionally they broke open, and we saw Andean ridges plunging toward the river on one side, thrusting toward heaven on the other.

Our trail led up to the edge of a flat meadow, the only significant respite we found from the vertical trend of the mountain. Here we met the man who had invited us up the night before; he was now leading a mule back down the trail. We chatted for a few minutes, but he was in a hurry: "It's market day across the river, at Hacienda Parcas," he told us. "I must get going." It was unusual haste for a man of the Andes, but then market day is an unusual magnet. Peasants flock down out of the hills with goods to sell and chicha to drink. It is a rousing, drunken, day-long party and a cheerful reunion for families and friends isolated by these soaring mountain ridges. The market itself is secondary.

We walked across the rolling meadows, now criss-crossed with broken lines of trees, dotted with cows and horses. A stone house and other buildings were isolated behind a rock wall, snuggled over against the hill. It was a gentle oasis nestled picturesquely among contentious mountain slopes.

Our trail rose again; the sun burned through the mist; and tropical heat gripped the land. We were thirsty now and sipped toward the end of our rationed water. We dared not drink from the occasional rivulets, because of the ever-present threat of disease. We grumbled to each other about the iodine kit being somewhere up the mountain with Dee. It had never occurred to me that he would go up the mountain alone, but I guess I should have known.

We began what seemed like an endless traverse around one of the spiraling ridges. The trail crossed slopes so steep that one would think them uncrossable. Our path reminded me of the great Inca trails around Machu Picchu—trails that skillfully use every fracture and weakness in the soaring cliffs they cross. I had thought that such art had died with the last Inca, but the trailblazer who designed this route for J. J. Núñez around the turn of the century had certainly retained the ancient skills; or perhaps they had found an overgrown Inca trail.

After we had passed beyond the steep ridge, we saw a few houses and sheds occupying tiny breaks in the terrain. One woman emerged with two children from a stately stone house, curious to find out who we were. We chatted a few minutes and passed on.

Fields here were tilled on land so steep that there would be some danger of losing one's footing and rolling to the bottom while working. The mountainside was far from crowded, in a physical sense, but I was surprised at the considerable number of people we did see. Hiram Bingham failed to mention anyone living on these slopes during his ascent in 1909. John Hemming, whose visit was apparently made in the 1960s, reported only two huts, both of which he slept in during the two-day ascent. Now there were easily twice that. It was a regular population boom. Four or five families on an entire mountain may not seem like much, yet all the choice spaces, the few flat areas, were gone. Each new settler must choose a steeper slope, farther from water, then clear the tenacious underbrush from erosion-prone land. It was clear no one would do very well up here, nor would the fragile, exposed soil. In this sense, the land is overcrowded and overused.

On the final approach to Choquequirao, on a ridge beyond the second stone house, we met Dee coming down the trail. He had only briefly visited the ruins. We got back the iodine kit and hurried to the next brooklet to quench our thirst.

At 10:30 the lowest of the stone terraces guarding Choquequirao loomed through the brush in front of us. Moss was clinging to the ancient walls, and vines dangled down from branches above. A clogged path had been trampled along the base. We walked along it to a point where stone steps ascended. They led up through several levels, then we hiked left through a more open clearing. At that point we approached a broad depression on the main ridge.

The geography of Choquequirao was typical of Inca fortresses in the Vilcabamba. Vitcos, Machu Picchu, Choquequirao—they were all built on the saddle of a steep and spectacular mountain ridge. The great ridge of Choquequirao plummets nearly 7,000 feet in 3 miles from the glaciers of the Yanacocha massif to the low saddle where we stood. From there it rises, as if in a last gasp, to a small knoll overlooking the valley, and then it shatters over vertical cliffs that plunge another 6,000 feet to the river below.

Several broken walls with doorways rose above the gentle slopes near the saddle of the ridge. The stones had been cut to fit snugly against one another, although with less care and precision than at Cuzco and Machu Picchu, which are closer to the heart of the Inca empire. This was truly an outpost, and while big, it was more roughly hewn. A few hundred yards up the main ridge we found buildings with higher walls, almost perfectly preserved, some seeming to lack only the grass-thatched roof to bring them and the Incas to life again.

Here we walked in through ancient doorways and were nearly smothered by vegetation. The growth inside, protected from the excesses of the climate by high walls, had grown luxuriantly. In one place we struggled through this indoor shrubbery to get to walls in which were cut perfect trapezoidal alcoves and from which protruded large pegs of pure rock with holes like the eye of a needle ground through them. A few stone artifacts were scattered around.

The still-perfect form of some of the walls renewed my sense of marvel at Inca genius. This is one of the most active earthquake regions in the world. The history of most great cathedrals and churches in Peru is a history of successive destructions by earthquakes and rebuildings afterwards. In Lima in 1974, my family had been wrenched through one of these heaving-crashing earthquakes—a Richter scale 7.8—and

The remains of Inca building at Choquequirao.
The walls are still intact after five centuries of earthquakes.

quickly came to know their shattering power. Nothing endures the centuries in this land, except the mountains, the rivers—and Inca walls.

We crossed the broad saddle and ascended the outermost knoll. We found its summit leveled—fashioned into a 100-foot table top. Had this once been a lookout station for the Incas? Indeed, it might have been. The view from the knoll was expansive and magnificent in all directions. This bit of terrain hung like a watchtower above the steep valley, revealing hillsides, ridges, and peaks in marvelous relief. Broken cliffs tumbled 6,000 feet to the Apurímac below, and the ribbon of the river could be seen eternally advancing through its stupendous canyon.

I sat down on the edge of the knoll near a clump of yellow flowers high above the river to prolong the view and to study our adversary. The incredible roar of the Apurímac rapids echoed up the canyon walls and filled the valley with its threats. I heard clearly its message, modulated only slightly by gusty mountain breezes that pulsed with different notes and intensities. It was eerie hearing such torment from this soaring, distant perch.

I turned my attention more fully to the origin of the noise, because there lay our future path. I was looking west—downstream. The Apurí-mac here changes its direction from west to northwest, as it comes curling around the mountain of Choquequirao. It then intercepts a deep side canyon gushing with water from Nevado Yanacocha, Sacsara-yoc, Kaico, and other peaks to the north. The tributary stream is called Río Choquequirao. From here the river trends west again through the Vilcabamba.

Where the river came into view beneath me, it was engaged in a cataract. It relented, then poured into an awesome drop against a cliff that pushed the river left. Three rapids followed before the river disappeared behind a canyon wall. It reappeared briefly, swinging sharply right, to the north, into a steep-walled gorge heading for union with the Río Choquequirao. It emerged more distant, more obscure, and faded gradually into the gray walls of its canyon. Altogether I could see maybe 3 miles of its length.

Where it was visible, the river could be passed. It wouldn't be easy, but it could be done. The cataracts would have to be portaged; at least they were more widely spaced than above. But I could not fathom the mysteries of that steep-walled gorge, nor of the canyons below. These puzzles would have to await our return to the river.

It was now 12:30. The day had been strenuous, and we lay down in the dry grass near the saddle of the ridge to rest. Where once trod armies and legions of men, we now heard only the gentle rustling of the breeze, the sweet songs of birds, and the buzzing of flies. No human sound. Here was the result of so great a human effort—seemingly all for naught.

But that was from our perspective, the narrow outlook of one-day visitors from another land and another century. From the Incas' view-point, this remote citadel may have guarded a frontier to the jungle and given happiness and a sense of security to the people of the moun-tains. It is, indeed, widely speculated that Choquequirao was an ancient fortress. But as I looked around, I wondered what route it might have guarded. The incredible hills and the rocky gorge of the river should be barrier enough. Yet Hemming's map shows an old Inca road climbing up behind the ruins, crossing the steep ravines of Río Choquequirao, and crossing the Cordillera Vilcabamba near Arma. We ourselves had followed a well-laid trail to the ruins. Who is to say what ancient byways may have threaded through these mountains or what forgotten armies may have labored across the ridges seeking plunder, threatening the empire?

B ecause we had far to go, we left Choquequirao at 1:30. We trudged down the trail, in and out of the shadows of puffball clouds drifting in a brilliant blue sky. We stopped when two eagles swept over our heads from a nearby ravine. We watched them circle higher until they were lost in the infinity of the horizon.

Reaching the river at 5:30, as the first heavy shadows of darkness began creeping over the Vilcabamba, we set up camp among the stones and rock shelves near the cable crossing, for there was no other place. Horses had been tethered here, waiting to cross the Apurímac. A rank barnyard odor suffused the air. There was no room for tents. It began to rain again.

We are now ready to start on our way down the great unknown.

John Wesley Powell

Nature pardons no mistakes. Her yea is yea and her nay, nay.

Emerson

I almost conclude to leave the river. But for years I have been contemplating the trip, to leave the exploration unfinished, to say that there is a part of the canyon which I cannot explore . . . is more than I am willing to do, and I determine to go on.

John Wesley Powell

≈ CAPSIZES!

I N THE DAMP, restless hours of the night, I contemplated our future. The route ahead lay through the most obscure canyons we had yet faced. The coverage by aerial photography vanished at this spot, near the bottom of the trail that wound to Choquequirao, and it did not resume again for 12–18 miles along the river. In this span of obscurity, the Apurímac made its final and most reckless sweep north into Vilca-bamba granite.

The aerial photographs had been indispensable in plotting the course of the trip. We had been able to see all the big problems coming up—the chasm of Acobamba, the cataracts above Choquequirao, and others up higher. Although the smaller problems, the single, foaming plunges, had shrunk to invisibility on the minuscule scale of the charts, and we couldn't see the rocks that split the current or the whirlpools or the depth of the falls, we could at least see where the cataracts were thick.

Before coming to Peru, I had allowed long days to bypass those storming cataracts above Choquequirao, based on the photographs. I was certainly shocked by the realities of our route, the monstrosity of the rocks and the thundering of the water. But the schedule inspired by the charts remained intact. From the photos we could see where the canyons opened and closed, where broad portage paths swept down the rocks on the bank, where they were shut off by cliffs. We could see the deep gorges. We had been forewarned about the Chasm of Aco-bamba. That alone made them worth their weight in gold.

This keystone of knowledge was now missing. We knew next to nothing about the canyon ahead. We had studied a few miles of the river from the heights of Choquequirao that day, but that was only a trace of the void. And my maps added little. The 1:200,000-scale map showed the river plunging through the unknown as a thin, tranquil line; nowhere did it reveal the steepness of the canyon walls nor the gradient of the river's descent. Even its curves and bends had proved inaccurate when compared to the wild twists of the Apurímac. The maps, in short, told us only that the river didn't fall through a hole in the earth and that it didn't evaporate. No, it continued down through the mountains on a course of rippling water and cut rock, a course whose details were unknown to us, and it emerged finally out of mystery onto another photograph downriver.

That was another problem, the reemergence. Where the trace of the river crawled back onto a glossy photo print, it received a little thread of a tributary from a canyon called Quebrada de Arma. Then the trace skipped half a centimeter and reappeared to scribble its way on through the mountains, where it looked okay. Where the river blanked out was my concern. Back home I had looked at this small skip a hundred times, changing light, changing angles, rearranging photo sheets beneath the double lens of the stereoscope, working and staring and thinking into the late hours of the night. In the end it was indecipherable, almost unbelievable. It appeared that a monumental block, perhaps several hundred meters across, had collapsed off a wall and fallen into the canyon, choking it off almost completely, except for a channel where the river wormed behind the block, out of sight. But was the river flowing in calmness or madness back there? Was there a shoreline to go along in that thin crack of flow? Could we get up over the top of the block if the river and its shore were impassable?

The photos had sat for hours at a time on my desk beneath the glare and the lenses, suffering my interrogation about what had happened to the river. But in the end they said nothing at all concerning the secret they hid in the gray of the rocks.

In the jarring battles with the Apurímac above Choquequirao, I had put all questions about the mysterious blockage of the canyon out of my mind. Now they returned in the dreariness of the night to trouble my sleep. I tossed on my bed of coarse sand and rocks, damp in the lingering rain, repulsed by the overpowering horse odor that the wetness drove out of the soil. I wondered how we had gotten stuck at a livestock crossing in the midst of a wilderness so vast and pure.

My thoughts turned then to my birthday, only four days away. Where would I be? If the river closed in on us down in the unknown stretch, we might be there a week. If it broke open—even a little—we'd be through, maybe even past the Quebrada de Arma. Suddenly that's what I wanted with a passion. I wanted to work past those question marks, through the unknown stretch and the blockage, and emerge on or before my birthday. That became my goal and my dream.

Morning came and I arose exhausted. Two sleepless nights added to days of toil had sapped my strength. I should have rested awhile that morning. But our small expedition was now rigid with a mood of artificial, inflexible haste.

Upon arising we automatically scurried around lighting a fire, boiling water, preparing breakfast, setting aside lunch, drying gear, sorting and packing, and loading our boats. We hurried and fretted, but we never really got our minds together to ask how we might move ahead better by helping each other. There were too many tensions. It seemed impossible to get the whole team to act to improve efficiency. At most two or three worked together. Those in the greatest haste constantly defeated their own purposes by splitting the team and leaving stragglers. This had slowed us down when Chuck undertook his solo swim up on Acobamba. When I fell behind and faced a rapid alone, even though someone waited down the river, I was hesitant and cautious. Rapids seem twice as big to me when I run them alone, and it is always slower.

So it is with exhaustion—sometimes it is faster to rest. It is certainly less dangerous. But to suggest it here, I felt, was useless. So I prepared for the river, saying nothing.

We worked down the tough canyon beneath Choquequirao, alternating between short runs and stretches of lining and portaging. The river had backed off a trifle from the terrible severity we found in the canyons above, but it was still full of threat and was in fact to be the site of a tragedy eight months later. Two Germans who had spent six months training in Switzerland launched two inflatable boats down the same canyon we struggled through that morning. The river was probably still high from winter rains, and in their attempt to navigate the treacherous rocks and rapids, only one of them survived.

At midmorning we faced a narrow chute of water that twisted and foamed over an abrupt drop near the right side of the river. Below the chute was a pool swirling with leftover streaks of foam, and below that a long, mean rapid. The drop looked tricky as I paddled around to the right, where I could look down on all its kinks. The others slipped through and disappeared below.

As I studied the chute it struck me suddenly that it was no worse than any of hundreds of the mad, contorted drops I had paddled in the highlands. Here it was a small chute at the edge of the big river, but it looked much the same as the main chutes in the young Apurímac far above us. I knew I could do those. I had done them again and again.

I swung out of my small pool of calm water into the current that swept to the edge; then I plunged with the water over the first abrupt drop. At the foot of the drop the current spun left. It was up to me to follow, and I dug my paddle into a mound of bubbling water and pulled hard to swing around into proper position. But that morning, my strength had deserted me. I managed to turn partway, but that was not enough. There was no second chance. The current carried my boat sideways into a second drop. As the craft hit bottom, its nose plunged down into the water and caught on a hidden rock. The current behind piled over me in a great choking mass; it pushed me underwater and jerked me out of my seating. I struggled to stay inside the kayak.

The exertion left me out of breath. I had little air—and thus little time. I fought to regain my position in the boat, to get my knees back under the deck, where they could give me leverage to eskimo roll. Then I realized that the boat was still trapped upside down in the rocks. Bubbles of air carried deep by the plunge of the current washed up across my face, scattering flashes of skylight and creating a dazzling light show to mock my troubles. My mind raced over the question of what to do next. Then the river decided.

The push of water crashing down over my boat and body tore us suddenly off the rocks. I bobbed free, still upside down, and was carried by the waves arching between the rocks down the remaining length of the chute. The seconds ticked by. My lungs felt as though they would burst. My senses became preoccupied with air and breathing and how good it would feel to inhale again. I wanted to claw out of my boat and up to the surface to gasp this wonderful, transparent stuff, this neglected miracle of our earth. But I knew at a more cerebral level that I must stay in the boat and try to get it upright. I must try to roll. The big rapid brawled ahead, and I could lose it all if I bailed out and faced the monstrosity of its turbulence as a helpless swimmer.

I gritted my teeth, concentrated on the currents, and got my paddle up through the jostling water into position for a roll, waiting for the thrashing to subside a little. Then I tried—perhaps a little too soon, a little off in timing—and the currents slapped me back under. My lungs began to shriek for air, and I could no longer ignore them; I could no longer hang upside down, carefully placing my paddle, awaiting the proper currents and the right feel of the water for a roll. I had to act now for air. I threw my weight on my paddle blade and tried to push myself far enough around to get my head out for a breath to tide me over for another attempt. But I was too weak now; I couldn't reach the air and slipped back under the surface. I tried again, now desperate, worried as the realization struck me that I had run out of time and that failure was upon me. The battle to stay in the boat was lost. It was time to face the river alone.

I exploded down out of my boat and fought desperately up through the water, my lungs aching and screaming for oxygen. I broke the surface and gasped air in rapid lungfuls, wishing it weren't so thin and lacking in substance. Then, before I was half satisfied, I accelerated into the rapid.

Everyone but Gerry had left the area. He was across the river when he saw me upside down, and he raced across to help me. His boat splashed above me, looking as big as a battleship from my position down in the water. But I couldn't reach the short loop of cord attached to his stern that could have pulled me to safety. Then the boat was gone in the next wave, and it was too late.

I was now sweeping down on the first protruding rock of the rapid, where the water split as if it were falling on an ax blade. The left stream reeled out into the maelstrom in the middle of the river, while the right stream spun choppily down a channel near shore, where I could still hope to swim out with my boat.

I swam desperately, awkwardly in that direction, my kicking feet hindered by tennis shoes, one hand occupied in holding my paddle and the kayak's end loop, my speed neutralized by the pull of the boat dragging upside down in the water after me. Then suddenly, we were in the swirling water above the rock. I lunged hard right and got to the shore side, but my boat didn't make it: it struck the rock broadside and stopped. I clung to the end loop, and the water washed me around against the rock. For a moment we came to an uneasy equilibrium; while I held on, my boat balanced precariously, one end sticking out to each side of the rock, the current pushing them equally. The thin shell shuddered and creaked, twisted and flexed, and looked as if it would break as the current drummed against its helpless, outstretched form.

I found a foothold deep in the water on the jagged edge of the rock and half-standing, half-swimming, I tried to balance the kayak, to maintain that rootless equilibrium, to buy a little more time. The boat shook and wobbled incessantly, threatening to break loose without warning. I swore shamelessly, infuriated at the current for buffeting my boat around and trying to pull it loose, allowing me no rest. I was angry at the river; angry at my failure to roll; mad at still being out of breath and strength.

And I swore because there was not much else to do. I needed above all else to get my breath and strength back, but the river wouldn't hold still for it. Without that, I couldn't get anywhere, do anything positive. All that was left was to try to hold the kayak in place, hoping for a miracle of respite, a breather, a little flow of lost energy, enough to try a final plunge to shore with my boat. In the meantime there was the possibility that Gerry—now up on the bank—could get a rope out to me.

But the river would have none of it. It shook and pulled and battered at the boat without mercy or rest. I fought to keep it balanced, straining without any real leverage, up to my armpits in the water. Then I felt the boat shift almost imperceptibly away from me. That was enough to undo the equilibrium. The kayak shuddered as the current pushed it hard, swinging the left side downstream, forcing my side upstream, and I knew I must act then, breathless or not, for a last slim chance to save my boat.

I lunged outward and pulled back on my end with every ounce of my weight. The boat slowly tilted on the pivot rock like a playground teeter-totter; it left me nothing to grab, no anchor to hold me back, and all my weight was canceled by a greater weight. There was nothing violent about it. I just found myself pulled inexorably away from my objective by a superior force. The only thing left was to jump free in time.

So I let go of my friend for the first time on the demon river. I had no real choice. If I had clung to the boat, I might have guided it through the rocks and turbulence, but I hadn't seen the rapid, had plotted no route. A swim with a crashing boat half-filled with water is dangerous enough in a known rapid, for one can be pinned, crushed, sucked into holes, trapped in rocks. Here above an unknown drop, deadened by fatigue, it would have been insanity.

My boat slipped out into the current. It began rocking like a baby in a cradle as it accelerated down into the waves, strangely peaceful, out toward the worst of the river. With it went my only transportation, my food, my clothes, my tent, my money, my papers, my maps, and my matches—all my means of survival. I felt helpless, desperate, and still angry as hell.

I slipped off the rock and swam through the choppy water toward shore, dragging my paddle with me. I staggered out on the rocks, panting wildly for breath. Yet I couldn't stop—must push on—must pursue the boat—get down the shore.

Then, in a sweeping glance, I spotted the blur of a human figure sitting high on a rock down below the rapid, on the opposite side of the river. It was Dee. He had worked through the rapid earlier and gone ashore. He seemed in a perfect position to intercept my boat as it emerged from the turbulence, before it disappeared into the emptiness of the canyon. He would surely help in this emergency, do all he could. I was hopeful now. I waited to see him move, and when he didn't, I thrust my paddle high in the air and waved the big white blade back and forth, to call his attention to the boat, to the need for help. But he didn't respond, didn't stir. I waved frantically now, but the figure on the rock was as still as the stone of the canyon wall.

Dee said later that he didn't see me. Maybe not. But I have never known a kayaker who would go to shore below a good rapid and fail to watch his comrades come through, especially in the wilderness, against new water. And in a land of such solitude and challenge as this, where there is no one to help but those of the common group, there is more involved than a question of curiosity at an outcome; there is a compelling moral obligation to watch out for comrades when the water flows fast about them.

I was completely thrown back by the silence on the rock. I lowered my paddle slowly, as if I was dragging it down out of molasses instead of air. I was stunned—I had never seen such inaction in the face of a crisis in all my experience outdoors. Perhaps this happens in the faceless cities, but in the wilderness, I have always observed mutual aid almost ferocious in its intensity, as if some old instinct of tribal preservation rekindled itself. So I stood in semishock while river water dripped off my body and formed a thin ring of liquid on the rock on which I found myself.

Then my thoughts came back to the boat. I looked for it out in the river, but my view of the rapid's main drop was blocked by rocks. I had lost track of it. I clambered up the bank to look over the big blocks in my line of sight. Then, as I came high enough to see, a ray of hope flowed back. Hidden from my view, Chuck had seen my boat crash by and gave chase. Soon Jim closed in too. But they could only follow and watch, as the boat spun crazily through the rapid. I watched it tumble through a hole and felt the water and rocks would surely grind it apart. But the demon river has always had a touch of softness just when it was about ready to snuff out a victim.

The boat narrowly missed a massive rock and plunged into a small eddy near the end of the rapid. There it lodged tenuously against another rock. Jim and Chuck circled below, into a big, deep eddy abutting the shore. They scrambled over the caboose-sized rocks dividing the two pools and pulled the kayak up tight. As they began to drag it over the barrier to safety, I swam out to help.

The boat had fared pretty well. Its nose had been crushed, but little else was wrong. The gear was still tied securely inside.

"Wow, I'm grateful, Bill Clark," I muttered under my breath. Bill was a world expert in kayak construction. He had built the boat, had engineered its toughness. Today had been the acid test. Today, Bill was my hero.

Then—my breath back again and the boat on shore—I turned to Jim and Chuck.

"You guys, a million, million thanks. You don't know how I appreciate this. You really saved the day. It would be a long walk out in bare legs and tennies, up in those thorns, and nothing to eat!"

Then I thought about the damn river and about going on with it. It just didn't make sense anymore. The accident had broken—better to say pulverized—my confidence. Its occurrence in a side channel of no unusual consequence showed the threat of my fatigue, heightened by our rush, by our scattering along the river, by what seemed a growing numbness to danger.

I stared downstream along the tops of rocks that cluttered the shore-line and the riverbed to the next bend. There they disappeared from sight, but my mind drew a picture of them marching on and on like the waves of the sea.

"You know," I said finally, "I don't think I can get down this canyon safely anymore. I'm just too tired. Besides, I don't want to hold you back. I think I'll give it up—try to walk out while we're still near the trail. I've had enough of this miserable river."

But all that soon passed. I'm too stubborn to cave in that way, to let the river run me off. Instead, I set my jaw against it. My journal cap-tured my determination:

I resolve that this trip is of my creation and orchestration and I will not abandon it now.

We proceed, and I go cautiously now—still shaken—lining some of the rapids that the others run. This takes time; it requires their patience . . . which is unfortunate. But I reason that I can no longer feel apologetic. One of the trip's well-stated goals was navigation of these canyons in a safe and conservative manner. There would be no trip—no possibility for success—without my concept, my planning, the long months gathering information. Everyone has signed an agreement that those going ahead will help those having difficulties. I do not mention this, because I never anticipated that I would be the recipient of such help. Jim and Gerry do in fact help where possible on some difficult carries and lines.

Dee complains tonight about the pace, my unwillingness to tackle the larger rapids. He is very impatient, very compulsive. Yet when help is needed it is Jim and Gerry—and sometimes Chuck . . .

Indeed, the rest of that day, I shunned a lot of rapids. I would pull ashore early when the pulse of the river quickened into whitewater. If the rapid was wild, I would lift and drag my boat up on shore, then wrestle it over the tops of the rocks to start past the thunderous parts. Jim and Gerry would run more of the rapid than I, in some cases all of it, then one of them would walk back up along shore to help me. They were tired, but they did it anyway, every time.

At the top of one difficult rapid, Jim asked me, "Do you want me to paddle your boat through this rapid for you? It would be a lot easier than carrying it."

"No thanks," I said. "I wouldn't feel like I was really getting down the canyon myself that way. I don't mind staggering along inch by inch as long as I can keep going. I'm certainly not going to give up that easily."

Then Jim and I each lifted up an end and lurched ahead, pulling and pushing each other, because our steps and jumps across the rocks never matched. I watched Jim take a long step up to the edge of a rock, to a precarious stance, and I fed him up the boat. He stood there straining, not very stable, pulling up the boat, trying to move it higher and lifting it awkwardly off to one side, then he got it to lean on another rock behind, as tall as an elephant. While I held the boat from below, he scrambled up around to get a new position to start another step. Tedious business. It gave me time to think about Jim's proposition.

It was well and good to hold the ideal of making it down the canyon myself, but, as I thought about it, I wasn't doing that anyhow. Nobody was. Each of us had had help from others carrying down the rough shore. Each of us had had help lining. Each of us had had parts of the canyon scouted out for us. We had all enjoyed someone else watching out for our safety in many bad spots. Most of us had been rescued from some pretty ugly predicaments by our companions. Some of us who had ended up swimmers had been dragged ashore by those still in boats. Some had been stuck in the rocks while lining and had been rescued. And we all relied every day on emergency gear, repair materials, and maps carried by the group as a whole.

Every one of us but Jim had had our boats flushed down segments of rapids upside down, swimming alongside, no more in control of our destiny than we were in control of the orbit of the earth. Surely none of us could claim credit for doing by ourselves those things over which we had lost all control, all ability to independently guide our fate. No, no one was getting down this high-tension canyon on his own. Jim was the only one who even came close.

Despite our grittiest stabs at it alone, we ended up a team. In a sense, so great was our isolation, so absolute our dependence, that we became something more than a team. Alone in these canyons, we seemed transformed into a loosely jointed organism—five limbs joined by invisible elastic bands. When the bands stretched too far, it became awkward, unsure in footing, prone to stumbles, to accidents, like a spider trying to run up a glass wall with each leg at its own pace. But when one leg slipped, the others luckily held, and we always pulled through.

Everyone had had his turn at a slip. No one was alone, and it made no sense to try to make it alone. Our boldest dashes—our most stubborn pursuits—were counterproductive if they didn't help the organism get safely down the canyon. So the sight of Jim setting himself for another tug on the boat, exhausting himself to help me gain another meter against a river as endless as the sky, drove the last nail in the coffin of whatever pretense of independence I had.

"Jim, wait a minute. You had the right idea. It would be ten times easier and faster for you to run the boat through. I can't handle the rapid now; you can. There's an eddy over there to start. Do you still want to do it?"

Jim said yes, and soon he was paddling through the big waves of the rapid. He pulled in below, got back in his own boat, and I took over. Occasionally we repeated this procedure, and our pace picked up. Still we fought long and hard to gain every bend in the canyon. Time after time we hit jaw-dropping, smothering torrents that forced us all to crawl like snails around the edge. We still had a battle to engage, all of us.

And we still had shocking reminders that we needed each other.

Not long after my capsize, Gerry had problems of his own:

I was beginning to feel pretty lousy, but didn't yet know it was due to an infection. Very tired from the hike [to Choquequirao] of the previous day, too . . .

Immediately below [the rapid in which I capsized], I misread a drop, tipped over above a giant hole and choked on water as I washed into the turbulence.

Damn it! I've got to learn to keep my mouth shut in these holes. Panicking, I say to hell with it and exit from the boat, which gets away from me (ejected from the hole before I am). It runs through a couple of drops before being retrieved by Jim and Chuck.

While [they] are chasing the boat, I'm having the ride of my life out in the river. Can't get to shore. Current too strong. Finally, Chuck sees me washing through and helps me out. Together we ride through a couple more drops, all the while working closer to shore. After one chute I am kicking furiously when I feel my sneaker torn from one foot.

Now the loss of a piece of footgear is no trivial matter in the middle of an Andean canyon, desolate, covered with stones, spiny plants, and thorns. It could be disastrous, so I manage to hold onto both boat and paddle with one hand, reach down with the other and grab the shoe.

What to do with it? Crunch, ouch, grunt, I'm dragged over another boulder. I need that hand. There's only one thing to do: into my mouth it goes. After much strenuous effort . . . we finally reach shore.

"What the hell are you doing with that thing in your mouth?" exclaims Jim. "I wish I had my camera handy."

"Want a doggie biscuit?" is Chuck's sole comment.

"Go to hell!" or some such expletive was all I had to offer to the conversation at the time.

Our camp that night was on an expansive beach strewn with the Apurímac's big rocks. Across the river a vigorous stream called the Río Ancascocha broke through the cliffs, pouring yet another complement of water into the mother river. In its ages of descent, the little river had cut a straight-walled, shadowed slot down into the rock, leaving behind a spectacular side canyon aimed like a gun barrel at our beach. Below, a waterfall splashed down the high canyon wall. Everywhere around us were broken walls and the breath of utter wildness.

The Río Ancascocha flowed in from the south, opposite the point where the cliff-shattered ridge of Choquequirao plummeted downward into the sand of our beach. At this point the canyon curved to the right around us, away from the Ancascocha, changing gradually from west to northwest. Here it began to encircle the mountain of Choquequirao like a boa constrictor encircling a wild pig. Halfway around, the Apurímac lashed straight out at the Vilcabamba peaks, in the deepest thrust it would ever make to the north.

We had gone only 4 miles that tortured day. We had come down a steep inner canyon that grazed 2 miles south of Choquequirao, but we had been hidden from the ruins by the deepness of the gorge. Tomorrow we would swing around the right bend, where the river cut away at the foot of the ruins, just over a mile horizontally and vertically from the old fortress. Then we would come under its surveillance. We would break into view on that stretch of the river that had roared its sullen threats high, high up the void of canyon to the old, gray, silent, abandoned, jungle-choked, dead city of Choquequirao.

A tough wrapping of tape had held my boat's crushed nose together since the accident. Now Jim and I set about making repairs. It was dark by then, so after dinner, after setting up camp, we gathered wood from the beach and lit a large fire for light. Its flickering glow brought color—it almost seemed to bring life—to the ageless rock sentinels standing in broken ranks in the sweep of sand guarding that shore and the ancient ramparts of ghostly Choquequirao.

In this little pocket of light—so singular and alone in the black cut of the canyon—we pursued our task like two actors onstage in an infinite dark theater. We stripped the boat clean, repaired some previous breaks in the seam, repositioned the end loop, and retaped the bow. Next we put the boat up on end like a small telephone pole, braced it up against the uneven rocks, and secured it by three guy ropes running out to stone anchors on the shore. We poured tough-setting epoxy resin from a paper cup deep into the bow—down where the tip of the eggshell structure had been mangled. Then we stoked the fire higher, using its heat to cure and harden the epoxy. With the rise of the flames, the old rocks guarding the mountain fairly danced on the stage of white sand.

The work went on into the deep of the night. Fatigue began to dog every step; I moved on to each new task slowly, methodically, like a robot. Jim, too, looked beaten and tired. I admired his grit in sticking with this task, not really his responsibility. That night underscored the dangerous cycle I had fallen into. My fatigue was causing me accidents, which caused extra work, which caused me deeper exhaustion. My weariness was forcing me to the shore, to immensely difficult portages, which further drained my energy, making each new rapid an even greater obstacle.

The trouble was, I saw no prospect for breaking out of the cycle. Only a change in the river could help me now.

On the twenty-fourth day we began the 3-mile leg of the river that trended northwest, under the ruins. We encountered several difficult rapids, which we all lined. Finally we worked our way into the stretches of river that we had seen from Choquequirao two days before.

At midmorning we ran into a large rapid crashing toward the right. The shoreline on that side pinched thin as the river converged on the wall. It vanished where the water thundered on by the cliff. The rapid had a vaguely familiar form; it might have been one that we had stared down on from Choquequirao. It had looked like a mutilated kink in the dark ribbon of river winding through the range. It was shredded by rocks and bleached white by innumerable bubbles whipped into its water.

I stopped on the right above the rapid. Jim and Dee, somewhat to my surprise, continued deep into the rapid along the right, then pulled into a wide eddy and landed on one of the last strands of beach before the river hit the wall. They climbed up to look at the center of the big kink of water. I could not imagine that they would run it. While they studied it, I paddled left across the river to begin a long portage down a rocky shore. Gerry and Chuck remained behind to see how the challenge worked out.

After a while, watching from the shore across the river, I saw Jim return to his boat and get in at the lapping edge of the water. He drifted back across the flat of the eddy, paddled out into the current, then began a descent of some of the most powerful chutes of water I have ever seen. It was a scary thing to watch, to see him graze past rocks of such massive size, to lose sight of him buried deep in holes, to glimpse him bobbing, bracing, fighting, washing on the flood. But he ran magnificently, and soon came to rest below, still upright and secure in his boat.

I continued to watch as Dee began to follow in Jim's path. I saw him swing out of the eddy, into the current. I saw him drop into a giant hole high in the rapid—saw him capsize—saw his roll fail—saw him come out of his boat to face the churning hydraulics. I saw the boat pitch through the next giant chute, flipping over lengthwise like a matchstick, Dee clinging desperately to one end.

Only Jim now stood between Dee and disaster in the river below. According to Jim:

> The rapid was obviously a big one, even from way above. I saw an eddy we could drop into just before the cliff, at the end of the boulder bar, and we ran down into it, beaching the boats

on the breadbox-size rocks. We climbed up to the cliff, and climbed up maybe 10 feet for a better view. The rapid was a beauty. It was maybe 50 yards long consisting of huge waves dropping through three distinct drops between boulders. It was obviously a handful—at the limit of what I was willing to tackle with our loaded boats. The alternative was to haul our boats back up the 25 yards of boulder bar, ferry to the other bank, and portage there, since the vertical cliff blocked further progress on our side. But, I picked a route I thought I could hold, running the first drop in the center, working right thru the set of big waves to hit the next drop right of center, and then going further right yet to hit the final and biggest drop at what looked like the best point.

We agreed to try it, I first, with Dee close enough to assist if needed. The thing that made it tenable was that beyond the final mess there was a decent pool where one could probably roll or collect the pieces and get ashore. We climbed down and crawled into our boats and I shoved off.

It was soon apparent that I had misjudged the rapid—I might have made the first drop as planned, but after that, my carefully chosen route was forgotten. The water carried me way to the left, and as I was fighting for control, it was apparent there was no chance I could get back to my chosen route. I got over the next drop somehow and was headed for just about the worst imaginable place in the final and biggest drop—way over near the left side of the river—when I chanced to see a break between two boulders into a large size eddy. I grabbed it in an instant! I was just sitting there at the wonder of being home free when I thought of Dee. There was no way I could warn him not to go, as I couldn't even see the top of the rapid from my little haven.

Then, as I looked out into the current, I saw him flash by, hit the big stuff, and capsize. He tried a roll, and then he was swimming in the water below beside his boat. I had to help, for I could see now that the pool was not really a pool, but rather fast, green water which was rapidly carrying Dee toward big and unknown rapids about 75 yards below. Looking downstream, I found that I could drop over a rocky ledge into the current below directly from my eddy without reentering the main current. I did so immediately and struck out to catch Dee. When I got to him, he was hanging onto his boat and paddle with one hand, his small waterproof bag which had washed out of the boat in his teeth, and was swimming toward the distant shore. I offered him my bow loop and started back-paddling with all my strength, doing a backferry toward the left bank against the fast current.

We were making progress, but not nearly fast enough, as the next rapid was fast approaching, and it was obvious even from where we were that it was not one to run in our compromised situation. There was no way we could reach shore in time, but there was one chance—a car-long rock was right at the head of the rapid. Fast-water chutes whistled around the ends, but directly in front the water was relatively smooth. I pulled like hell and broadsided both boats against the rock and there we were.

But where were we? We could perhaps hold our position for a while, but how could we dump Dee's boat and get him back in it? The stern one-third of my boat stuck out in the chute left of the rock already, and half of Dee's boat was in the fast current on the right side of the rock. Our position was stable, but we could not seem to improve it, for I could not get a purchase on either rock or water to pull Dee and his boat out of the current, and it was obvious he could not hold it forever. . . .

I would have to somehow get up on the top of the rock without losing my own boat! The rock stuck out of the water maybe three or four feet, and the upstream face, against which we were sitting, sloped up at about 60 degrees to the top, with a smooth flat surface. The water in front was deep, offering no footing.

I got off my spray skirt, and somehow managed to claw my way carefully out of my boat and up the rock, hanging on to my own boat with my toe, then grabbing the boat and wrenching it up to balance it on the top of the rock.

Back to Dee, who was still clinging desperately to the boat with one hand, the rock with the other, while the fast current tugged relentlessly at the exposed end [of his boat] sticking out in the chute. He had lost a little ground during my struggle, and the water was getting a bigger bite on his boat. He was tiring fast, and I had to do something quickly. But I soon found out I was no better off here than I had been in my boat. The rock was rounded and smooth on top, no hand or toe-holds to be had. To reach his boat at all, I had to lean out, and had nothing to hold on to. I could keep from falling in, but could add almost nothing to the effort to pull the boat up or in.

"I'm losing it," he said. "It's gonna go."

"Any chance you can get me your line?" I asked. There was no chance. To avoid the possibility of entanglement, he had tied the painter up into a fistlike knot onto which he was now holding for dear life to keep the river from claiming his boat.

I was desperately looking for a way to help when he said, "I can't hold it. I have to let it go."

And away it went, wheeling down the chute and into the rapid. I extended my hand and helped him up on the rounded rock where he sat for a moment, exhausted. We watched the boat crunch over the next drop and Dee said, "Somebody has to get it. Somebody has to go after it." I knew that I was the only possibility as the others were still upstream of the huge rapid and after our problems, certainly not about to run it. They would be at least 20 or 30 minutes portaging. The rapid below looked nasty enough that we would probably normally scout it, with an uncertain-looking chute directly below our rock. I thought aloud, "If we lose two boats, we will be worse off than we are now." I looked upstream and saw a distant figure or two halfway past the big rapid, with no boats yet in sight. I climbed into my boat and slid-splashed off our big rock into the current.

Thirty feet downstream I hit the uncertain-looking chute and tipped over. Roll. Roll. Got to roll. I cranked [the paddle] hard, the boat righted, and on I went.

A row of boulders was now dividing the river into a right and a left channel. I was in the right channel now, headed for another, bigger drop which I probably would not dare chance without scouting when I saw a flash of white off to the left in the other channel—the boat! Stuck on a rock close to the left bank. Very lucky I had managed to pull it so far left above or it would have certainly gone on down the right side into the chute I was facing and destroyed itself. I ducked in between the row of boulders and paddled across the current to the boat, sunk, broached in a little channel, and stuck very tentatively in this position.

I rammed my boat up onto the rocks, jumped out on a boulder and dived for the loose painter, tying my longer lining rope onto it immediately, and then climbed back up on the rock to rest a minute. I yelled and whooped, hoping to let Dee and maybe the others know I had the boat. I got the boat up and was dumping it when I saw Dee swimming along the sheer left bank with paddle and wetbag in hand. The boat was a mess, deseamed from the bow back almost to the cockpit on both sides.

We collapsed on the rock. . . . We lay there recovering as we waited for the boat to dry so we could tape it. Soon after, the rest of the party arrived.

Pandemonium and concern had electrified those of us left above. I had been searching out a portage-lining route on the left when the accident happened. I saw Jim and Dee stuck hopelessly on the rock, two blocks downstream. I rushed back to my boat to get my rope and started running down the rocky shore. At this point Jim and Dee were out of sight. Then Chuck—still across the river—signaled me that everything was okay. I rested for a few minutes, then clambered to the top of a nearby boulder to see the final outcome. To my horror, they were still in the midst of the tug-of-war with the overturned boat. I don't know why the signal was ever made. But I was too late now: Dee's boat washed away shortly thereafter. From then on, we could only watch and pray. It would have been, as Jim had estimated, a good half-hour before any of us could get our boats into the river below to offer aid.

Dee had been lucky he hadn't run this rapid alone. He had been lucky that Jim gave all his heart to the rescue. Any lesser effort would certainly have seen his boat lost in the canyons—the end of the expedition for Dee. Had there been any diminution in Jim's skill or grit, Dee would very possibly have lost his life. We were not alone. None of us. We had seen firsthand the increasing hazards of a capsize in these waters. Three times in the last two days we had risked the loss of a boat. Rescue had become difficult, risky business. So far we had been lucky.

The enormous volume of water in these canyons had ballooned our risks beyond reason. When a boat capsized—first heavy with gear, then heavier with washed-in water—it literally swept on its own course down the river, toward subsequent rapids and probable destruction.

Other elements now favored the demon river. Day by day the fatigue and strain of the trip made our judgment a little more suspect. It made our boating a little less consistent, so that we were a little more subject to capsizing and slower to recover when we were tipped over. We were descending the river, but were we winning?

≈ T H I R T E E N

If there is magic on this planet it is contained in water.
Loren Eiseley

Toughness is false. The real tough people in this world don't go around bragging about it.
Arthur Jones

≈ UNCHARTED WATERS

I N THE DAYS THAT followed, we pushed through the canyon below Cho-quequirao and out into the range, out where we had seen only pieces of river from the ruins—pieces of a dark thread weaving in and out of angled walls. Out there it was a jigsaw puzzle, a labyrinth of twists and bends and side canyons. For us, sitting dwarfed like ants in its midst, our view blocked by vertical stone, it seemed like a country unrooted, isolated, unconnected to the world we knew. We might as well have been on an unknown planet.

Our only shepherd through this land was the relentless current. Somehow, by an old, old secret, the drifting water knew its way through the mountain fastness, to the jungle, to the ocean. But what did it drop over? What did it thunder between? That was part of the secret. So we followed the path, so broad and well marked and certain in its destina-tion, so unsure in its route. Our senses came alive in fear and hope, in anticipation of each new edge of the secret as we rounded each bend.

The canyon unfolded rock by rock and cliff by cliff, displaying with each new angle of wall and water another vista of raw, vibrant, shim-mering splendor. There was a special excitement, added to all the rest, in feeling the pulse of a land that was truly uncatalogued—in full bloom mystery.

But what of the maps? Didn't they take the mystery out of the river? Well, they showed its direction through the range. The thin line of the river turned from northwest to west in a course of gentle curves. But as to detail, the river we traveled thrashed and twisted in the agony of its geology; its true character could not be recognized from the maps.

Such a dream, the map-river! No gorges, no cataracts, no plunging bends, no roaring like thunder. It flowed on, less than a millimeter wide, a pure blue thread streaking through mountain contour lines. Not one growling fleck of white marred its flawless course—its noise-less flight of fancy.

I was tired now. I wished there were such a river in this land.

≈ A view of the Apurímac River from the heights of Choquequirao. The river is over a vertical mile below the ruins but still can be heard roaring its way through the Vilcabamba Range.

Following Dee's accident, the rest of us moved down to the rapids where Jim had rescued the overturned boat. Dee seemed momentarily transformed by his bad experience; he appeared humble, civil, even helpful. At one point he came back upstream and offered to help me carry my boat down a portage. I could remember nothing like that happening since the first days of the trip. I would not see it happen again. Immediately below this portage, Jim filmed some movie footage of the canyon. He put his movie camera on a rock, then kneeled down to rearrange gear in his boat. Soon afterwards we paddled across the river and began a rough portage downstream.

Later, as I carried my boat over my shoulder through the rocks, Jim came scrambling up the shore toward me. I could see that he was upset, so I stopped and waited. "I left my movie camera somewhere up there," he said as he topped the last rock, and swept his hand upriver in a sign of disgust. "Can I borrow your boat? I need it to go back up there and cross the river to look. Damn! I'm not even sure where I left it."

"I remember you setting it down on a rock just before we came over the river," I said. "Did you pick it up afterwards?"

"No, now that I think about it, I don't believe I did," he replied. "That'll be easy to find if I take your boat back up and cross at the same place. Is that okay?"

"Sure. But here, let me help you carry it back up. "

Then I got the kind of answer so typical of Jim, a simple and sincere remark without a trace of the balance-sheet mentality that so many people use to dole out and call in favors:

"Why do you want to help me?" Jim asked quizzically.

I stumbled for words. "My God," I stuttered, "You've pulled my boat out of the water; you've helped me get around rapids; you stayed up half of last night helping me fix my boat! Of course I'll help you! That's the idea of the trip anyway, isn't it?"

We worked together back up the shore. Jim crossed the river and soon found his camera. All we had lost was a few minutes of time. We weren't always so lucky.

Things kept slipping away from us as we went down the canyon. An item was forgotten here, left behind a rock there, or washed away in the river during a capsize. All were irreplaceable.

A simple household sponge was worth more than gold to us because of leaks in the boats. Often we found too much water inside and had to empty. Without a sponge we had to paddle to shore, get out, roll the boat over, and tilt it up one end after the other to spill out its water. With a sponge we could continue drifting along, just reach inside, sop up some spongefuls, and squeeze them back into the river, where they belonged. It hardly interrupted our progress at all.

And we were full of leaks now. My boat was the worst. On top of the cracks and perforations created in ten thousand impacts with rocks, it had a faulty seam. Small faucets of water leaked in around its perimeter. Every few blocks I had to sponge it out. I would wait for a calm stretch of water, then lay my paddle in front of me across the rim of the cockpit. I would strip back the spraycover, reach in, and pull the sponge out of the crack where it was jammed beside the seat. Plip! Plip! I'd drop the sponge in the pool in the bottom of the boat and flip it over. Then I'd pull it up dripping a stream across my legs and squeeze it dry off the side. Ten or fifteen such spongefuls relieved the bathtub feeling of the boat. The pool in the center wouldn't actually dry up, but the deep sloshing would stop, and my speed would pick up noticeably. Then I'd shove the sponge back in its crack, stretch the spraycover up front over the cockpit rim, grab the paddle, and hurry along.

I had brought three sponges to Peru so that I wouldn't risk going without. One went to Chuck, who had forgotten to bring a sponge of his own. Another went to Gerry, who had lost his in the river. The last one I clung to and protected as though it were my baby. When I put it back in its crack after each use, I tucked it tight so that it wouldn't wash out if I capsized and the boat got away again. When I used it to clean away sand or mud that I tracked into the boat, I swished it out in the river before squeezing it so no microscopic particles would remain to cut and wear it from within. Yet with each plip! plip! tiny pieces of sponge sloughed off, and the tears across its sides widened. The poor thing was not designed to fight off such a river for a month, and it looked awful. Still, shabby as it was, if it should ever start to wash away, I would swim through almost anything to get it back.

I had inexplicably lost a water purification kit back near Quebrada Huaynacachora. Then—in one day—two plastic bottles disappeared on a beach, and my widest search turned up not a trace. One had been used for water and the other for sugar. I could get by without the sugar; luckily, I had a spare for water. But I was getting near the end of my tether.

Step by step we advanced deeper into the unknown canyon that afternoon. My journal takes up the story:

Progress is somewhat better than a few days ago because there are block long stretches of quiet water between the giant drops. There are a few runnable rapids. The cataracts are more amenable to lining our boats through, although nearly always there are sections where they must be laboriously carried over giant boulders.

I reflect on the terrible difficulties of this trip, beyond what any map or aerial photography would suggest: day after day of lifting and pulling these awkward boats around unbelievable cataracts; exhaustion by midday, yet we must push on; no time to enjoy the scenery, the wildlife, the spectacular vistas and geology. We are in a routine of monotonous plodding from dawn to dusk. Endless, grinding struggle.

How long can it last? We read our altimeter after each day's progress. The altimeter! It is our harbinger of hope and despair, for our progress is measured in feet of altitude lost—not in miles. It is those terrible rock-laced drops, the vertical components of the cataract, that enslave us. On difficult days we drop 100 feet or less. On good days we do 200 feet or more. The entire trip requires 7,000 feet of descent, and I have allowed for about forty days. We need almost 200 feet per day, but when we carry so much, it is impossible.

But there is hope. We are now at about 4,300 feet of elevation, and we need lose only about 2,500 more to reach San Francisco, or nearby Hacienda Luisiana, where our trip ends. We have already dropped 4,700 feet through Apurímac whitewater. About one-third left.

This steep canyon lasts another 30 miles, to a point where the Río Pampas enters. [We were now almost exactly halfway through the great Vilcabamba Canyons as measured in miles of horizontal distance. We had spent over eleven days from Cunyac—ten days not counting the hike to Choquequirao.] *Our best evidence suggests that this crucial junction—this place where the gorge breaks open to jungle canyon—lies at about 4,000 feet. We are getting near that, vertically. This horrible monotony cannot persist, can it?*

Of course, one narrow gorge with a 10-foot waterfall and no portage route could, by itself, bring the whole expedition to an end. Such could possibly exist in this uncharted section of canyon where the Apurímac makes its most daring, most northward charge against the snow-capped Vilcabamba Range.

We choose our camp tonight on the right bank, in a straight section of river. Three blocks below I notice the river making a sharp right bend into a rock-walled gorge. Curious, I paddle to the left bank from where I can walk down past another giant cataract toward this gorge. As I draw closer, I see that it begins with a large but runnable rapid. But once through this rapid, return along the banks is impossible. Water occupies the chasm from one vertical wall to another. Will this contain the 10-foot waterfall that will end our trip? I push on but the gorge curves too far right to see its full course. I do see a large rapid crashing against the left wall. Can one get by on the right? I have no way to tell—it is out of view and cannot be seen without climbing much higher and making a difficult traverse out onto a short ledge.

With this burden of doubt on my mind, I return to camp for much needed rest.

The night was black and filled with water sounds. Intermittently, a curtain of rain would descend and a million of its little spheres of water would splatter on the sand and the gear and the dark forms of rocks scattered around camp. Nearby, hidden in the void of darkness, the water of the Great Speaker rippled and gurgled and flowed, flowed, flowed, down into the cataract, sending a rumble booming back up the canyon. The water, coming out of the cataract, flowed and pushed and undulated down around the bend into the gorge, where the walls swallowed its voice. The silence of the gorge was the loudest sound of the night.

I awoke at intervals and rolled over on my mattress of sand. I wiggled into a state of comfort, then lay quietly to soak in the night. Even after all these battles, I still loved the night voice—so dreamlike and full of melody alongside the harsh resonances that began with the sun. I found it comforting even though it roared with cataracts; no matter that it imprisoned the message around the bend. I strained to hear every echo and to sort out a dozen intermixed booms and crystalline pulses of bubbles breaking free from deep water, the rippling noises near shore, and the raindrops on fabric, rock, and sand. A symphony, but a short one, for soon all sounds grew fuzzy; the tones converged to one voice and were suddenly lost in the canyon, as I was overtaken by sleep.

I awoke to a clearing sky and the promise of sunlight for day twenty-five. The scattered camp began to stir. Suddenly Chuck called out from behind some rocks, "Hey, what's this?" Down in his gear he had found the deadly form of a scorpion. It had crawled there in the night over some unknown path—maybe over Chuck himself—seeking shelter and warmth. Its venom-filled tail and stinger were cocked above it like a loaded gun. If it had been differently positioned, a little better hidden, it might have unleashed its venom into Chuck. He would have been sick and our expedition would have been delayed for days. We were lucky again.

As we ate breakfast our conversation drifted toward the gorge around the corner. We talked about the concrete things: the approach, the timing, the canyon, the choices. As usual no one expressed any feelings, any questions, any doubts.

I fell silent, wondering why it was so uncommon for men to speak their uncertainties. The canyon was bigger than any of us, and that would not change for all the denial in the world. It was not a thing to get despondent over, but to admit uncertainty was to admit that it was adventure. That is something worth sharing, something I missed.

Sometimes when the chores of the day were done, Jim and I would sit around camp and talk quietly about the question marks that littered our path through the canyon. But rarely did anyone else voice any doubts. To the contrary, our camp banter often exuded smugness, even cockiness. On that morning we faced a classic of uncertainty, an unknown gorge. As far as anyone knew, it might end our expedition. Not surprisingly, no one said a word about this. Nonetheless I was taken aback by a simple comment that Dee made regarding his prospects of getting through the gorge: "It would take a lot to stop the kid."

I could only reflect on the irony of this attitude, coming as it did less than twenty-four hours after Dee had been floundering helplessly beside his boat, his kayak and maybe his life hanging on Jim's extraordinary strength. Then I ended up wondering what Dee was really trying to say, trying to act out. I tried to understand how anyone so well educated could appear so immune to the mathematical certainty that enough close brushes inevitably lead toward disaster. But for all I know, he may inwardly have been seeking self-destruction, as he certainly appeared to be doing the next year when, according to press accounts, he intended to ski down from the shoulder of Mount Everest on a pair of old Japanese skis.

For a long time I think I had misinterpreted the hints of bravado I heard, from whatever source. I took them as a sign of strength and formed the wrong expectations because of them. I remember once thinking Chuck was invincible, so I had asked him if he would bring up the rear going down the Chasm of Acobamba. The rear in that gorge was a lonely place. If you got hung up on the big rocks midway through, no one could ever get back to help you out. I thought Chuck could handle that, both mentally and physically. But once inside the gorge, he pushed ahead. Gerry then volunteered to come out last.

I believe Gerry's fearlessness was real. He told me once, and I believed him, that he had no fear or trepidation about any of the big rapids he ran. He showed a sense of survival and adrenaline, but not a sense of outright fear. The major rapids were clearly a temptation: he would run them for the thrill of it, and he would run them to avoid the labor of portage. Not to run them required all his willpower added to my admonishments. I think I had more fear for his life than he did.

As for me, I was less influenced by fear than by a distaste for risk. I could do what I had to do when my back was against the wall, and I never felt panic. But I thought often of my children and their need for me. I knew that any number of things could go wrong on an expedition like this, and I was determined to avoid every one of them I possibly could. I confess to being awed by the river and its canyon; the Apurímac was too big and relentless, and I felt ill at ease about its seizure of our destinies.

The canyon was indeed beautiful, but it was a wild place; it had not aged and ground off its rough corners to become a gentle wilderness like a New Hampshire mountainside or a forest beside an Idaho river. It was not a place to relax beneath a pine tree and contemplate the tiptoeing of clouds. It was more a place where you might come to hear nature's thunder, to dodge rockfalls and shake with earthquakes, to attempt to stay above the flood lapping and roaring at your feet, and to avoid the sting of scorpions. The canyon, for all its glory, had an alien feel to it that went to the core of my being, and I felt an overwhelming aversion to the thought that I might die there so far from home and loved ones.

Jim, it was clear, was little influenced by fear of the canyon. He recognized the reality of its risks, but I sensed in him abundant confidence in his own strength, confidence that proved to be valid. There was no bravado about it, no rushing ahead to prove anything, but a willingness to work with others and bite off the toughest assignment, including coming through last when that was called for.

But Dee's feelings about fear puzzled me most. I think I missed them by a mile at the beginning, looking only at the surface. Outwardly his emotions seemed as hard as the rock of the canyon. Yet later I came to realize that this was a veneer. Somehow I felt that Dee had a lot of fear beneath his brash exterior, and that his challenge was to deny it to himself, at great personal cost, and go on anyhow, flinging himself against all challenges. I became aware of this through an accumulation of small clues—actions and reactions, scraps of conversation, puzzling contradictions—that increasingly came together as the trip progressed. Some of these clues were only impressions of mine, but when I took them apart and thought about them, they grew stronger, and they kept falling back together the same way. Some were very simple, such as the impression that when Dee capsized in the midst of his most daring runs, he would panic and come out of his boat prematurely, often too early for an eskimo roll. Maybe, in all fairness, something else went wrong all those times, but one way or another, Dee ended up swimming too often in some nasty places. The hazard of it was worrisome.

I also had the impression—and I couldn't understand it at first in view of his actions on the river—that Dee had been glad that I had planned the trip to be safe and conservative. Then it occurred to me that this type of trip may have promised a safe refuge if his bold confrontation failed. And then there was my feeling that Dee sometimes froze when help was needed and the feeling, as he talked of past trips, that he had often been badly frightened—which did not seem to square with his present appearance of forwardness and boldness.

Maybe these impressions were wrong. But if they were true, the goad of an underlying fear might explain his incessant drive down the canyon. It might also explain the anomalous change of personality that seemed to come over him in the face of the threat of the river. Jim, too, had noted a remarkable contrast in his manner: "Self-centered and self-serving is how I remember him during the actual on-river part of the expedition. Personable and likable in Cuzco and other off-river parts of the trip."

I can remember almost nothing Dee said in the whole length of the trip that addressed what drove him from the inside or how he truly felt. Only when the expedition was over did any suggestion emerge regarding his feelings at confronting an entity more powerful than himself. Reflecting on the journey and on our side trip to Choquequirao, Dee wrote that the visit to the ruins "was a genuinely needed break from the fear, pain, and terror of the river gorge itself."

t was time to organize for action on the gorge. "Who's willing to go down there and climb up in the ledges for a look?" I asked.

"I might as well go down," Jim volunteered. "I'll send an arms-up signal if it's okay."

"I'll go too," Chuck added. "It shouldn't take very long."

Jim and Chuck packed their gear and paddled out across the river. They landed on the opposite shore and proceeded on foot past the cataract, toward the chasm. I watched the two figures grow smaller as they walked down along the beach, weaving in and out of rocks, scrambling over the canyon debris. Soon they reached the point where the canyon wall thrust itself out from the beach to form the gateway of the gorge. They began moving up the sloping ledges toward the overlook. Their distance and smallness made it seem that they were barely moving at all, that they would never get to the answer. They climbed to the foot of the final ledge, which appeared to be steep and shiny; it seemed to offer no holds, no fractures to cling to or walk on. They stepped out on the rock, slowly, carefully, then stopped altogether, to stare down the gorge. I knew they weren't far enough out on the ledge to see around the bend, and it suddenly occurred to me that the steepness of the ledge might stop them altogether. The seconds ticked by.

Again motion started, a very careful and methodical shuffling along the sloping rock. Step by step the two figures inched out to the ultimate point of the ledge, beyond which it plunged over the cliff into the river. They would never see any more than they could see from there. They were motionless now, staring, analyzing. Nothing seemed to be happening. The seconds ticked by, seeming like hours.

I grew apprehensive at the deathly uncertainty that seemed to fill the air of the canyon, and it struck me as strange that we had not even brought up the topic of what we would do if we couldn't get through the chasm. This would be one hell of a place to get out of. We couldn't get back up the canyon because of the water sweeping back and forth against the walls. We couldn't climb to Choquequirao from this side,

even if we had had a month. If ever Choquequirao took on the aspect
of a fortress, it was from the west, from the foot of those fractured
mile-high cliffs. And it seemed unlikely that we could go north of Choquequirao, over the frozen Vilcabamba.

We could only hope to get out by scaling the southern wall of the
canyon, by going up the faces and the scree and the cactus-choked
ravines, hoping to get to the broken tableland far above, hoping to find
a remote hacienda or village to get us on the trail back home. It would
be excruciating, hot and dry as an oven, worse torture than the river,
but suddenly it loomed as a big prospect in our lives, for clearly the
gorge was a problem, or else they would never hesitate so long. Either
they saw a difficulty, or they were bothered by something they couldn't
see. And so they stood like statues on that distant ledge. I swore under
my breath at the tension in the air.

Then, without warning, the arms of the statues unfroze and shot
directly in the air: it was the "go" signal. But it was not a relief now.
What question mark lay beneath those shadowed walls? What new risks
would we face?

I started across the river, anxious to see Jim, to find out what they
had seen. We met partway down the shore. Jim told me that the rapid
down at the bottom of the gorge could probably be run on the left,
along the cliff. They couldn't tell for sure. But if it couldn't be run,
there was a possibility that we could land in a small eddy in the rocks
on the right. From there we could line down to the bottom of the rapid,
where the gorge ended. There were still some questions, but Jim felt
good about it, felt that it would really go. I accepted his judgment. We
began the long, hard portage toward the chasm.

The sun baked us and the canyon air smothered us with a motionless
blanket of heat and steam. We edged down the margin of rocks near
the shore, toward the tailwater of the cataract. Here the current still
churned in the rocks, then spewed left into a deep pool near its last
beach. After that the water picked up momentum for another rapid
below, and in so doing it sped past the gateway of rock—the point of
no return.

I dragged my boat down to the small beach above the gateway and
climbed in.

In my journal I wrote: "It is with a feeling of finality, of ultimate
commitment, that we paddle into the first rapid—into water that will,

under no circumstances, let us back. The rapid ahead [at the end of the gorge] now looks unrunnable . . ."

Once between the walls, in the heart of the gorge, the water swirled down past big rocks, acting neither lazy nor rushed. I maneuvered around to get some pictures, and saw that we were in a deep trough between gray cliffs, broken and rough, intense and impressive, untamed and untamable. The current was fighting my efforts at photography, and most of the group was moving ahead, seeming to have no interest in the form and mood of this corner of wild earth, so I tucked my camera back into my life vest and hurried to catch up.

The main rapid, thundering down the left cliff at the bottom of the gorge, was indeed formidable. We hugged the right wall to stay away from it as long as we could. There the water coursed nervously through big rocks, itself preparing to twist left and plunge down onto the flank of the rapid. We had no choice but to follow it toward the lip.

Suddenly the thin tip of a peninsula of rocks appeared among the scattered debris choking the right. It was our first sighting of an assured safe exit from the gorge. We cut swiftly out of the current to land on the peninsula and avoid the plunge of the river. From here we could breathe easy. We worked our boats down along the edge of the water across the rocks, then back to the main stream below the worst of the rapid. One more obstacle fell behind us.

Immediately past the gorge, the river began to swing westward. Here we were approaching the northern corner of our trajectory. From there the Apurímac thrust 6 to 10 miles west, along the northernmost frontier of its Vilcabamba penetration. If we got through this stretch, we would be done with our uncharted canyon and would be face to face with the mystery at Quebrada de Arma.

We continued on past several more rapids that were so big they forced everyone to line down the shore. The struggle fell into its old monotony. We stopped for lunch by still another huge rapid, this one where the Río Choquequirao broke into the Apurímac. This tributary had cut a deep side canyon from the north. A considerable stream rumbled down its depths, then fanned out over rocks where it joined the Apurímac. The arriving water had begun at the top of a drainage system that circled up behind the Inca ruins to capture the melting snows of a row of mountain giants. Now their collective glacial waters ran silty gray over their last drop, plunging madly across our path.

Sometime in the past, enormous floods had rolled off the mountain slopes beneath the icy peaks. Room-sized boulders had tumbled like pebbles down the Río Choquequirao and washed out into the Apurímac, where they had created a dreadful, frothing barrier across the river.

Clearly, we couldn't run the rapid, nor could we go down the south shore, because that side was blocked by cliffs. We had no choice but to stay on the north shore—to go directly across the mouth of that raging little river!

Up higher, where the testy river flows in one channel, it would have been a nightmare to cross. But down here it spread its strength over dozens of lesser passages, and we could tackle them one at a time. So we waded out into the glacial runoff, stumbling waist-deep in entwined chutes snaking among the boulders, bracing against the power of the rushing water, lifting and dragging our boats against the current and up across the water-washed boulders. Soon we reached the other side of the stream and continued to line down past the cataract it had created in the river.

With this passage, still another hurdle fell away. It had been easier than some, and I thought again about how lucky we were. If the Río Choquequirao had been swollen by rain, or had been anywhere out of its dry cycle of flow, we would have been trapped up above, scratching our heads and wondering when the water would go down and let us by.

Beyond the Río Choquequirao, the Apurímac eased up a degree. My confidence, shattered when I had capsized and nearly lost my boat two days before, began to flow back. I noted in my journal that "I have been feeling more comfortable in this big water and find the rapids more and more enjoyable."

With the change in the river, we began paddling more and portaging less. Soon we were staying on the river nearly all the time. Big, runnable, joyful rapids took the place of brawling, gut-rending cataracts, and small rapids took the place of big ones. Then all at once we found ourselves on a stretch of river so quiet we thought we must be lost. We had not seen anything like it in ten days of struggle. It seemed unreal that this was the same river; that the plastic, gurgling, peaceful water beneath our hulls had just ripped through hell.

Elation began to well up from our souls, elation mixed with the caution and respect that this river deserved. We rounded a bend and then another, and nothing shattered the peaceful vision. Could it be true? Had we really outlasted the demon through its darkest canyons? It looked like maybe we had.

With this realization we went wild with joy. A huge, crushing burden was lifted off our shoulders. It was like coming out of a dungeon to light, to clean, open air where we could breathe deeply, where we could lay down our paddles and float awhile, watching the walls drift by and not counting the seconds until the jailer came back to throw us once more into the pit. It was ecstasy.

My journal recounts our passage through this section and beyond:

. . . suddenly, we are in a narrow canyon—virtually a gorge—with smooth, flat water as far as the next distant corner. A small rapid, then more of the same. A beautiful canyon. A beautiful feeling. Have we finally broken the back of this monstrous river—ended our terrible burden? We hope so, and whoop in joy. We stop to photograph this beautiful canyon. Dee and Chuck have pushed impatiently ahead.

Near four o'clock we approach the end of the photo gap. We have gone 6 miles and dropped nearly 300 feet. We approach the Quebrada de Arma, a side stream from the snowcapped peaks of the north. My aerial photography begins again here, and shows a giant slab of rock in the canyon forcing the river through a narrow slot to the right. We don't know if navigation is possible. Another question mark to face in this endless series of unknowns. Tomorrow.

We line a big rapid, and as Jim is tired, he and Gerry suggest making camp. Dee tells them that we can make still more progress, and he pushes on. Jim is upset: he came here to see and enjoy this spectacular land—not to undergo a forced march. Dee is very arbitrary, and is making decisions he has no right to make.

Jim, Gerry, and I find a beautiful sandbar across the river to the right. We set up tents. It rains with a vengeance.

Our campsite sat on a plain of sand elevated above the river, dotted by towering rocks. Enormous, graceful curving sheets of whitish sand had spilled over the flat and encircled the rocks in waves, making them appear to float like tall ships at sea. And now little tents of yellow and orange went up on the plain, and the tongues of our campfire lit the air, creating dazzling points of color in the peaceful sweep of sand. It struck me as the most beautiful, ethereal campsite I had ever seen, and

I just sat and watched its flow of form while the water heated for tea.

When I raised my eyes above the arches of sand and the capstones of the sailing rocks, I saw a land whose heart had been gnawed out, whose loveliness had been mutilated by erosion. Its green mantle of life had been stripped away by the elements, leaving pendant, formless walls of rocks embedded in cliffs of ugly mud. We had entered an incredible, alien landscape, seemingly at war even in the midst of such peacefulness, reflecting violence, promising violence. We had entered the domain of the Quebrada de Arma. In the morning we would have to leave our sand-shrouded paradise and find out for ourselves just what the forces of nature had done to the canyon. But for now, the tea water was ready.

We were wanderers on a prehistoric earth, on an earth
that wore the aspect of an unknown planet . . .

Joseph Conrad

All the rivers run into the sea; yet the sea is not full; unto
the place from whence the rivers come, thither they return again.

Ecclesiastes 1:7

≈ QUEBRADA DE ARMA

THE RÍO ARMA IS born in perpetual snows clinging high to the wind-swept slopes of the Vilcabamba Range. Its birthplace is surrounded by Vilcabamba titans Pumasillo (6,246 meters, 20,492 feet) and Panta (5,840 meters, 19,160 feet), 12 miles north of the Apurímac. Halfway through its earthward plunge, the little river spins through a valley beneath the watchful eye of Choquetira (5,070 meters, 19,160 feet). It then cuts like a machete deep into the cordillera, carving out its own gorge, Quebrada de Arma, as it makes its final precipitous descent to the mother of the Amazon. The Río Arma joins the Apurímac on the far western corner of its northern reign, just before the big river retreats southwest to brawl with other mountains.

The Apurímac's canyon is criss-crossed with tense formations that telegraph a grim warning to intruders: "Stay away from here. I have lost my spirit to the torture of wind, my grace to the violence of water, my calmness to a million years of upheaval; I care for nothing—the starlight that kisses me, the birds that sing me melodies, or puny hu-mans, who bring nothing here except immense ego. Beware of my con-vulsions of madness." This message is everywhere. It echoes off the walls of the highland gorges, it thunders out of the water screaming over rocks at the middle elevations, it precipitates with the rain of loose rocks falling on the Acobamba shore. But nowhere in the recesses of this Amazonian chasm is the land under so much tension as it is at the mouth of the Río Arma.

Some cataclysm once swept over the land where the little river comes down out of its quebrada to join the Apurímac. It left a terrain so desolate that it seems improper for our earth. Walls of unconsolidated rock stand stark and weathered at the quebrada rim, guarding Río Arma as it breaks out of the cordillera. The walls have been sliced and carved by the elements to form fluted towers, barren, eroded, beyond seduction by the human spirit. Now the quebrada stood above us, its walls dried mud and baked-in rock, sculptured into evil, friable cliffs. And below there remained the fallen slab so large that it filled the main canyon. My aerial photographs suggested that a block of mountain had fallen off the right wall of the canyon just below the entry of Río Arma, perhaps after millennia of undercutting by the Apurímac. After the fall the river must have bored its channel down the fissure left between the block and the canyon wall. But whether fury or calmness had been left behind by the unknown ages of erosion could not be fathomed. The river in my photographs was out of sight behind pendant walls. Nor could we see anything of it from our camp.

The torn landscape suggested violent geological events. But its two parts, the slab and the eroded walls, were probably not connected. A colossal mud and rock slide could have poured out of the Quebrada de Arma (Gerry thought in the last ten years) to fill the main canyon to a depth of hundreds of feet. But perhaps the unconsolidated walls dated back to the last ice age, when glacial debris poured into Andean canyons on rivers of ice. The slab was likely to be much older still. Had each been initiated by some great earthquake in the past? And could the slab possibly be at the spot where in 1555, according to Garcilaso de la Vega, ". . . a piece of the mountain fell into the river, of such size . . . that it blocked the stream up from one side to the other, insomuch that not a single drop of water passed for three days . . ." But this place fit the description even less than the slide in the canyon above Choquequirao, for we were now 2,000 vertical feet, more or less, below the site of the Bridge of San Luis Rey. Water that deep cannot be imagined backed up behind a slide, even in this canyon. There is some basic error, I am convinced, in Garcilaso's memory of the great 1555 Apurímac slide. Some day I hope to fathom the mystery.

I awoke to my forty-fifth birthday on day twenty-six of the expedition. Thousands of other Americans shared their birthday with me that September twenty-sixth. Most had parties, birthday cakes, cards, telephone calls, gifts. I would have none of that. But if we could get past Quebrada de Arma that day, it would be a birthday present more dear than all other gifts of the world.

Early that morning Gerry hiked up among the scattered rocks that lay in the wasteland above the Río Arma. He sought a view of the cataclysm of the slab, but soon his path ahead became steep and loose with crumbled rock, and he had to turn back without any real penetration of the mystery of the canyon.

We ate breakfast and packed our boats. After lining and paddling only a block, we came to the camp on the left bank where Chuck and Dee had stayed the night. Dee had already left. Chuck told us what he had seen climbing high on his side.

"It looks like we can get through," he said. "There's a big rapid at the bottom we can run. The one at the top is way too tough. We'll have to try a portage."

Dee and Chuck had made their camp at the bottom of a thorny slope on the left bank at the head of the gorge. From here we could reach out and touch the first spur of the slab as it began to enclose the river. As we paddled by this point, we again handed our fate to the river. We worked down through big rocks peppering the wide channel, as the walls closed in like a funnel. The raw face of the slab, low near its beginning, soared to increasing heights above the river. The opposite wall, perhaps the mother of the slab, loomed above its child like an obsessed guardian, plunging the river into shadows beneath its great mass.

We arrived at a low island of rocks. This was not an island with soil and shrubs and birds and flowers at peace with the river. It was, instead, a mere surfacing of a wall of rocks blocking the angry river from shore to shore. Apurímac floods had pounded over it, tearing free and washing away every object smaller than a 3-foot boulder. Most of its rocks were 10 feet high, with their bases buried in swirling water. On each side of the island the river roared down over the wall in fiendish cataracts. The vertical faces of the deepening gorge blocked hopes for a portage on shore. Our only route was across the island.

We clambered atop the behemoths of stone, pulling our boats behind. Moving from rock to rock, we stepped across channels of turbulent water, maneuvering our boats along with us. Midway we dropped ten feet over the brink of the rock wall under a splashing waterfall. At the bottom, mere shreds of the island remained, surrounded by tongues of galloping water. We moved as close to its rocky end as we could.

Here was our new launching point. Here it was that we must climb back in our boats as they bobbed in the turbulence. This would be an easy matter with someone's help, but a devilish task alone. The last man to leave would carry the full risk of this exercise for everyone.

"I think I can do it," Jim said. "I'll come last."

One by one we climbed into our kayaks and secured the spray covers, while someone else held them against the wrenching force of the water. Gerry and I dropped down to clusters of rocks to watch and photograph the launchings and to prepare to help Jim if he needed it. As we waited, several rocks came pinging into the water from some great height. This startled me, as we were almost 200 feet away from the base of the main wall to the right. I glanced upward and saw the overhanging eyebrow of the parent cliff looming directly overhead, jutting out over the river. It was dropping loose rocks into the gorge below like a giant shedding dandruff.

Finally only Jim was left on the island. We got ready for rescue, half expecting him to wash by, out of his boat. But he calmly slid into the rocking, wavering craft and flipped his spray cover into place. He soon joined us among the deposits of rocks below where we had landed to plan his rescue.

The entire river now veered right, to escape the banks of rocks. It plunged into a deep channel against the base of the main wall and rolled through a rapid toward the deep haunts of the gorge. We followed. Below the rapid the world grew calm. The water deepened and slowed. The winds were still. The noise of the rapids quieted behind us. Two dark walls not 50 feet apart thrust skyward and echoed back the rhythmic sound of dipping paddles. A remarkable tranquillity descended to the core of the canyon, and a feeling of peacefulness dropped over us. This pocket of calm was a real anomaly in an environment born in violence and surrounded by wildness.

Below, the gorge widened and discharged us into a rough drop. Gerry and I scraped down a narrow channel on the right, while the others went left. At the bottom I felt incredible joy and elation! We had made it past Quebrada de Arma, and my birthday prayers were answered. We were now past the uncharted northern frontier of the Apurímac, past the cataracts of Choquequirao. We were now swerving south, away from Vilcabamba's peaks.

Our bondage to the river was dissolving. "We seem to have overcome the major obstacles," I wrote. "My schedule for this was liberal, and we are somewhat ahead of schedule—well ahead now on a vertical

The author lowering himself over a waterfall at the center of the river in a gorge below the Quebrada de Arma (photo by Gerry Plummer).

≈ Jim Sindelar helping Chuck Carpenter launch his kayak below a short, rugged waterfall in a gorge near the Quebrada de Arma.

Jim Sindelar, after helping everyone else, prepares for his own launch below a
waterfall in a gorge near the Quebrada de Arma.

drop basis. The plan is working well despite the incredible hardships
we have endured."

With the Quebrada de Arma safely behind us now, we plunged on
at an accelerated pace. My journal contains this description:

*The canyon has indeed leveled and moderated. Rapids still occur at
frequent intervals, but they are more direct, with a more even gradient,
lacking the waterfalls and mazes of giant rocks as occurred above. In some
rapids there are giant waves and hydraulics, but they are fairly direct.*

*We pass through narrow gorges most of the day. These gorges are not
deep like some above, and their walls angle back to provide occasional
egress, if needed. But they are walls of solid rock, and they have been
polished fifty feet high by the raging Apurímac.*

*The high slopes become greener during the afternoon, at first patches of
green, then solid green. We are in the jungle! In this short interval we have
passed from semiarid Andean slopes to semitropical Andean slopes. This
abrupt transition occurs elsewhere; one sees it prominently on the road
from Lima to Tingo María.*

We haven't seen Dee or Chuck all afternoon. They have raced ahead. We camp at 5 without sight of them . . .

We have gone nearly 10 miles this afternoon and are comfortably ahead of schedule. We dropped probably 300–400 feet, and must now be 3,800–3,900 feet [in elevation]. *We don't know exactly because the altimeter has been slightly erratic—perhaps responding to some changes in weather.*

Dehydrated beef stew for my birthday dinner! Very tasty. And I treat myself to two candy bars. I never touch these normally, but on this trip we have developed a great affinity for carbohydrates.

Camp that night was established in a large field of rocks packed one against the other, barely broken by a few pockets of sand. Jim and Gerry, who shared a tent, found a flat spit between two rocks; I found another by the cliff. The night was dark and the sky ominous, but our campfire threw it back. We bathed in its glow and in the warmth of friendship and fresh optimism.

Day twenty-seven began with rain from 3 A.M. on. When time to break camp arrived, at 7:00, the rain still fell in erratic bursts. The exquisite pattern of rainless nights and star-filled skies of the high canyons was apparently gone for good.

Waiting for the rain to cease seemed futile, so I packed my things still wet and was ready to go shortly after 8:00. Then I saw a forlorn and drenched figure stumbling over a mound of rocks from the direction of the other camp. It was Jim. He had been sick during the night and was still weak and pale. Neither he nor Gerry had packed. Their tent still stood, a sodden orange patch among the gray rocks strewn along the beach. So I sat in the drizzle, watching clouds blow across the canyon walls. While my two companions packed their gear, I wandered out across slippery rocks toward the river. I stopped by a large rapid that we would face as soon as we launched. It had big waves and holes, but bore a navigable channel down its center. I noted the clarity of the streamers of water as they rushed toward the first drop, before breaking into spray. After watching awhile, I wandered back to camp.

Nearly an hour later, we brought our first load of gear to the river. As I struggled to the bank, I was startled to see a dramatic change in the appearance of the water. The opposite half of the river, flowing clear an hour before, was now flowing brown, the color of flood! We knew the chocolatelike water had entered the Apurímac nearby, because it had not yet had time to mix across the breadth of the river. A likely source was a stream we had passed the afternoon before, at a sharp left bend in the canyon, a stream running off the flanks of the Nevado Choquetira. The ugly water now streamed down the Apurímac into the rapid, making big brown waves flecked in foam, an appearance unlike anything we had seen along the length of the river.

What did it mean? Was this the beginning of the annual flood? If so, how long would we be able to navigate the surging waters? We did not have enough information to answer these questions. We had heard no weather report in weeks, and so knew nothing of precipitation patterns outside our narrow valley. We knew only two facts: we were advancing toward a jungle rain belt, and we were approaching the season of rains.

The critical question, about which we had few clues, was whether the increase in rainfall in the last few days was due to our approach to the jungle, or whether it signaled the early onset of the rains of the Andes. If it was jungle influence, the river would gain volume normally as we moved downstream past new tributaries; there would be no flood from above. If it was the early onset of the Andean rains, however, we might soon find high water thundering down the canyon from the highlands. The brown water gave some credibility to the arrival of the rainy season, for the sudden presence of mud in this clear-water canyon suggested an abrupt seasonal change. But then it might be only another of nature's infinite fluctuations.

I shuddered as I glanced up at the canyon walls, swept clean high above our heads by rain-swollen floods. We launched quickly. Jim was still pale from sickness.

The rapids that morning were frequent, but all runnable, and we made good time. We soon joined Chuck and Dee, although they stayed with us only intermittently during the day. Later a sidestream—perhaps the Río Chamanayoc—entered from the right, and a severe rapid ensued. We portaged and lined its upper parts, then looked for a place to reenter the river.

Choosing a good point of reentry is sometimes difficult, but it can be crucial. The cataracts of the demon river rarely die abruptly. Even beyond the biggest of their drops, the water lashes through boulders like the tail of a dying serpent. When laboring down the bank on a portage, one must make a decision about where to attack the serpent's tail, where to challenge the river again. Enter too high, and its remaining vigor can crush a boat on the rocks. Enter too low, and you needlessly extend the excruciating portage. Such choices are hard and always subject to fleeting moods of caution, confidence, or fatigue. None of us seemed to choose consistently from rapid to rapid or from day to day; there is just too much subjectivity to danger and backache.

Midway in this powerful rapid, Jim saw a route he felt he could follow. He entered his boat in a narrow recess between towering rocks along the right shore. Immediately below, the water crashed into a maze of rocks meshed tightly like teeth in a shark's jaw. Jim would have to skirt above these, fighting strong currents to a channel beyond, near the center of the river.

As he swung out from the shore, the strong current seized his bow and levered it sideways. This kept him from attaining the position facing upstream that he needed to contend with the current charging down from above. He pulled desperately, but in an instant it was too late. He was dragged inexorably toward the sharklike teeth. His boat struck some rocks sideways, and there it became pinned, only to begin to tip upstream. I feared for his life, for it looked as though he might be overturned and remain pinned underwater.

Instantly Gerry dove into a boiling channel near shore, trying to swim out to the row of rocks below Jim. I raced to get the rope out of my boat. When I returned, Gerry had reached the opposite side of the channel. He clambered up on the row of rocks and bounded toward Jim, leaping from rock to rock across the frothing chutes. He arrived beside the tilted boat, reached down, gripped an end loop, and broke it free. The boat bumped and slipped down a narrow chute, past the remaining teeth on the jaw and into a pool, followed by the final convulsions of the serpent's tail. A minute later and Jim had fought free to the end. A tough run for a man still weakened by a night of illness.

I threw the end of the rope to Gerry and pulled him back to shore. The rest of us then completed the portage. I was filled with admiration for what Gerry had done. I wrote this brief tribute in my journal: "Gerry has been a tower of strength and quickness in emergencies. He has no fear of turbulent water. He has quick reflexes and a deep concern for his fellow passengers on this hazardous venture. He is the kind of man who makes an expedition a success."

Soon another turbulent rapid loomed ahead, perhaps a quarter of a mile long. I started it badly; a narrow chute at the top twisted me into the current too far to the right. Directly ahead a massive rock squatted midright in the riverbed, deflecting angry water to both sides. I paddled desperately left to avoid it, but the chaos of water tossed me about like a twig, as if I had not paddled at all. I plunged into a deep hole and emerged backwards. I fought to keep my balance, but was swept past one large rock and dropped into another hole backwards. I was fighting now to keep my balance—and my breath.

Into another one backwards; the river was relentless. Blinded by spray, immersed in deep troughs and holes, I had lost track of the squatting rock into which I thought I would soon crash. But the fickle currents had swept me left, and I saw the mammoth rock speed by, just out of range. I scraped over a stony shelf lurking beneath the surface, then rode the tail waves of the rapid to the bottom. It had been horrible, and I was shaken, gasping for air.

"Better than watching a circus," Jim said, amused at my gyrations. It was the first smile I had seen cross his pale face all day long.

"Yeah, I did it just as a stunt," I sputtered, "trying to humor the sick!"

The drops that followed were shorter but even more severe, as the river steadily gained power from the inflow of sidestreams. I estimated that its flow was approaching 10,000 cubic feet per second. Such a flow is equivalent to over 300 tons of water shoving by in the tick of a second; over a million tons in an hour.

The demon seemed fully determined to become the greatest river on earth.

The canyon is very tortuous, the river very rapid and many lateral canyons on either side . . . Piles of broken rock lie against these walls; crags and tower-shaped peaks are seen everywhere and away above them long lines of broken cliffs. . . . We are minded to call this the Canyon of Desolation

John Wesley Powell

. . . the attempt to navigate the Apurímac . . . brought us to a rock defile—a true inferno, where in a torrent worthy of the end of the world the water was broken up against the rocks and projected 6 meters into the air in a white explosion. It took us half a day of painstaking work to climb back to Pasaje.

Michel Perrin

≈ WINDS FROM HELL

JIM, GERRY, AND I, left behind again by the other two, pulled to shore at the head of a large rapid to scout it. It looked so ferocious that I resolved to portage the main drop. Jim decided to run. It was a rough descent. Gerry followed. He dropped into a choppy pool through which the currents raged. As he fought his way around to face the last drop, his paddle snapped in two. He let go the short end and grasped the longer half like a canoe paddle. He braced down into a sucking hole, and it began to swallow his remaining paddle blade like a pit of quicksand. The paddle sank slowly out of sight, followed by Gerry—up to his elbow, up to his shoulder, and the last thing I saw was water coming up across his beard, across his startled face. Gerry was torn out of his cockpit, as the boat was wrenched from his grasp. He was then swept violently onto a partly submerged boulder and over it into a frothing hole. The undertow pulled him deep beneath the surface and held him for seconds that seemed like hours, before the tug of his life preserver brought him back to air.

For a moment my activity on shore was more hectic than Gerry's. As he began his troubled run of the rapid, a man and woman came up to me on shore. They had spotted us coming down the river and had brought us a bundle of bananas and a pineapple. They deserved the full dignity and concentration of formal Andean greetings. Meanwhile my dear friend was being swallowed by water. Even worse, at least for the maintenance of my composure, the sight of his suddenly broken paddle and his perplexed look upon immersion was momentarily funny beyond description—and even in the context of danger, I could not suppress an explosion of laughter.

And so, all at one time, I faced the most hilarious sight I had seen for a month, an Andean introduction, and a penetrating concern for Gerry. The awkwardness of my predicament and the danger of Gerry's unplanned swim quickly cured the hilarity.

"Buenas tardes" (good afternoon), said my visitors.

"Buenas tardes," I blurted back, and I shook their hands, but my eyes were following Gerry's fate through the rapid.

In fact there was little else I could do from shore but watch. My apprehension about Gerry's safe passage through these canyons now resurfaced with a jolt. In my journal I wrote: "I am especially concerned about Gerry. Absolutely unafraid, he will tackle almost any rapid. He has made many nice rolls when capsized, but he has had several hazardous swims in the last three days. I hope he gets through this trip safely."

In a moment Gerry washed on through the rapid, and Jim gathered up the pieces in the quiet water below. I could then turn more respectful attention to my visitors. They had remained courteous throughout the ordeal, but if ever there was a time when the words "crazy gringos" flashed through native minds, it must have been here.

The meeting itself was a remarkable reunion with humanity. These were the first people we had encountered since Choquequirao, five days and 30 miles ago, and the first I had seen near the river since San José, almost nine days back. When one considers how the Indians of Peru use every cultivable patch of land in every niche in the mountain vastness, this hiatus was mute testament to the desolation of the canyon we had traversed.

"Where do you come from?" I asked.

"Up on the hill," the man replied in Spanish, pointing to the thorny slopes above the right bank. "We live at Hacienda Apurímac."

Hacienda Apurímac! Here, again, we had stumbled across the path of the British expedition led by John Ridgeway. In the fall of 1970 his party had labored on foot and by road parallel to the Apurímac, seeking a place they could begin navigation in the valleys far below. Two expeditions—Ridgeway's and ours—had each sought in its own way to explore Apurímac country, they up on the mountain, we down in the gorge. Yet such is the immensity of the canyon that our paths rarely intersected.

While we had watched the river grow drop by drop, the British party had not seen the river, except when they crossed by bus at Cunyac, for almost 150 miles. The change was startling to them. "No longer were we faced with a playful stream," John Ridgeway wrote. "Now fifty yards wide, the flow was a rich brown torrent frothing yellow through roaring rapids and gliding dark and sinister across pools." I wondered what

Ridgeway's impression would have been if he had seen the monstrous cataracts above!

Our river—for the moment—was still clear. His party had crossed here on October 31, 1970, a month later in the season.

"Do you remember the expedition from England?" I asked the man and his wife.

"Oh yes, of course. I took them across the river here," he replied. "I am the balsero at this crossing. I take many people across, but I remember them well." Then he added, gazing with curiosity at my odd river-running outfit, "There are not many outsiders that come this way."

I thanked them for the bananas and pineapple and rejoined Jim and Gerry.

Somewhat later in the afternoon we entered a narrow gorge with deep, swirling rapids. Ahead the south wall of the canyon turned red with brilliant rock. For a moment I had to blink away the unbelievable sight. I felt I was drifting along in some deep redrock gorge back in Utah. The splashy color, so new amid the grays and greens that had dominated this canyon, was as refreshing as strawberry ice cream.

Beyond the red wall, a sizable tributary entered from a narrow cleft, its water clear and blue. This was the Río Pachachaca, a major tributary arising in snow-capped peaks 100 miles south of us. My journal noted:

We are steadily winning the war against this giant of a river—but it is even larger now, by maybe 1,000 cubic feet per second—due to the entry of this new tributary. It seems even more augmented in volume and power.

We camp on sand patches high on a bank of rippled rock. Chuck and Dee have rejoined us.

There are more insects now. The yellow gnats are as bad as ever. Flying antlike creatures have joined the insect circus. Small mites are crawling all over. And we see more spiders now, some of them very large, that dart in and out of rocks at river level.

This evening, while talking with me, Jim spots a large scorpion going under the rock serving as my tent stake. He is a full three inches long, from nose to tail. We must be more on the alert for these deadly creatures, for they seem to be cropping up with increasing frequency.

There are more birds, too. Our campsite is alive with the squawking of parrots, and water birds abound.

There are many bats flying about at night, but I don't think we have yet

*entered the realm of the dreaded vampire bat. This will occur somewhat
downstream.*

*Tomorrow, back to the tragic trail of Perrin and the female companion
who drowned in the Apurímac further downstream. He visited the river
below Hacienda Pasaje, at a trail we shall cross in one mile.*

On day twenty-eight I was awakened by the chirping of thousands
of birds. It was spring here, south of the equator, a vocal time of
year. The voices were unfamiliar, exotic and wonderful. I looked
around and realized how arid the canyon had become since our brush
with the jungle. The dry walls and buttes were again covered only thinly
with clumps of thorns and cacti. Only two days ago, I thought that we
had entered permanent jungle, that there would be no break in solid
green all the way to the Atlantic Ocean.

We had discussed hiking up to Hacienda Pasaje that morning, but I
decided I should stay by the river and avoid cutting deeper into my
reserves of strength. I told Jim of my decision. "Would you like us to
go?" he offered. "I'll walk up if you think it will help document our
trip."

"If you like," I responded. "I would like to know what has happened
there—if anything—in the twenty-two years since Perrin's visit."

Michel Perrin and Teresa Gutiérrez arrived at Hacienda Pasaje near
the end of July 1953, after a difficult passage overland, away from the
river. They had traveled from Hacienda Carmen, in the vicinity of the
Cunyac Bridge. "The Hacienda," Perrin wrote, "which had been left to
complete neglect . . . did not inspire us to stay." They moved on to the
river, but soon returned to stay a few days.

Chuck and Dee accompanied Jim to the hacienda that morning.
They hiked up the steep hillside to the left, following an ill-maintained
trail lined with sentinel cacti. As Jim later told me:

> The trail near the hacienda was lined with crumbling rock
> walls and some . . . citrus trees. It looked like it had once been
> a place of some splendor, but now run-down, little more than
> a dreary workcamp. We opened the gate and entered an en-
> closed courtyard littered with crushed sugarcane. A couple of
> horses were near the wall. A handsome Indian with a wad of
> coca in his mouth met us, told us in Spanish that he owned

the place along with his eight brothers and that we were welcome to look around. They had a large herd of goats and were just taking the kids to the mothers for feeding. There was a big overshot waterwheel run by irrigation water for power. It was maybe 18 feet in diameter. There had been electricity earlier but the previous owner had made off with the dynamo when he left.

It appeared, from Jim's description, that Pasaje had only drifted further into decay in the twenty-two years since Perrin's visit.

Gerry and I prepared for our departure at a leisurely pace. We left at 9:30 and immediately began looking for the place where Perrin had come to the river. His description was brief: "the attempt to navigate the Apurímac . . . brought us to a rock defile—a true inferno, where in a torrent worthy of the end of the world the water was broken up against the rocks and projected 6 meters into the air in a white explosion. It took us half a day of painstaking work to climb back to Pasaje."

Gerry and I encountered two large, navigable rapids, but neither one seemed likely to be the rapid so sketchily described. Then around a right bend below the trail to the hacienda, we found a cauldron of water dropping between low cliffs. It was a formidable place, impossible to run, almost impossible to portage. We waited for our companions a while, then slowly worked down the left shore, lowering our boats over rock shelves, down to a narrow gravel bar by the river. Below us the water ran against the cliff and our portage ran out.

The biggest drop was now behind us, and we puzzled over the best way to navigate the remaining rapid. We disagreed. Gerry thought it best to start high, working out to an interior channel obstructed by a big rock. I felt unsure that we could avoid the rock. I preferred to start in a steep channel next to the cliff, where a jet of water impinged against the wall. Gerry was uncertain about getting through the jet without capsizing. We each decided to follow our own path, watching out for the other from our parallel courses. We twisted through our respective passages and dropped over the final fall of water without any problem.

This was certainly Perrin's rapid. We found no water shooting 6 meters into the air—at least at the present level of river flow. We did find, however, a formidable rapid that would discourage anyone with a heavier boat and an inexperienced companion. It was the worst rapid in this part of the canyon—one of the worst anywhere. Perrin had unluckily stumbled onto it as he began. Yet in a sense it was good that he was warned away here, because a lot of rough water was still to follow.

As we worked through the rapid, our companions returned from their visit to Hacienda Pasaje and came downriver to join us. As they ran a short rapid at the entrance of the cauldron, Dee capsized. I shuddered at the thought that his roll might fail again, that he might be swept over the vicious drops below. But he succeeded, and all three pulled in to shore. While they portaged the major drop, Gerry and I went ahead to look for the Río Pampas.

The rapids below Pasaje and the twisted rapid that we portaged were big and clear, wild with waves and spray. We sped through 3 miles of river punctuated by these roller coasters of water. Below this stretch a side canyon broke in abruptly from the left. Here the Río Pampas, a major tributary and landmark for this expedition, flowed in, loosing a torrent of muddy water into the blue Apurímac. We watched the waters mingle and the blue succumb to the brown. Our clear-water Apurímac was gone for good. Step by step the Apurímac was becoming the Amazon. Here it changed its color and took on still another increment of volume and power.

We stopped at 1 P.M. by the mouth of the Pampas. Here we would eat lunch and wait for the others. I looked around. The valley widened below and the hills fell back. The Apurímac Canyon was shaking off the Vilcabamba Range, losing some of the incredible steepness that had blocked so much sky for two tense weeks. I wrote: "We are jubilant, for this marks the end of the great Apurímac Gorge. It is the major break point of this canyon. We feel we have won the battle now. Still, at about 3,200 feet elevation, we know that we must drop another 1,400 feet or so to reach our roadhead near San Francisco, 100 miles or more downstream. And now the river is much larger and more powerful. There are, then, still question marks on the severity of the route ahead."

The others arrived, and I asked the group how they wanted to proceed. "We are a week ahead of schedule," I noted. "We have plenty of food and our gear still works okay. We can speed down the river or slow down and look at things of interest. For myself, I would like to

take time to photograph the Campa Indians down below." No strong
opinions were offered. We would thus move along at a reasonable pace,
and stop whenever something interesting turned up.

We launched after a brief lunch. The river below the Pampas was
much wider than before, about 300 feet across. It seemed somehow
even larger than one would expect from the addition of the brown
waters of the Pampas. It was a bigger river now than the Colorado
River through the Grand Canyon. It was becoming a great river, more
than ten times larger in flow than the rocky stream we had started on
a month ago.

Wide banks paralleled the river now. Patches of grass grew near the
waterline, although a barren slope of rocks above the river spoke of the
annual cleansing of the flood. A few thorny shrubs clung to life in the
rubble above the highest reach of the floodwaters. Strips of sand lent a
desert atmosphere to the canyon floor. Above loomed gray and rust-
colored cliffs of crumbling rock. The wildness of these badlands fascinated me, and the bleakness made me shiver. A brisk wind blowing up
the canyon magnified the appearance of desolation and enhanced my
feeling of solitude in confronting its vastness.

Late that morning, above the Río Pampas, the wind had arisen almost imperceptibly. A breeze blew in our faces, pushing upcanyon, and
it strengthened as the day passed. A few miles below the Río Pampas,
it exploded into a gale. Upcanyon winds are common in the mountains
and deserts. They originate in layers of heated air that chase up the
canyons and peak in the afternoon. Many boatmen have cursed them
on western rivers in the United States, for they are brisk and annoying,
and they multiply the difficulty of paddling or rowing downstream.

In all my years of paddling western rivers, I had never seen a river
wind like this before. Sheets of spray were whipped off the water and
sent screaming up the canyon. Enormous gusts struck us, ripped at our
paddles, and pushed our boats sideways. Jim, immediately ahead of me,
was blown off course in a rapid and capsized. He rolled up and struggled across to the right-hand bank. The others, also troubled by the
wind, rounded a corner and disappeared from sight.

I stopped above Jim on the opposite bank and dragged my boat
ashore. Though it was still loaded heavily, it rocked ominously in the
gusts and threatened to become airborne. I filled the cockpit with large
rocks to hold it down, then struggled up the bank searching for shelter.

Nowhere was the terrain free of wind, and I sat huddled among the rocks watching rainbows of spray race by. As time passed I told myself it couldn't last. These things always let up, especially late in the day. Then a brief respite in the wind would give me momentary encouragement. But soon a new sheet of windblown spray would race and tumble up the river, almost reeling me out of the rocks. I began to realize that I might have to sit here all night.

Jim was huddled in rocks on the other side of the river, a few blocks away. Occasionally I would see him move around, then settle out of sight again. I hoped I could at least get across to him by nightfall.

After a seeming eternity, the wind subsided ever so slightly, and I decided to try to cross. I threw the rocks out of my cockpit, dragged the boat to the water's edge, and started out, hugging the left shore. Gusts still rocked me as I weaved down through the channel of a small rapid, then started to pull across the river toward Jim. It was tougher than I had thought. The wind showed unexpected vigor, and I fought for every inch. I concentrated on staying upright against the gusts, for I was on my own now. At each new stroke, I forced the blade of the paddle deep in the water, for here was my only anchor of stability; the air above was a sea of chaos. The demon water was now my friend—the air had become my enemy. I made the moment between strokes forcefully brief, for in changing sides, the flat of the blades turned fleetingly to the wind. The struggle seemed interminable.

I reached shore out of breath. Jim helped me pull my boat up and anchor it. We ducked down behind low rocks, and Jim told me about his experience:

"I was paddling very hard and going almost nowhere, thinking how stupid it was to push on and burn all that energy for no gain, when we could make up for lost time and more the next morning if we made camp. Even with the good current and paddling very hard, little progress was possible. Every time I took a new stroke, the bite the wind got on the upper blade was easily enough to cause a capsize. It was by far the worst wind I have ever tried to paddle in, and nearly the worst I have ever been out in.

"To me it seemed senseless and stupid, but Dee and Gerry and Chuck were ahead, so I put down my head, gritted my teeth, and continued. I passed through a couple of minor rapids. The windblown spray and dust were so bad that I could not see far enough for safe boating in unknown water. Then I came to the rapid above the bend here. It looked as though I should run it on river right, and I headed there. The windblown spray and dust stung my eyes so bad that I could not really see the rapid. Then the wind caught me, blew me over to the left side of the river where I had decided I did not want to be, and I could do nothing to prevent it. The wind then blew me into a hole, and the hole plus the wind on my paddle tipped me over. I rolled up in the hole. At this point the others were just turning the corner, out of earshot, completely unaware of my tipover.

"When I got squared away finally, they were out of sight completely. At that point I decided that further boating was not safe, and that I didn't give a damn if Dee and company paddled to hell, that I was going to camp right there. I fought my way back to the right bank and pulled out. I lay down on the shore here in the shelter of this boulder, reflecting on the stupidity of the others going on, of the useless god-damn wind in which one could not hope to build a cooking fire or pitch a tent, of the disgusting prospect of having the party split up again with nothing I could do about it, and figuring that I might as well just eat nuts and dried fruit for supper and sleep right where I lay, for at least there I was somewhat out of the stupid wind, and the only prospective campsites were up over the bank of the sandflat with wind like hell and sand blowing everywhere.

"God, how I hate this wind. Do you suppose it'll let up by dark?"

"I thought it would let up long ago," I said. "It's pushing 5:00. Nothing to do but sit and wait."

My journal continues the tale:

We wait, but these erratic gusts do not subside. We decide to stay the night, but we know a tent cannot be put up now without being blown across the canyon. We eat a cold dinner, for a fire is not possible either. Finally, about dark, the winds lessen, and we stake out the tent. Gusty impulses still blow across this wasteland of rock, sand, and thorny bushes.

As I work on the tent, I look up and catch a glimpse of a flash of light—a reflection from the beam of my headlamp. I look intensely way out on the windswept rocks, and two large furtive eyes stare back from the void. The creature moves nimbly over the rocks, then stares again. It is too far away to be distinguishable by my beam. Perhaps a large fox? Or a puma? Pumas reputedly abound in Apurímac canyon country, preying relentlessly on the region's livestock. I doubt that one need fear attack from

*the pumas, but the effect in this lonely place of knowing that something
has us under surveillance is electrifying.*

*We probe the darkness of this rock-strewn beach with our weak beams
of light, but nothing more reveals itself. The creature is gone, and we
succumb to sleep.*

Our twenty-ninth day dawned clear and windless. I looked for the
tracks of our unknown visitor in the pockets of sand between
thorny bushes, but they had been erased by the wind. My thoughts
turned to the river, and later I wrote:

*We should be in the clear now, in the open canyon down below the
Pampas, but the Apurímac seems determined to throw every possible hurdle in front of us. High water. Gusty winds. What next?*

*We start at 8:00. After several drops, we come to a giant rapid, full of
frothing holes and protruding rocks. I elect to line, but Jim runs. He capsizes, and is upside down through much of its terrible turbulence. Finally
he rolls—certainly the most dependable roll under adverse conditions that
I have seen. We found later that his was the only run through the rapid.
Everyone else had lined it.*

*Another large rapid in this enormous water, and I begin to think I had
grossly underestimated the Apurímac in this section.*

*We reach the others at 9:30 and proceed. We start less than auspiciously.
In the first rapid, which we all run, Dee flips and must swim out. In the
next big rapid, a large hole, into which the entire river funnels, flips the
other four of us, and we must all eskimo roll.*

After showing us who was master, the demon river improved its
behavior. The rapids below were big and clean, with large standing
waves and easily avoided rocks. We passed several tributaries, including
the Mapillo Grande, which arises on a 16,700-foot ice-bound giant 10
miles to the northeast. The mountains weren't all dead yet.

At midday we rounded a bend and saw ahead a mountain that
looked torn in half—a slide had ripped one side away. Gray rock and
earth clung together on the remaining side in pendant agony. Left behind was a barren face of pits and gullies perhaps half a mile across.
Plumes of dust whipped free and fled in the wind. Nothing green, nothing alive, could be seen on its whole foreboding expanse. The mountain
looked freshly destroyed, as though it had happened that morning.

"My God!" Gerry muttered. "If the slides above put such big cataracts in the river, this must've filled the canyon up with waterfalls!"

Our view of the meeting place of the mountain and the river was blocked by a curtain of low embankments; we couldn't see what had happened at river level. Expecting trouble, we followed the river along its twisting course to the mountain. But when we finally saw where the eroding face plunged into the water, to our surprise, barely a ripple stirred. A small rapid at the tail end of the mountain was the river's sole acknowledgment of the catastrophe. And yet the demon had probably precipitated the whole thing by undercutting.

We speculated that the slide—and who knows when it occurred?—had consisted of clay and rock so fine that it had been washed away in the floods. I estimated that at least 100 million tons of debris had poured into the river, and maybe ten times that much. It is all in Amazonia now, or on the delta at the edge of the ocean.

The end of a mountain—faster than most.

The harshness of the canyon began to relent, and human influence crept back, in hesitating steps. A dozen miles below the Pampas, a trail cut down one hillside and up the other. We found a cable and a balsa raft where travelers crossed. Just below a youngster, fourteen or so, stood on a cliff, looking ready to flee. We coaxed him down to the river. "Do you want some bananas?" the youth offered.

Starved for fresh food, we chorused "Yes! Where can we find them?"

"Nearby!"

Three of us beached and followed the boy up the hillside. Big cactus plants dotted the slopes, with trees and thorn-clad bushes scattered between. I stopped to watch a herd of goats being let out of a corral. Then barefoot children erupted from the small house adjacent to the corral. They brought with them three large and magnificent dogs—perhaps livestock guard dogs. They were a far cry from the typical mongrels of the Andes! Well-groomed and well-fed, light-brown in color, one looked like it might have been a purebred Anatolian shepherd, a large guard dog from Turkey. This dog was someone's anomalous but proud possession in a land of toil and poverty. I thought I might go ask the children where the dogs had come from, but then I thought better of it. The dogs' dispositions were—after all—unknown. Most

243

dogs in these mountains are aggressive and yappy, but too small to be a threat. These weren't. I let them disappear in peace over the hill, following the goats.

Gerry and Chuck had gone on toward the promised banana patch, so I returned to the river to wait. They went quite some distance and were gone over an hour. Nearby, indeed! But the bananas were worth the wait!

At 4:00 that afternoon we came to a long rapid, which at the end curved around a bend to the right. Beyond the bend the river bored into low cliffs and plunged into an enormous cataract. It was an awesome scene, so much water pouring through the broken chutes. It was one of the most violent floods of water on the Apurímac. We beached and made camp. The next day we would face the portage. We had gone about 20 miles that day, thus moving another increment ahead of schedule.

This place, too, was coming under human influence. Some workmen were clearing brush from a slope above the river. A sugarcane plantation would arise here if everything went according to plan.

At dusk a Quechua Indian and his son—maybe twelve years old—arrived at our camp. We had no language in common, but we motioned them to share our campfire. We exchanged food: our nuts, sausage, and tea for a large portion of their cooked cassava root. They rolled out two blankets and prepared to stay the night.

I crawled into my tent to sleep at 8:30. I had been unusually tired, probably from the sustained stresses of the trip. It seemed so long ago that it had started, so far away, so different a land. Only the river played a constant theme. The night air resonated with the roar of impassable rapids.

On day thirty, we were awakened by rain while it was still pitch dark. A small puddle of rainwater deepened in the corner of my tent, which was not waterproof enough to keep out tropical downpours. Finally the day dawned gray. We started a fire with some difficulty and came alive with hot tea. I reflected on the inconvenience of the primitive life and hardships we faced daily and wrote in my journal: "We live here in a world without common conveniences. We have only lightweight tents and clothing, simple medical supplies, cooking pots, flashlight, repair materials, and the like. But our new friends, the Quechua Indians, have only their blankets, a cooking pot, and some food. It is four in the morning and has been raining two hours. I can imagine them out there, huddled in their wet blankets. Yet it must always be so for them—lack of shelter and even simple medical supplies. They have almost nothing, and our limited supplies seem rich by comparison."

We started the portage early, through a field of rocks and up over an embankment of cliffs with downsloping shelves to the water. Everyone seemed to be in so much of a rush that I had no opportunity to photograph the Indians fishing down by the main waterfall. The struggle with gear lasted almost two hours. I arrived already tired, the last to start. Jim had waited, and we proceeded down the canyon. Gerry joined us.

We worked through three or four enormous rapids, then the river began to ease up. Soon we arrived at an overhead cable—an aroya—with a wheeled conveyance for transport across the river. We were nearing the final staging site of Michel Perrin's tragic expedition.

. . . the tranquil waterway leading to the uttermost ends
of the earth flowed sombre under an overcast sky—
seemed to lead into the heart of an immense darkness.

Joseph Conrad

Deep, dark and cold the current flows,
Unto the sea where no wind blows,
Seeking the land which no one knows.

Ebenezer Elliot

≈ CANYON OF TRAGEDY

HACIENDA CHAPI WAS SOMEWHERE above us, hidden in the folds of the hills. In Perrin's time, Chapi was the last outpost on the western slope of the valley of the Apurímac, above the settlements of the jungle. The cobweb of trails that laced the hills and connected the pueblos had no known strands through the canyon to the sylvan land below. So it was that Perrin, weary with frustration, came to Chapi to resume his voyage. It would have to work this time, because no overland routes of travel down the canyon remained.

Michel Perrin and Teresa Gutiérrez had left Pasaje, higher up in the Apurímac Canyon, on July 31, 1953. Defeated a second time by the river, they struggled down the canyon on muleback and on foot. They crossed the Apurímac by raft, swimming the mules behind on a tether. Here they gained the right bank and, avoiding the deep canyon of the gorge, followed a trail high above the Apurímac, back in the hills. They passed through one settlement after another: Pacaypata, Piquipata, San Martín. No one would give or sell them food, and they nearly starved. They crossed the tributary Mapillo Grande, which we had passed the day before. Then they proceeded to Hacienda Huarancalpi, where a kind family, the Rosas, took them in and fed them. They, like the others, said the Apurímac was navigable below.

"You can descend safely," they assured the worn travelers.

Perrin and Gutiérrez turned now toward the Apurímac, embedded in the stone of its canyon over 6 miles away. They reached the river and camped on a sandy beach, then discharged their guides and mules. They were alone again with the demon river. "At this point," Perrin wrote, "the river is as wide as the Oise, as swift and deep as the Rhône, as encased as the Verdon. A torrent, but on the American scale which multiplies everything." He added that compared to stretches above, "Its violence is unimpaired . . . its turbulences are only more powerful." But Perrin would not relent in his quest; they prepared to embark the next day. Teresa gave him her trust.

Three times they attempted to launch. Each time the boat filled with water and had to be brought to shore and emptied. Alongside one of the rapids, Perrin waded and floundered with the boat in tow, Teresa seated inside. In another he sat astride the boat, guiding it through the shallows. Progress was slow.

At 4:00 they heard a tumultuous noise and pulled to the bank. The rapid ahead was long, unrunnable. Days would be required to carry their boat and gear over the rocks on its shore to reach its other end. Once again they were defeated. Once again they had been deceived into believing that the Apurímac was tranquil. But now a net of circumstances tightened around them. They could not go back, for the route was blocked by walls and rapids. They must somehow continue in the direction of the river.

They decided to strike an overland route toward Chapi, now some 3 to 5 miles away in the hills down the canyon. They began to climb out of the gorge, but their path was soon blocked by cliffs and thorns. They tried another place the next day, and were turned back again. An attempt to go up a stream bed failed. They were trapped now in the canyon, unable to go forward or backward. That night they sat around a fire, pondering their fate and their hopelessness.

Then Teresa said a strange thing: "We will probably get out of this somehow, because I have a feeling that we will encounter worse things further downstream . . ."

The next morning they awoke to hear strange voices on the beach. Three Quechuas had followed an obscure path through the growth and the tangle of the canyonside on a once-monthly sojourn to tend some fields. The voyagers raced after the natives, learning the secret of the trail. Soon they were on their way to Chapi. They arrived at the hacienda on August 9.

At Chapi they were received by one Miguel Carrillo, member of a prominent Lima family who owned the hacienda. He was a muscular, somber man, who claimed to possess wide knowledge of the river and its rapids. Slowly an atmosphere of tension and distrust developed between Carrillo and Perrin. Carrillo was overbearing, never wrong. Inexplicably he sent Perrin to the river alone to recover the kayak and gear, and Perrin came to suspect that Carrillo had done so in order to be alone with Teresa and to make advances toward her. He later thought Carrillo sought revenge for her rebuff.

Over the next few days, the explorers prepared their gear and began planning for the next stage of their adventure. One choice was to go far inland, away from the river, on a long safe journey to a Benedictine mission in the jungle called Simariva, down where the river was flat. But Carrillo thought little of the idea.

"From Simariva, the Apurímac is not terribly interesting," Carrillo said. "It is known fairly well. What is unknown is the passage from here to Simariva. The river has been run in this stretch, but only by natives who don't know what to look out for, never by an explorer. . . . I can help you."

Carrillo then described the canyon. He detailed how he would find native balseros to go along in a raft and carry equipment; how he would provide food. He presented his plan for navigation. They would start from Mandor, a beach down the valley from Chapi. From there they would navigate the river to the Canyon of the Donkey, reputedly impassable. The balseros would help cut a path around by machete. The rest would be simple. Carrillo then sought to scatter the hardened caution that had grown in Perrin from the deceptions, misinformation, and near disasters upstream.

"The trip will be easy," he assured. "There are no more chutes, no more blockades, not a single difficult passage except for a canyon much further downstream, two days navigation. . . . After Mandor, the river is so calm that a seaplane was landed down there two years ago."

Carrillo's arguments were made with an air of conviction and sincerity, so that the two explorers were won over to his plan and the generosity of his offer. After all, had they not come to explore the river?

Some days later, on August 14, they descended to the river at Mandor and established camp on the beach. But the river told them it was not yet dead. Perrin wrote:

> Two familiar threats could be heard: a rapid above and a rapid below.
>
> "This doesn't look much different from what I have been looking at for the past months," I say to Carrillo.
>
> "It's the last rapid and it's not a bad one," he answers. "You can go through without fear. Afterwards there is nothing but river all the way to the Canyon [of the Donkey]."

The day of the Assumption broke over the canyon. Elsewhere in the world it was the day to feast in honor of the reception of the Virgin Mary into heaven. At Mandor it was the day of the river, a day to start by adding balsa logs to the raft to strengthen it for the support of the journey. It was to start as a day of happiness—of realization—for Michel Perrin and Teresa Gutiérrez. It was the day to launch.

At 4:00 the kayak bore the two explorers out onto the water, and the raft followed, carrying three balseros and a mound of equipment.

At the first rapid, Teresa was put ashore to film the passage and remain clear of any danger. The balseros lined the raft down the side. They were past the rapid by 5:00. Teresa reboarded. Perrin guided the kayak over calm water behind the raft. Before long they noticed the raft pulled over on the left shore. The balseros, who spoke Quechua and not Spanish, signaled a rapid ahead.

"Another one?" Perrin wondered. "Carrillo had said that the one I had negotiated . . . was the last one. . . . He undoubtedly never mentioned the one I am facing right now because of its insignificance."

They drifted forward, assured by Carrillo's authority that there was no rapid, increasingly alarmed by the strength of the waves that seemed to grow bigger in front of them. Teresa refused a last opportunity to go ashore. They accelerated into the lively current that prefaces every rapid and passed the point where the current was so strong that they could never return.

"At the center of the river, a dorsal spine, a wall of crests of waves, toward which we are swept irresistibly. Two feet high, no three, no four or five; a liquid curtain boiling and menacing. We are swept there broadside. I realize that for the first time in the trip we would capsize—I find myself in the water, near the kayak, its keel in the air."

Teresa, rigid with fear, had become trapped in the overturned boat. Three times Perrin dived beneath the surface to free her.

"I am horrified," he wrote. "I am blinded by the surrounding waters which gallop by in a furious, foaming torrent."

He finally got her loose, but then she clung to him and pulled him under. He kicked her free and got her arms up on the keel, where she could cling and breathe. They passed over another drop. This time the boat was ripped from Perrin's grasp. He was thrown against a rock, then pulled by the current so deep beneath the water that it became dark. He came to the surface only to be drawn under again, to be tumbled and drenched by the walls of water.

"I struggle not to die. . . ," he wrote, but moments later, on the brink of hopelessness, "I have no strength left. I let myself go."

"The thoughts stream through my head at an increasingly rapid pace. . . . Her life vest will bring her out of it providing she does not lose her breathing rhythm. Where is she? Is this never going to end? It takes too long, much too long. Is this the way death strikes . . ."

Finally the water cast Perrin, half-dead, up on the left shore. Slowly he regained consciousness, aware of his continued existence but realizing that Teresa was no longer with him. He looked out on the river for her, but she was gone; she had continued the voyage that they both had dreamed of. It was her last.

Perrin, not knowing Teresa's fate, searched for her from shore, then from Chapi. The quest was hindered by obstacles of terrain and the walls that guarded the secrecy of the river. The search party got as far down as a big tributary called Río Pampaconas, but they did not find Teresa.

Perrin, filled with bitterness toward Carrillo's deception, returned to Lima. There he arranged transportation to Teresita, a jungle outpost 60 miles below Chapi, near Simariva. From there he struggled upriver against the current and the jungle. The tortures of heat, ants, rapids, cliffs, and jungle growth beset him, but his resolve to find Teresa was unbendable. Nearly two weeks later, he again reached the Río Pampaconas, where the search from Chapi had ended.

The remains of Teresa were finally found drifting aimlessly in an eddy of the Apurímac near its confluence with the Pampaconas. A companion brought the news to Perrin. They buried her on the bank of the river.

Michel Perrin has explored great sweeps of the earth since Peru, but his memories of the tragedy on the Apurímac still burn. In a letter written to me he stated, "The tragic events related to my expedition have been, and still are, the most important thing in my life. . . . The few autochthons [natives] who helped me to give a sepulture to Teresa Gutierrez told me, after having performed some superstitious rite, that that would bring punishment on the perpetrator of her death. A few years ago I was informed that on the occasion of a local revolt of his 'peones' (or serfs), Miguel Carrillo had been arrested, brought before a popular tribunal, condemned for a number of crimes, and put to death on the spot."

The cable beneath which we lingered was at the end of the trail from Chapi, where Perrin and the others had descended the hills to the river. We drifted into a stretch of calm water that followed the cable crossing. Soon we passed through a small rapid and saw three men standing on a beach. One prepared a lasso to pull us from the grip of the river.

We stopped and found that the three were cane cutters from Cuzco. They offered us pieces of a cake of brown sugar that they carried for food. One of them showed us how he had intended to rescue us as we floated by helplessly. He had remembered the tragedy of Teresa. I asked them about the incident, and they responded with considerable knowledge. They confirmed that the expedition had started at the trail above. One of them motioned to the next rapid, half a kilometer away, where low cliffs emerged again, and said, "that is the place where the girl drowned."

I asked more questions to make sure that I had understood and translated them correctly. Then we climbed back in our boats. In my journal I wrote: "We advance to the tragic rapid under an overcast sky. From the far right bank I take pictures of my companions descending two by two, and I think of the two unfortunates in that frail craft of Perrin's twenty-two years ago. It is a big rapid although not a giant cataract like those we have seen above. At the center, past the main drop, it divides past a prow-shaped rock, then, shortly, over another drop. It occurs in a rather restricted canyon, walled by low cliffs. This is a depressing place when the sky is so gray."

We continued through a low-walled canyon that was swept by currents and waves. Here Teresa had drifted off into oblivion. If she was still alive during that stretch, it would have been starkly terrifying—to be alone, a stranger to the motions and hydraulics of rivers, washed from one rapid to the next through an unknown land. The drops she encountered were sizable, despite Miguel Carrillo's assurance that all water was calm below. Our boats were rocked repeatedly by 8-foot-high waves.

Suddenly, we felt the sweet breath of jungle. Above us we had found thick vegetation only in pockets, but here it rooted everywhere. The canyonsides turned green, in an endless sheet of leaves and blades bent to the contours of rock. Trees and vines, mosses and epiphytes, shrubs and bamboo—their profusion cloaked the land. Orchids glowed from the trees. Strange sounds and smells entranced us, and parrots quarreled overhead.

New tributaries joined the Apurímac. Some tumbled down over cliffsides in streams unbroken and as smooth as ribbons of sand. Silent alcoves oozed water, grew moss, harbored rainbow butterflies.

At 4:00 we spotted a grass-thatched hut overlooking the river from a knolltop high on the right bank. No one was home. We waited awhile on the beach below, hoping to see the occupants, but the hills kept their silence.

It was still early, but we decided to camp there. We had gone another 10 miles that day. We were ahead of schedule on this leg of the journey as on every segment preceding it. Our odyssey would end in a few days. This magnificent land, and this incredible adventure, were slipping through our fingers much too fast.

After kindling a fire on the beach, we ate dinner and prepared our tents for the night. That evening Dee announced that he would push on by himself in the morning. He didn't say much else, nor did anyone argue. He simply expressed his dissatisfaction with the pace of the trip and his desire to get done with the canyon.

Our voyage would not be much different without him. He had not stayed with us much on the river. We would not significantly lose the strength of our numbers, because we had not worked well together in any event.

At dusk the family from above came to visit, curiosity having conquered fear. They had evidently decided that our actions carried no mark of aggression or ill intent toward them. They stepped timidly onto the beach, where we greeted them warmly. With them they bore a blanket; they spread it open on the sand and motioned us to take the bananas—delicious bananas!—they had carried in it from their garden. We gave them nuts, matches, and nylon cord in return.

253

Jim showed them how to whip the frayed ends of the cord by melting them with a match. They stared in fascination, but their faces clouded over when he cautioned them by means of gestures not to burn themselves on the hot nylon.

They were a family of five, a man, a woman, two boys, and a mongrel dog. They were small, meek, unpretentious people, aglow with smiles. They spoke a native tongue, but always talked in subdued tones, as if they were afraid the hills would hear. Although the man mumbled one or two words in Spanish, verbal communication was not possible. We used gestures and pictures scratched in the sand.

The man wore a tattered shirt, patched together from rags. A cloth belt held up threadbare pants. He wore leather sandals, and his felt hat was brimless, like an inverted flower pot sloping over his forehead and neck. From beneath it gleamed big, dark eyes and features both striking and charismatic. The wide grin on his face revealed a gap of lost front teeth. He stood no more than 5 feet all.

The woman, shorter still, wore a blue sweater and a full skirt. Her hat was of felt, but wide-brimmed. Her face was cut of soft lines, rather pretty.

The older son, about thirteen, looked like his mother. He wore a woven cap and an almost new shirt, yellow- and black-checked flannel. His oversized pants were held up and cinched in by a thin leather belt. They had probably been his father's.

The younger child was five. He was dressed in sweater and pants, and wore a woven hat with ear flaps—a type common high in the mountains, but rare in the jungle.

The man muttered "Quechua" and thus identified their roots. They were descendants of the highlands. But when, how, and why had he—or his ancestors—migrated here, to this solitary plot in the jungle canyon? To a land hot, rainy, and perpetually green, like another planet beside his ancestral home in the heights beyond the haze of the hills. We could not ask and would never know.

As darkness approached they departed our beach abruptly, showing all at once tenseness and fear. They melted into the forest as silently as they had come. It grew so dark we could not see them mount the trail where it led through the open garden at the foot of the knoll beneath their hut. The nights for the people of this land are full of strange sounds and unfathomed meaning. The family above us would reach their shelter and huddle together behind its thin veneer of grass and poles, while their little mongrel dog became their ears and eyes.

I wrote: "A gentle, generous family—seeming so shy, so small, so frail to contend with this untamed land. We hope to visit them tomorrow, to learn more of their means of existence in this canyon environment. Our location has been getting steadily more remote . . . it is a canyon wilderness as far from the influence of civilization as one is ever likely to encounter. We hope to learn how people have adapted to this in comparison to the supercivilization from which we come."

It rained all night. It was not a driving rain, but just a fluctuating drizzle that never fully stopped. My tent was like a sieve in the face of so persistent a rain. Patches of wetness grew on my tent floor, soaked into my clothing. At first I felt around for the driest spots to lie on, then said to hell with it and went back to sleep. In the warmth of the jungle night it didn't really matter. Being wet here was only a nuisance, not the agony of sleepless shivering that it would have been above, in the cold of the highlands.

The Quechua family came to visit us before the full light of day. The five of them trudged out onto our beach (rather, their beach) and opened the blanket once more. Within were more bananas and a papaya. We reciprocated this time with safety pins, rubber bands, aluminum pans, plastic bags, and margarine. Then we attacked the papaya.

Overnight the family's curiosity had grown to the point of explosion. They advanced now from tent to tent, looking inside, feeling the materials, inspecting every contrivance. Each object would be turned over, around, or inside out, followed by moments of vacant staring. At such times I could sense their imagination spinning out through space to another world.

Then they turned their attention to the boats. The highlander, in an impulse of humor, slipped on a helmet, seized a paddle, and pretended to paddle away. We all laughed. Everyone was in good spirits and totally warm.

The family then asked us, in the "language" we had developed, to visit their home. We stepped into the margin of jungle and walked through the banana grove, beyond the young papaya trees, and across rows of vegetables and some plants I didn't recognize. Up farther and steeper now, climbing and slipping on a practically vertical trail worn to mud that led to their hut on the top of the hill.

The Quechua home was a simple and crude shelter held up by poles, thatched on top. It had no walls. Without walls the family would be drenched by blowing rain and frightened more by night sounds, but they would not get cold; they had left behind the chill of the highlands. On muggy days they would welcome the crossbreeze blowing over the knoll.

The scene we saw within was one of shocking austerity: a cowhide lying stiffly on the floor for a bed, two worn blankets, cooking pots and a garden tool, corn drying beneath the eaves, two small animal skins. And last we saw, beneath the gables and strangely out of place, a small rectangular bottle bearing a label that looked very old and read "Sloan's Liniment." It was half-full of some unknown liquid, which in all probability, was not liniment nor anything else from the outside world. I still can't conceive of where that bottle might have come from, unless it washed down to them on the river and survived the rapids.

One of the animal hides, or shells, hanging from the eaves had once belonged to an armadillo. The other looked like a ringtailed cat. We pointed to them and asked where they came from. The man beamed and pointed at their mongrel and was saying with his eyes, "he caught them," or, "he treed them." That little dog was a proud fifth member of the family.

But of course, their gain was our loss, and maybe their loss too, in the long run. I had seen no wildlife since the eyes in the night, and higher up the fox and an otter. The people in the valleys and hills killed what wildlife they could see and catch, or if they had a gun, what they could hit. On the whole journey I never saw a wild mammal near any human habitation.

It was time to leave. The four of us returned to the beach with the Quechuas; Dee had departed earlier that morning. Now we folded, stuffed, and organized our own gear for departure and hauled it down to the boats by the water. The Quechuas followed our every move.

I kneeled beside my boat and began to load gear, piece by piece. Near me on the sand I had a widemouthed plastic bottle, in which I had put my daytime supplies: lunch, knife, repellent, film, matches. It was a discarded gallon pickle jar, perfect for my purposes. It would go in last, directly behind my seat, where I could quickly get to it. The woman, who had been watching me, kneeled too, picked up the container, inspected it, fondled it. A longing developed in her eyes of a depth I had never seen. She pointed to the jar, then to herself.

"Can I have it?" her eyes said.

I thought about it a moment. It was a programmed part of my gear. Without it my lunch would have to squeeze into the camera bag, and I would have to make room by taking out my tripod and lenses and putting them in the overnight bag. But the overnight bag was already fastened shut; it would be too inconvenient.

"No," I said in our language. "I'm sorry, I need it."

Rarely have I regretted a decision so much. I often think of that gentle Quechua woman and the way she looked at me and pleaded with her eyes. I remember how she caressed the plastic, gently turned the lid. A simple plastic bottle. So rare a treasure for her, so abundant in the overflow of our dumps.

And so we left the gentle family of the Apurímac. We left them to their toil and their harvest; to follow the clock of sun and rain. We left them to whatever ancestral traditions directed their steps and their fears. We left them to get along without medicines, without books, without formal education. We left them in their smallness and frailty to face the wildness of the canyon. We left them to get along alone.

Yet in self-sufficiency was their strength; they and others like them have created a society that can endure forever. They use no fossil fuels, sicken no one with pollution. They need no steel plants, no copper ore. They require no bulldozers, for their garden is contoured to the land, a part of ancient hills. Their world can survive as it is; ours cannot. It is our world—wallowing in a wealth built on sandcastles of wasted resources—that must change. Our children and grandchildren are the ones who must face the shocking transition to a new society.

I think I would as soon have my children roaming free in those hills as facing the nuclear-fossil uncertainty of Western civilization. Perhaps someday collective society will strike a middle ground, one in which the poor Quechua woman can have her plastic bottle, but in which we do not burden the earth with ours.

A vigorous current drove us down the river. Small waterfalls tumbled over walls flecked green and black with moss. The jungle intensified its grip on the land. (*See* Plate 11)

We reached a cable crossing that we surmised led to Osambre, a fabled hacienda in the mountains. The 1970 British expedition had rested there, calling it a "Garden of Eden." Refreshed, they came down to cross the river, probably at this spot. Osambre had been hewn from the jungle by a legendary Norwegian-Peruvian named Berg, around 1945. He had helped Perrin in his search for Teresa in 1953. The three cane cutters from Cuzco had told us the day before that Señor Berg had succumbed only recently to a heart attack. This had stifled our desire to hike the long trail up to Osambre. We hoped as we passed that this garden of Eden would not spiral into the decay we had found at Pasaje.

Much of the morning went by in a shallow gorge. The demon, it seemed, could not shake off its tradition of gorges, even in the jungle. But here it had created a gorge of beauty, not terror. The river was encased in 30-foot-high cliffs, polished smooth by floods. Trees and vines clung to its rim. The water flowed black with depth, hurrying softly in tumbling undulations—a magic carpet through wonderland.

We reached the Pampaconas River at about noon. It raced into the Apurímac from the right, through a shallow bank of gravel, bringing maybe 1,000 cubic feet per second of new water to the swelling Amazon. With the water came another flood of thick silt. The Apurímac—still light brown from the assault of Río Pampas waters—now became gray and ugly, covered with flotsam and froth. No trace remained of the mountain freshness we knew so well. It was just another dirty jungle river.

The rapid below the Pampaconas was the biggest of the day. Enormous crests broke down the left side of the river, but the channel was unobstructed, exhilarating to run.

Later we entered another shallow canyon. The water tore through at a ferocious pace, up to 10 miles per hour. Little alcoves in the walls formed quiet eddies, sheltered from the mad rush of current. This gorge fit the description given by Perrin of the Cañon de Asnorotcha, Canyon of the Donkey. Incredibly, he and a Campa Indian named

Polycarpo had worked a balsa raft up this canyon in the search for Teresa. At this point they inched from alcove to alcove, hugging the cliffs, clawing at rock for shreds of leverage against the current. Only to find Teresa dead above.

We left behind now the canyon where Teresa Gutiérrez had faced her ultimate torment—and reached her final peace.

The Campas [are] the largest and historically most important tribal group in the Peruvian montaña.

The demons of the river . . . live in the whirlpools and bad passes of the river, where they wait to drown and eat voyagers passing by.

It is the main river system flowing through Campa territory that gives orientation to Campa notions of geography. The only general directional terms for the surface of the earth are katónko (upriver) and kirínka (downriver).

Gerald Weiss

≈ CAMPA LAND

W E WERE NOW ENTERING the land of the Campa Indians, but the casual visitor to this region does not see much of the wealth of Campa culture. The Campa mind closes like a clamshell to outsiders. Truth to tell, the Campas have never been given much reason to trust us. Like other native peoples of the Americas, much has been stolen away and little given back to them since the white man came. They continue to be uprooted by the endless encroachment of our civilization.

The family of Arawak languages occupies a crescent swath from the lower Apurímac eastward into Brazil, then northward to Venezuela and the Caribbean. The Campa Indians make up a number of tribes speaking languages of the Arawak family. They represent the western extreme of Arawak influence: the far rim of the jungle against the mountains.

The time of Arawak settlement in Campa country is unknown. Presumably it was long ago, for their traditions contain nothing about immigration. To the contrary, their traditions teach that humankind was created in Campa land.

We were now approaching this navel of the world. Here I hoped to catch a glimpse of Campa adaptation to Western influence. But change cannot be fathomed unless one knows where it began, unless one knows the heritage of the tribe. Campa tribal knowledge is scattered in historical documents and mission reports. A recent monograph by Gerald Weiss (*Campa Cosmology*) has summarized Campa lore and has pushed back the horizons of knowledge of Campa customs. The perspective I give is largely adapted from Weiss.

The Campas, at least the tribe called the River Campas, dwell along the watercourses of the lower Apurímac and its extensions and tributaries downstream: the Ene, Perene, and Tambo. These rivers, though flatter than those above, are not yet sluggish, like the jungle rivers that dominate the expanse of Amazonia. They are still alive and thrashing with rapids as they emerge from the Andes; they still run through valleys and canyons rimmed by mountains. This canyon setting distinguishes Campa geography from that of the bulk of Amazonian tribes.

Rarely is a culture so dominated by a rapidly flowing river. The Campas live on its bank, listen to the music of its motion, navigate its whirlpools and rapids in balsa rafts, catch fish from its waters, and grow crops on its alluvial soils. Their focus is so exclusively on the river that it has come to rule their concept of the surface of the earth. The world, in Campa belief, is defined by two cardinal points. Intatóni is where the river begins, and Ocitiríko is where it ends—where it falls through a hole in the earth. The only directions recognized in the land between are those oriented either to or from these poles: *katónko* means "upriver," toward Intatóni, while *kirínka* is "downriver," toward the hole. The passage of time, too, is often described in terms of the river. The principal seasons are the cycles of wet and dry. The rainy season, *komohánci*, derives from another Campa word meaning "big water."

As if the flow of the Apurímac were not enough to dominate the mind, the Campa have invented a river flowing in the sky. It is an invisible stream, filled with fish. It is called Hananerite, River of Eternal Youth. It is where the good spirits bathe to maintain their immortality.

The Campa world overflows with spirits, demons, and gods; much of the Weiss monograph is spent describing them. They have remarkable powers of invisibility, transformation, flight, and strength. The human soul joins the spirits upon death. The spirits acquire visibility clothed in the bodies of birds, animals, plants, insects, and so on. They may be seen in lightning, heard in thunder. They crowd the earth, the sky, and the mountain ridges. They are everywhere.

Nor do the spirits neglect the river. Sacred birds and others reside at Ocitiríko. They clear away the logjams with their great strength. They burn the debris, and the smoke can be seen coming up the canyon. The spirits own the fish as well. Each year after the big water, they bring the fish upriver for the Campa.

The evil spirits—the demons—are as numerous as the good spirits, but they hover more ominously, posing a constant threat of illness and accident. They are found everywhere, some of them infesting the rivers. The elite among them, the Mankóite, inhabit the cliffs and outcrops above the waterways. Two of the river demons are Impositóniro and Sonkatiníro. They lurk in the whirlpools and the rapids along the river, where they wait to drown and eat Campa voyagers. Comvuníro, another river demon, has for a stomach a large shoulder bag, into which he puts the souls of the drowned. Their bodies are discarded to the buzzards. Kacivoréri is a demon of a different stripe. It is out flying on the rivers at night, a small black creature dripping blood, emitting a strange light. It is a powerful demon and will attack humans. It is much feared by the Campas.

The most powerful of the spirits are the Campa gods. The sun is the supreme god of the universe. The moon, too, is a god. In these latter respects, Campa belief parallels Inca belief.

The god that most deeply intrigues me—and that bears direct influence on Campa adaptation to Western technology—is called Inka. With Inka, we discover how the Campas maintain their pride, their ethnocentricity, in the face of a superior foreign technology. Inka clearly followed the Spanish to Campa land, but the Campas think he came much earlier. According to the Campas, he is a technological genius. He once ruled the land of the Campas. When the whites came, they produced a great flood from below. Inka saved himself on a raft and drifted into white captivity. There he was held at river's end and forced to manufacture goods for his captors.

According to Weiss, "*Inka* remains a captive downriver to this day, wishing to return to his people but restrained by the Caucasians. If he ever did return, the existing relationship between Campa and Caucasian would, of course, be reversed."

Jungle clearings and grass-thatched huts became common below the Canyon of the Donkey. Most were a few hundred yards above the river, on inclined shelves clinging to the canyonside. As we passed, a vacuum of silence descended over the canyon. We saw no one working the sloping patches of fields, no one by the huts, no one on the river bank. No smoke emerged above the thatch. No life was apparent anywhere. Had the people somehow known of our coming and fled? Or was it a dormancy forced by the heavy warmth of the afternoon air?

Our disappointment at the silence grew. Somewhat exasperated, we stopped at one hut near the right bank. No one. Then we walked up a jungle trail to a neighboring hut. It too was cold, unoccupied. We paddled on, wondering if we would see any of the natives of the canyon.

Toward the end of the afternoon, we saw some huts on a high beach, then a few human figures farther down the river. We paddled past the huts, toward the figures. I glanced back and saw several women and girls, who had emerged from the huts to stare at us. They stood out like beacons. The brilliant red colors of their clothing blazed strikingly against the dull shades of the endless jungle. The figures below were those of a Campa Indian and his three sons. A crude balsa raft was pulled up beside them on the beach.

The man had thick black hair—not long—and a short beard. A red stripe had been painted high on each cheek. His clothing was old and torn, dull in color, Western in style. I would guess the boys to have been about eight, twelve, and fourteen years old. They were barefoot, shirtless, dressed in tattered pants.

Two women walked slowly, hesitantly, down the beach from the hut. Their clothing made up for the shreds on the males. The older woman wore a shin-length skirt of scarlet red, encircled by two white bands at knee height. Her blouse was brilliant rose pink, full-sleeved, bearing a design of blues and reds at the neck. Two red dashes marked her cheeks, beneath a canopy of black hair. The younger woman, perhaps still in her teens, was similarly dressed, but her skirt was blue-gray, her blouse scarlet. She wore a necklace of beads.

The bright clothing stood in stark contrast to the unexpressive manner of its owners. I handed the woman some safety pins, and she reached out and took them without a smile, without any gesture of acknowledgment. They stood motionless for minutes on end, hands folded across their chests, staring vacantly down the river. Only the boys seemed capable of some joviality.

They made no attempt to communicate. The Quechua Indians we had met above had told us their story of survival, largely by gestures and expressions, but these people told us nothing.

Some spark of Andean hospitality finally won out in the end. One of the boys brought us some cassava and, later, some bananas.

A Campa Indian family on the shore of the Apurímac. ≈

We continued down the canyon. Around a bend, and rather unexpectedly, a stunning change broke the horizon. Fold after fold of dark forest rolled away from the riverbank and was lost to a hazy, distant obscurity. Craggy mountains erupted from the distant green hills. Their stone faces were streaked with clouds, illuminated by fingers of sunlight. We blinked in disbelief at the expanse, like prisoners emerging from a dark dungeon.

We had been buried in canyons for weeks. Here and there glacial pinnacles had peered at us over the rimrock. We had seen no distant mountain, no far-off forests. Not since Choquequirao had we seen the land flow unbroken from the cut of the river to the mountain crests. It was a welcome sight for canyon-weary travelers.

We hauled in at a beach opposite the vista. Film clicked through the cameras. And then we set up camp. As soon as I had landed, I began eating. My appetite had grown uncontrollably. I felt perpetually hungry now. I often thought about food while paddling on the river. I had a hard time waiting for lunch stops. It required my entire resources of willpower to resist eating up my supply of candy bars, and especially the peanut-butter bars made for us by Iris Sindelar, Jim's wife. At home I almost never eat any kind of candy, but the demands of the trip had made their appeal incredibly magnetic.

While hunger grew, another annoyance relented. The black and yellow gnats that had plagued us from the beginning gradually disappeared from the scene. Other insects, flying ants and biting flies, entered the void, but they could not match the profusion and persistence of the gnats. We were better off for the exchange. We had seen only a few mosquitoes on the entire trip.

That night I wrote about a vacuum of knowledge as to our whereabouts: "We have passed beyond all reasonable maps and are having increasing difficulties in locating ourselves and identifying the distance remaining. Sooner or later we should encounter someone who speaks Spanish to inform us. Until then we will simply paddle down the jungle river and enjoy the extreme richness of its environs. It starts to rain again at 10:30 . . ."

The problem of our location was solved abruptly the next morning. We broke camp early and paddled around a bend through a substantial rapid. At its bottom was anchored an enormous wooden canoe. A 40-horsepower Evinrude outboard engine awaited the day's work—propelling the 50-foot cargo craft up and down the waterway. The river had suddenly become a commercial artery. The Apurímac was tamed at last!

The mighty river had started with over 5,000 meters (about 16,400 feet) to drop, and it had plunged down through most of them angrily. Its descent was over 80 percent done now, and it was beginning to mellow. It would roar again spottily in the jungle canyons below, but it was changing moods, preparing for its tranquil march across the continent to the Atlantic. The rapid above the canoe was in fact no larger than some below, but several big rocks divided the current, creating a difficult course for the awkward cargo canoes. They all stopped here.

"Here" was Quillabamba. "Here" was the upper reach of civilization, almost literally the end of the road. Quillabamba was a village of bamboo walls and thatched roofs, lying at the edge of a peanut field on the wide west bank of the river. It looked clean and cared for. The people were well-clothed and spoke Spanish. They wore Western clothing. No one appeared hungry. Altogether there was an aura of prosperity to the settlement.

Quillabamba even had a small store. We had not seen a store near the river since Nayhua, nearly 200 miles above, and had bought nothing new since resupply in Cuzco. The monotony of our diet was making us irritable. Our eyes bulged at the sight of a store. Cold beer! Ice cream!

Manufactured goods had been carried by canoe up the river. Items such as flashlight batteries, soap, canned tuna, vermouth, and soda lined the shelves. Local items, such as sacks of cereal grains and beans, sat on the floor. But no beer—in fact, nothing cold. There was no electricity in the village. We drank warm soda in the stifling morning heat.

Quillabamba is an oasis of opulence in this land. That is, it is opulent by native standards. It was barely on the fringe of civilization for us. Suddenly we had entered a zone of colonization. All the land down the canyon was being cleared. Fires dotted the hillside as the jungle was turned to ashes and new fields were cultivated. All this broke the reign of one of the most intricate ecologies on earth.

Michel Perrin had said that these great jungle valleys would support 20 or 30 million people. He had said it twenty-two years before, when the Campas and the jungle ruled the land. We now saw an incredible momentum toward his prophecy. All along the river we would find new villages. Lechemayo was four years old. San Martín was ten. All were cut out of the virgin wilderness. Or, more accurately, they were cut out of Campa land. The Campas, the original inhabitants, were now being drawn into the inextricable web of civilization. Their story is that of primitive cultures all over our globe.

At noon Gerry and I spotted a fish trap and a crude shelter over near the right bank of the river. We paddled over. The fish traps here are like corrals into which fish are rounded up from the nearby shallows. A tight reed fence keeps them inside. A reed gate controls the movement of fish in and out.

These traps are built by Quechuas as well as by Campas, now that the Quechuas have invaded the canyon. They are often attended by one or more women. Sometimes the women sit on the shore talking or knitting; the lucky ones have a small shelter in which they can take refuge from sun and rain. These temporary shelters lie on beaches swept by yearly floods.

As we approached the fish trap, a Campa woman with a baby in her arms emerged from the shelter, alarmed at the sight of strangers. She clutched the baby under one arm and fled across the rock-studded beach toward the edge of the jungle. Soon she had melted into its foliage. Her flight was no surprise. Our arrival was abrupt, and our boats, clothing, and demeanor were strange. Yet there might have been a deeper reason. Campa myths held that whites are aquatic; their natural habitat was within the water, especially that in the lakes. To quote Weiss, "From one of these lakes the Spaniards emerged. The havoc they caused is . . . still remembered in Campa mythology."

"I'd like to see more of them," I told Gerry. "Maybe if we sit on the beach awhile, they'll come out of hiding." I paused, noted a characteristic feeling of emptiness in my stomach, then added, "It's lunchtime anyhow." Gerry agreed, and we paddled ashore to eat and wait.

In about an hour a man and a husky teenage boy stepped out of the jungle and walked toward us. We greeted one another, and the man surprised me with some broken Spanish. He asked about our origins and purpose, as all the rest had done.

We talked awhile, then I asked if we could visit his house. "No, I must return to my work." He disappeared back into the tangle of trees. I was surprised by his abruptness, so unlike that of other inhabitants of these parts. Here was a man halfway between two worlds—neocolonist and native Campa. His clothes and language spoke of his ragged adaptation to the new order. His customs and his family spoke of his roots in the old.

The teenager was thoroughly Campa. He spoke no Spanish. His hair was long, and he wore blue jeans with a large hunting knife tucked into his belt. A native shoulder pack was flung over a shredded flannel shirt. The youth walked over to the reed shelter to fold a fishing net. I busied myself taking pictures of this activity. Suddenly he motioned me to follow him into the jungle. Chuck, who had just come up, joined in.

There was no time to invite Jim and Gerry, who were down by the river.

The youth walked across the rough stones of the beach with an incredible gait. His steps were short, but they hammered after one another with lightning quickness. He sped into the jungle growth, followed a trail up a steep embankment, and emerged on a flat tableland overlooking the river. I followed, puffing and doubting. I had no idea where we were going or what his intentions were. We walked through a banana grove and emerged in Campa land. Here the jungle had been torn away to grow peanuts. The land beneath was still rough and uneven, broken by dead roots. It was still dotted with the trunks of jungle leviathans crudely hacked down, charred black by fire, bleached gray by sun and wind.

The Campa family lived in a spacious shelter at the edge of the peanut field. Their house was made of poles, thatched in coarse grass. There were no walls to hinder the breeze. Only women and children occupied the shelter when we arrived. We were seated in a corner and largely ignored. The children played on the dirt floor with sticks and other trifling items, casting occasional glances our way. One woman worked over a cooking pot and a fire pit at the far end of the shelter. She wore typical Campa clothes, but colored in pastel orange and green rather than glaring shades of red. A necklace of fang-shaped bones or teeth hung loosely around her neck.

The other woman, similarly dressed, was statuesque, endowed with refreshing Indian beauty. A few minutes after we arrived, she walked briskly out of the shelter, then strode out across the peanut field and disappeared in a maze of trees and tree trunks.

After a while she walked back. Following her at some distance was the man who had greeted us on the beach. Over his shoulder was slung a heavy field hoe. He had apparently been working, despite the heat of the day. I wondered what his reaction would be, finding us here in his home after refusing to let us visit a short while back. His cursory manner had suggested a distaste for strangers.

But his greeting took me aback. He welcomed us like long-lost friends—shook our hands and embraced us.

The woman disappeared again. This time she fetched a man who looked like a bearded guru, clothed in a cinnamon-colored garment that hung like a sack from his shoulders to his shins. He was a man of striking appearance and proud bearing. He sat on the ground among the children; he talked to them in Campa, holding them close and feeding them morsels of food.

The first woman brought us some cassava, which she had cooked in the giant pot. Later I asked the man with the hoe to show us how they cultivate and weed their peanut field. Both men walked out onto the sun-drenched field. The half-westernized man stood upright, chopping away weeds with his hoe. The man of strange dress—the aborigine—bent deeply toward the ground and thrust at weeds with a massive knife.

This family would make it. They were industrious. They were adaptable and adapting. They were responding to the siren call of civilization. They would soon merge with the mainstream of the valley, but their children would gradually lose their Campa traditions. Their grandchildren would no longer be Campas.

Other Campas will fail. They will retreat into the jungle. Civilization will grind after them. Finally there will be no place left to flee.

The Apurímac cuts deeply into the human soul. No one on its shores can escape its grip. It is not merely an element in fears, hopes, and conversations; it governs the course of human lives. In the high canyons, the river is a great barrier to free movement; its rapids and gorges cleave the world in two. People move freely in every direction over the land—across mountain ridges and deep valleys—but when they come to the riverbank, they must stop. Only rarely does a strand of cable or a bridge join together the two halves of their world.

In the jungle below Quillabamba, the river takes on a different role. Suddenly it is a link between people rather than a wedge dividing them. It is both highway and trail. Commerce and friendship float on it equally. Workmen cross it for employment. Markets grow closer. Centralized schools become practical. Wealth grows and people move in. The jungle and its traditions fall.

For the new culture, the river is a bright ribbon of progress. But for the Campas, whose roots in this valley go deep into the blackness of unrecorded antiquity, the change is shockingly fast. The Campas are Indians of the river. Forever they have sought nourishment in its water.

Now the Apurímac has brought progress that will destroy their river-based culture.

In another half-century, no one here is likely to remember how the Campas lived, loved, and dreamed over the millennia of their stewardship of the jungle and the river. Only in books—perhaps printed on pages pulped from the fallen jungle trees—will the mute statistics bear witness to their incredible reign.

A nd as I ate my supper by the fire I grieved for the clean
. . . country that I was leaving, for I knew, even then,
that nothing could ever bring back, or give again, the
wonder of that vanished summer.

R. M. Patterson

F ar better it is to dare mighty things, to win glorious tri-
umphs, even though checkered by failure, than to take
rank with those poor spirits who neither enjoy much nor
suffer much, because they live in the gray twilight that
knows not victory nor defeat.

Theodore Roosevelt

≈ LUISIANA

End of the Road

D AY THIRTY-THREE OF OUR EXPEDITION. The usual rain last night. Dogs came and barked outside our tents in the blackness.

Our beach soon became a thoroughfare. Workers passed up and down, staring curiously at our boats. In the river there were more balsas now. These were small rafts, maybe 4 meters long, slightly tapered forward, to form a rudimentary bow. They were made somewhat concave, so as to resemble a boat. They carried one or two workers—sometimes a small family. The balsero moved them up and down the river with only a pole.

We left our beach at 8:30, following the river into thickening civilization. Intermittent rapids still growled at the newly colonized world. The big cargo canoes, some 18 meters long, drove straight up through their midst. The balseros stayed clear. The 1970 British expedition had passed this way in a motorized canoe. They had trekked laboriously out of the hills to Villa Virgen, up near Quillabamba, and at this point had sped down the river in unaccustomed ease. They would follow the Amazon down to its mouth, at Belem. Michel Perrin had passed through here going upriver. Toiling against the currents and the shallows, long before the river was tamed by motors, he fought his way toward the canyons where Teresa had been lost.

We stopped for lunch by a long rapid. Soon a motorized aluminum boat churned up through its tailwaters, bouncing along the crests of waves. The owner saw us and swerved his craft out of the current and into an eddy nearby. We exchanged greetings. He wanted to buy one of our boats, but our selling was a little premature.

"How far to Luisiana?" I asked.

"Oh, only a half hour coming upriver in this boat. Maybe 6 or 7 kilometers . . ."

Another hour of paddling, some further inquiries, and we located Luisiana. It was beyond a wide gravel bar, hidden back in the trees. We drew ashore and beached our boats for the last time.

J im and I walked across the stony beach to the fringe of trees. A corridor hacked through the forest giants accommodated a dirt road leading to the main buildings. Here, then, was the farthest reach of the road upriver. Here was our ultimate goal, years in the making. Perhaps I should have knelt down to kiss it.

Instead, as we walked up the road, I felt uneasy. It was too wide for a trail. It was too straight and even. It lacked the intimacy with the jungle of native trails. It seemed out of place in this ancient, tribal valley. This was the beginning of the symptoms of withdrawal from a land where nature rules to one where she has been—temporarily—scorned and trampled.

We entered the hacienda's large clearing. As we approached the buildings, we spotted a swimming pool, and our eyes gleamed. Maybe we would be able to soak and relax in fresh, warm water. But no; as we drew closer, we saw that the pool was unfinished.

We met a worker, who escorted us to a large wooden building, ventilated on all sides with screens.

"Señor Parodi?" I asked, facing a tanned, mustached gentleman seated at a table.

"El mismo" (the same), he offered.

"We have come down the Apurímac River from Cunyac—and earlier from Pillpinto. We would like to stop here. We would like your help in getting out of the valley."

Señor Parodi rose to his feet, eyes afire. He had lived by this river for twenty-five years. He knew its moods. He had helped Michel Perrin organize the fruitless search for Teresa.

"That is fantastic!" he said. "Here, you must stay at my place. You will be my guest. Later we will arrange your transportation out."

We walked back to the beach for our other two companions and our boats. Bruised and battered, the boats would remain at Luisiana. Dee had gone on downriver without stopping.

J osé Parodi had hacked his way here through the jungle a quarter of a century ago. He had wrested Hacienda Luisiana from the vines and the trees. His was the first beachhead of commerce in the Apurímac Valley. Working with limited tools and supplies brought in with great

The bustling river city of San Francisco. ≈

difficulty, he established a waterwheel for electricity, a brewery, a distill-
ery, a marmalade facility, and a large farming operation. Now he was
building a resort complex.

In addition to his successes as a businessman, he had acquired a
reputation as an explorer and an adventurer. He had trekked to far-off
Apurímac tributaries, discovered waterfalls, unearthed Inca ruins. José
Parodi: effervescent, friendly, shrewd. One of the last of the true pio-
neers.

W e rested for two days. We slept in real beds and ate almost all of
José Parodi's food. Then we taught him to kayak in the fish pond.
Drenching fun.

On Saturday, the day after our arrival, Jim and I caught a ride with
one of José's workers to San Francisco. Here, 8 or so miles down the
river, was the raucous river town about which I had read. Here there

was a fiesta, a band in the street, a soccer game, and a round of bull-baiting in the soccer field. Across the soccer field we saw Dee. No one tried to make contact; we left the field without a word exchanged.

We walked out onto the bridge, a massive structure of steel and concrete. This river would not be spanned by another in its entire march across the lowlands of South America on its way to the Atlantic. From the railing we looked down on some cargo canoes clustered on the beach, bathed by late afternoon sun. Multicolored, ungainly in appearance, they looked small and insignificant against the backdrop of endless green hills. But tomorrow they would continue to play their part in changing them.

"It is 10 hours by road from here to Ayacucho," José explained. "It is rough. You may have to wait a few days to catch a ride. I can get a plane in here on Sunday. It will cost you 500 soles each."

That amounted to less than $12 per person, and it was hassle-free. We accepted at once.

On Sunday I penned my final journal entry:

We leave Luisiana . . . at 11 A.M., headed for Ayacucho, then Cuzco. The plane bounces noisily down the cleared canefield, and is aloft. Towering clouds cover the mountains to the left, between us and Ayacucho. These mountains, now eroded down to about 14,000 feet, leave the Apurímac in a wide gentle valley, its fight gone. Still, in total depth, it is . . . over 10,000 feet, for here the Apurímac flows less than 2,000 feet above the level of the sea.

And so we begin the long process of gaining elevation to get over the mountains and clouds. We fly way down the Apurímac Valley, creeping ever higher, over river, jungle, and dots of civilization. . . .

Down 30 miles to where the Montaro enters, and where these two giant rivers combine waters to form the Ene.

We are 11,000 feet high, and we make a broad, sweeping circle . . . to gain more elevation. Then, at the place where the Apurímac becomes diluted into another river and ends its official reign of the upper Amazon, we point toward the clouds, and this great river disappears from view. I shall never return.

For four years the Apurímac has held me spellbound—a giant, unnavigated canyon full of mysteries. 'Go and explore it,' my inner-self urged, 'go try the unheard-of.' And when I tried, I found a fascinating and strange people and vistas of beauty never seen before. And I found hard Andean rock and crashing water and almost unendurable toil.

Triumphant? No, not in the least. Humble. Thankful. More appreciative of the grandeur of our Earth.

Glad to be headed home!

APPENDIX 1

Apurímac, Inca River

THE MOST DISTANT WATERS of the Amazon River thaw reluctantly from a sweeping snowfield 17,000 feet high in the cold, thin air of the Andes of Southern Peru. The dripping meltwater soon becomes a tiny rivulet of clear water. From that point, the stream grows incessantly. It crosses a flat pampa between bare windswept hills. Then, at 13,000 feet, it begins one of the most spectacular descents of any river in the world. Slicing into the Vilcabamba Range of the Andes, pulsing through narrow gorges and unparalleled canyons, it crashes its way toward the jungle. It travels more than 4,000 miles before entering the Atlantic, a distance unrivaled by river water anywhere in the world except by that of the Nile, a close second.

The river in which this wild water flows is called the Apurímac. The name was given to the river in ancient times by the Indians of southern Peru. This river is great in its own right because of its magnificent deep canyons and its distinction of being the source of the Amazon. It gains further stature, or notoriety as the case may be, because it sliced and hacked its way through the core of the ancient Inca civilization, blocking expansion to the northern coast. The Río Apurímac thus had enormous influence on the development of Inca culture and the Inca empire.

The Apurímac has a sister river, the Urubamba, that follows a parallel but shorter course. Both start in the highlands and, heading generally northwest, cut canyons through the Vilcabamba Mountains.

The lofty strip of land between the Apurímac and the Urubamba Rivers was referred to as the "Cradle of the Incas" by Hiram Bingham, the American explorer. This "land between the rivers" begins as a barren highland plain, broken by rolling hills. Following the rivers, it descends to fertile tree-lined valleys, surrounded now by mountains of respectable but not spectacular proportions. In this region is found the ancient capital, Cuzco, along with other Inca villages and fortresses, such as Ollaytaytambo and Pisac.

Farther downstream, the great Vilcabamba Mountains thrust out of the strip between the two rivers. Salcantay looms to 20,574 feet. The Apurímac and Urubamba Rivers slice deep at the roots of these mountains, cutting some of the greatest canyons of the Andes in the process.

Thousands of visitors have adventured down the Urubamba Canyon by rail. Their destination has been the great citadel fortress of Machu Picchu, perched on the lofty flanks of the canyon above the river. Discovered in 1911 by Hiram Bingham, this monument has become a mecca both for its archeological wonders and for the exquisite beauty of the canyons and mountains surrounding it. Visitors have been rewarded not only by the sight of the great Inca ruins, but also by a trip down one of South America's great canyons and by glimpses back into enclaves of the marvelous Vilcabamba Range.

Few visitors ever see, short of remote glimpses from the air, the still more rugged splendor of the Apurímac's canyons. One can only imagine that which cannot be seen in full splendor—the magnificence of the aerial view if one could soar silently with the great condor of the Andes from the Urubamba Canyon to the Apurímac depths. But imagination can give us at least an idea of that awesome reality.

Proceeding southwest, up to and beyond Machu Picchu, green-clad slopes and ascending ridges gradually give way to the snow-clad giants of the Vilcabamba Range. Then, continuing southwest, across the backbone of the Vilcabamba, the surface of the earth plunges abruptly downward into the Apurímac drainage. It descends through sweeping fields of ice and snow past the melt line; down rock-strewn scree slopes and over infinite gray cliffs; down long green carpets of tangled jungle growth; down to a dusty eroded land barbed with cactus and thorny bushes; down, finally, over the rim of an inner canyon, plunging over dizzying precipices of polished rock to a ribbon of furious surging water. Here, 15,000 feet below the apex of the Vilcabamba, entombed in sunless gorges, the great river Apurímac crashes toward the Amazon jungle and the distant Atlantic.

INCA CIVILIZATION CAME to life about eight hundred years ago, in this strip of land between the great rivers. It took form around Cuzco, which became the Inca capital. Wealth accumulated, frontiers were pushed back. Cuzco became the center of one of the greatest kingdoms known to the ancient world, extending 2,500 miles from the southern reaches of Colombia to central Chile. The empire was laced together by 10,000 miles of roadway that crossed terrain of incredible difficulty.

Inca civilization also came to an end in this strip of terrain. Overrun by gold-crazed Spaniards, the Incas sought refuge in this rugged land, beyond Machu Picchu, deep in the Vilcabamba Mountains. There, isolated by the turbulent waters and sheer canyons of the Apurímac and Urubamba, protected by jungle growth and tumbling tributaries in a land tipped on edge, the shattered Inca empire clung to existence for four decades after the fall of Cuzco. Then, in 1572, the Spaniards captured Tupac Amaru, the last Inca, promised him safe conduct, and took him to Cuzco, where they garroted him in front of cheering throngs.

The Incas had mastered a severe land. They terraced and farmed the steep hillsides. They built magnificent roads through the highlands. They crossed flooding torrents on bridges of rope. And, ultimately, they broke through the great Apurímac's canyon barrier that had confined their northward expansion. In about 1450, ruled by the great Inca leader Pachacuti, they erected a marvelous suspension bridge across the gorge of the Apurímac. Across this swaying platform they surged north and west, up through present-day Peru and Ecuador to Colombia. With the Apurímac barrier breached, they conquered vast new lands for their empire.

The bridge has long since crumbled and washed into the Atlantic, but its memory has been kept alive by a great literary work, Thornton Wilder's novel *The Bridge of San Luis Rey*.

DEEPER INSIGHT INTO the great importance of the Apurímac River to the Incas is found in the words of the sixteenth-century chronicler Garcilaso de la Vega. Garcilaso, born in Cuzco in 1539, was the son of an Inca princess and a Spanish conquistador. According to him, in the depths of antiquity the great river bore the Inca name Ccapac Mayu, "to show that it was the prince of all the rivers in the world." The river was also called Apurímac, "which means the chief or prince who speaks." It still bears that name, which is often translated as "The Great Speaker."

Garcilaso also wrote that "[e]ven very close to its source it cannot be forded, for it carries much water, and is very rapid, flowing between very lofty mountains. . . . It is the largest river there is in Peru."

Considering that the river's source, to which Garcilaso refers, is the true source of the Amazon, the ancient name of Prince of all the Rivers in the World seems remarkably insightful. After all, the highland Indians could never follow the river into the hostility of the jungle and saw no more than a fifth of its great length.

While the Apurímac was a princely river in much of Inca thought, it was considered to be a demonic river at other times and among other cultures. In the elaborate entranceway to the Bridge of San Luis Rey the Incas, according to Victor von Hagen's *Highway of the Sun*, lodged their idol of the Apurímac on a thick beam. Other idols were placed there as well; they were all bathed in blood and clothed in golden robes. Through the larger idol, the Idol of the Apurímac, the demon of the river would speak to the Incas.

Farther downriver, where the Apurímac cuts through jungle valleys occupied by the Campa Indians, more demons arise. According to Gerald Weiss in his book *Campa Cosmology*, "[t]he demons of the river include the *impositóniro*, the *sonkatiníro*, and *Comiriníro*. The *impositóniro* and *sonkatiníro* live in the whirlpools and bad passes of the river, where they wait to drown and eat voyagers passing by. . . . Comiriníro is a spirit with a large . . . shoulder bag which is his stomach, into which he puts the souls of those who drown. The bodies are discarded to reappear at the surface and be eaten by buzzards . . ."

APPENDIX 2

Apurímac Explorers

A RIVER SO PROMINENT IN Inca history and so central in Amazon geography is an invitation for explorers to pour across its length and breadth; to search out its gorges, valleys, side canyons, shoreline, ruins, and ancient bridges. Indeed, many had visited the Apurímac at its most accessible locations. And yet, unlike the friendlier Urubamba Valley, no one had ever followed the Apurímac Canyon and its ribbon of water for any significant distance. The French explorer Michel Perrin, using a collapsible kayak, had navigated a few miles near the site of the Bridge of San Luis Rey, in 1953. He was driven off by big rapids. He then left the valley and bypassed the great Vilcabamba canyons, some of the deepest on earth. He probed the river again, above where the Río Pampas enters, and was again repulsed by rapids. He reentered the river a final time below the Pampas. The boat almost immediately capsized, and his female companion, Teresa Gutiérrez, was drowned. This tragic event is described in Perrin's book *Tragedy of the High Amazon*.

In 1970 a British expedition sought to follow the entire course of the Amazon. They started on foot and muleback. They walked down along the Apurímac Canyon in a few places, but were hindered by deep tributary ravines. Only infrequently could they see the river, buried in its timeless gorge. They bypassed entirely, as had Perrin, the deepest parts of the Apurímac Valley, entrenched at the heart of the Vilcabamba Range.

Loren McIntyre, a *National Geographic* explorer, writer, and photographer, has flown along the length of the Apurímac and explored its icy beginnings on foot. He first explained to me why the river was largely unexplored. He described an incredibly deep and narrow canyon in the Vilcabamba Mountains, beset by big rapids. "It is perhaps the deepest cut in South America," he explained. He made it clear he would not recommend anyone entering the canyon, because of its dangerous gorge and cataracts.

My two encounters with the Apurímac—down at the bottom of its gorges, adrift on its wild waters—took place in 1974 and 1975. I organized two expeditions, one in each of those years, that together successfully navigated the Vilcabamba canyons and other major segments of the Apurímac. A brief account appeared in *Mariah* magazine, in the fall issue of 1976.

Other attempts were made to navigate the Apurímac after our expeditions of 1974–75. In September of 1977, the American river guide John Tichenor and four companions entered the formidable canyons of the Vilcabamba on a single raft. He thought that three to five days would suffice to navigate the estimated 20 miles from the Cunyac bridge to the Inca ruins at Choquequirao, but the run was tougher than expected. On their fifth day, out of food and still 5 miles short of their goal, the rafters stumbled across the cable crossing at San José and exited the canyon by trail to the nearby village of Cachora. But John Tichenor, far from discouraged, organized two subsequent raft expeditions, in 1978 and 1979. He passed through lower and less difficult stretches of the Apurímac below the Río Pampas. The Tichenor expeditions are described in the book *Rivergods*, by Richard Bangs and Christian Kallen.

In 1985, a full decade after our expedition, a mixed kayak-raft expedition, led by François Odendaal, succeeded in following the Amazon from source to sea. The Odendaal party navigated many of the same canyons we first explored, along with some other segments of the Apurímac. Their venture was widely publicized. One account of the expedition was written by Piotr Chmielinski and appeared in *National Geographic* magazine. But the *National Geographic* article failed to mention our expedition. It was only with great prodding that the magazine eventually published a letter by my colleague Jim Sindelar, setting straight the fact that the most challenging part of their expedition—through the canyons of the Vilcabamba Range—followed in our footsteps.

Two books, one by Odendaal and the other by Joe Kane, were written about the 1985 passage. These books brought to the fore the bitter internal controversies that plagued the expedition, controversies foreshadowed at lesser intensity by our own interpersonal difficulties on the demon river.

APPENDIX 3

Elements of Kayaking and River Running

To BEGIN WITH, a *kayak* is a small slender boat, about 2 feet wide and 12 feet long (our kayaks were exactly 4 meters, or 13 feet, 2 inches long). It usually holds one person, but some longer ones accommodate two. The front end of the boat is the *bow*, the rear the *stern*. Kayaks are decked in (enclosed) except for a small *cockpit opening*, where the paddler enters. Once inside the *cockpit* of the boat, the paddler becomes mechanically part of the kayak, by using attachments to the boat called *foot braces*, *knee braces*, *thigh braces*, *hip braces*, and a well-fitting seat with, in some cases, a low back brace.

From a sitting position, braced firmly inside the kayak, the paddler makes powerful use of a *double-bladed paddle*, which has a broad blade on both ends of a shaft. Because of its streamlined shape, the kayak can be moved rapidly forward (or backward) by executing alternate left-right strokes with the two paddle blades. It can be quickly turned by a few strokes on one side. If a wave or other hydraulic feature begins to tip the kayak on its side, a quick *paddle brace*, in which the kayaker uses the blade on the side being tipped to in order to push off against the water, is employed to regain balance.

The possibility for instantly regaining horizontal alignment, or otherwise controlling the body-boat lean angle through weight shifts and paddle braces, gives unexpected stability. Although the kayak is narrow and thus tippy, it takes minimal effort in skilled hands to keep the boat upright, because it is so streamlined and easily controlled. The expert kayaker learns to integrate partial paddle braces into normal kayak strokes by subtle changes in blade angle, so the boat appears to become magically stabilized in the roughest water.

Inevitably the whitewater kayaker will run into rocks or turbulence so rough that capsizing is unavoidable. The boater must wear a sound helmet to protect him or her from underwater collisions with rocks. The *spray cover* is an elasticized cover that extends over the cockpit and is held in place by strong elastic cords stretched around the cockpit rim. The kayaker slips into a hole in the spraycover that is provided with an elasticized band to fit around the waist. With a well-fitted spraycover, very little water enters the cockpit despite severe splashing or capsizing.

With the aid of a spraycover, an *eskimo roll* becomes possible. Quite simply, an eskimo roll is a method of using a kayak paddle to turn a kayak and its occupant upright after a capsize. The eskimo roll is important because, under most circumstances, the only other option is to burst out of the kayak, surface for air, then swim to shore. It is easy to get out of the kayak, and sometimes easy to swim to shore. More often, on difficult rivers, the capsize occurs amid great turbulence, and the swim can be hazardous to life and limb. While a *life preserver* (or PFD) is always used, a swim through big rocks and powerful currents is still dangerous and can lead to being drowned, either directly or by being pinned against rocks, or having bones broken. It is better to eskimo roll and paddle out of the rapid. If one is forced to swim, it is usually best to hold on to the kayak, which can be a shield against rocks. Also, if the kayak is properly equipped with large bow and stern *flotation bags* inserted under the decks, the boat can keep the swimmer higher in the water, farther from hazards, and can keep some waves from washing over the head. While the boat protects the swimmer, the swimmer also protects the kayak, by guiding it around rocks that might otherwise cause damage to the craft.

DESPITE THE NIMBLENESS and stability displayed by an expert kayaker, the violent twisting, turning, and plunging of currents in rivers that are undergoing severe elevation loss is a challenge. Most problems arise as stream segments drop over or between large rocks, or less often across spurs jutting out from shoreline cliffs. One or more such drops is a *rapid* or *rapids*. An abrupt powerful drop is called a *cataract.*

As a stream of water flushes over a big rock, it often plunges deep into the water on the backside of the rock, forming a substantial *hole.* The water rises powerfully to the surface downstream from the hole, but the depth of the hole, combined with gravity, pulls some of the water back across the surface into it. Thus a recirculation pattern is set up, with a strong backcurrent right below the hole. A kayak dropping into a big hole can be stopped dead by the sharp wall of water and back-circulating current crashing down from in front. The kayak might be flipped end over end, and it will likely *broach* (turn sideways) into the hole. Eskimo rolls can be difficult and sometimes useless in this situation, because one can remain pinned in the hole by the recirculation. In the worst case, it is necessary to swim out.

There are a million sizes and shapes of holes, all fitting the above description. Sometimes they are called *reversals*, sometimes *keepers*, and sometimes merely *hydraulics*. They can be so small as to offer no threat at all, or so powerful as to pose a risk to life. Long even ones, like those found below weirs and low dams, are particularly dangerous, because they especially tend to trap boaters and swimmers.

Other river hazards include narrow twisting channels, in which boats can become pinned sideways on rocks or even logs. A pinned boat is difficult to break loose. In the worst case, the cockpit can rotate upstream and, if the boater is pinned inside, drowning can result.

Other dangers exist, particularly on remote expeditions, where illness or a broken bone on shore can lead to enormous complications in view of the uncertainty of evacuation. Generally, however, if a kayaker can stay upright in the boat, or at least avoid nasty swims through rapids by eskimo rolling after a capsize, chances of survival go up enormously.

As rapids become more difficult and the risk of a hazardous swim or pinned boat increases, the kayaker must decide whether to go around the rapid on or near shore. If the boats and gear are carried a ways along the shore, the event is a *portage*. Sometimes the kayak can be wholly or partially floated down side channels, with the paddler walking or clambering along, controlling the descent by selectively pulling on a *bow line* (attached to a bow loop) or *stern line*. This operation is called *lining*.

A dilemma can arise when cliffs plunge down into the water on both sides, forming a narrow gorge. The options of portaging or lining along shore are then lost. If the gorge is unsafe to run because of a waterfall or impossible rapid, the only safe route may be a very difficult (in some cases not even feasible) portage, going up and around the gorge. This dilemma was of great concern to us on the Apurímac, because it was reputed to have many difficult gorges. Luckily, we were never trapped in this way.

APPENDIX 4

1975 Expedition Document

SEVERAL MONTHS PRIOR to the launching on September 1, 1975, of Apurímac Expedition II, the author, as expedition organizer, wrote and distributed a document, critical in defining the nature and conduct of the 1975 expedition, outlining the background, goals, rules, schedule, and strategy of the expedition. The eleven parts of this document are briefly outlined here for historical perspective.

1. History of Apurímac Navigation. This part dealt briefly with Perrin's expedition (see Appendix 2), but focused more on the 1974 expedition and the subsequent gathering of information relating to the feasibility of a 1975 expedition.

2. Apurímac River. Here the vast stretch of the Apurímac was broken down into several sections that we would attempt to navigate. Details were given for each section, based on the author's research, of anticipated elevation changes, technical difficulties, mileages, climate, waterflows, streamside vegetation, and possibilities for resupply. The depth and potential difficulty of the great Apurímac Canyon where it passes through the Vilcabamba Mountains was discussed.

3. Trip Leadership and Participation. Here I noted that most of my trips have been run by consensus, and that this expedition would be similarly run insofar as possible. However, I clarified that this expedition was more complicated than ordinary trips and would require somewhat more defined leadership. I consequently reserved the right to make trip decisions, particularly where they related to safety and scheduling. I emphasized the cooperative nature of the expedition and the necessity for teamwork. "Most importantly, this will be a cooperative venture, a team effort in which each member will be expected to help each other whenever needed." I made it clear that each team member was expected to help others during portages or rescues from rocks, etc.

4. Safety and Navigation. Here I emphasized the hazards of severe rapids in remote country and noted how these hazards are multiplied in gorges, because one cannot always leave the river in such places. I made clear that "the emphasis of this trip will be on the safe approach. We

will enter no gorge without positive knowledge that an exit of some kind exists. If no safe passage exists, we will portage the gorge. Likewise we will portage difficult rapids if there is any question about safety." I continued by observing that "those of you who have portaged or otherwise carried loaded boats know that it is torture. But it must be clear to anyone interested in this trip that when safety is a significant question, we will choose this tedious option. We should be mentally prepared for this, which is half the battle. If we all understand this basic premise at the beginning, we should be able to avoid divisive arguments and disappointments."

5. Schedule. Here I outlined a tentative schedule that I felt allowed sufficient time for safety and for enjoyment of the river environment. Total trip time was projected at six weeks, with two weeks allowed to reach the Cunyac Crossing, three weeks allowed to proceed through the Vilcabamba Mountains down to the Pampas River, and one week to proceed through the jungle canyons below. Our actual trip time was thirty-three days. We came out ahead of schedule on all three trip segments.

6. Preparation. The emphasis here was on our need to obtain superior equipment (boats, paddles, patching equipment, camp gear, and clothing) that was functional, durable, and lightweight. All trip members were invited to make suggestions for obtaining improved equipment.

7. Transportation. This part dealt with getting our kayaks aboard the aircraft for transport to Peru.

8. Special Problems. Expedition members were urged to prepare to put up with short equatorial days, extremes of temperature, insects, and the possible theft of equipment.

9. Costs. The approximate costs of the expedition were outlined in this part of the document.

10. Writing and Photography. Because the National Geographic Society had expressed interest in publishing an article on our expedition, it was noted that extra time would be taken for photography. Everyone's cooperation was requested in this regard.

11. Sign-up and Deposit. An application form was provided, asking applicants to list their special talents and any items of group equipment they could bring. Applicants were further asked for a fifty-dollar nonrefundable application fee. The signature on the application form confirmed that the applicant would "agree to abide by the guidelines and conditions presented in the preceding writeup."